CW01509756

Heaven
his goal

TREVOR SAVIDENT

DayOne

© Day One Publications 2024
ISBN 978-1-84625-784-1

British Library Cataloguing in Publication Data available
Published by Day One Publications
Ryelands Road, Leominster, HR6 8NZ
Telephone 01568 613 740 FAX 01568 611 473
email—sales@dayone.co.uk
web site—www.dayone.co.uk
Cover design by Kathryn Chedgzoy
Printed by 4edge

Dedication

I dedicate this book to my lovely daughter, Beverley, who passed to Glory in June 2024, having been stricken with an aggressive cancer. She spent many hours deciphering my handwriting and typing up my notes. Without her input, this book would not have come to fruition. This book will be a memoriam of her, to me and our family.

CHAPTER 1

'**I**s that you Luke?' Alice shouted.

'Yes Mum,' Luke replied.

'You're late!'

'Yeah, just a bit I s'pose. I was chatting and forgot the time.'

'Well hurry up and get changed and do your paper round so you will have time to do your homework before dinner. Dad has fixed your bike, so all the gears are working now.'

Luke had, in fact, been home for the last ten minutes but had crept in through the back door, unseen, so that he could clean his shoes before his mum saw them; he then went around the house and came in the front door as usual.

Luke had indulged in a game of football on the way home from his Grammar School just a mile down the road. His mum had threatened him with serious consequences if she ever caught him playing football in his good school shoes again.

Luke is fourteen years old, tall for his age and the son of the Reverend Colin Tewkes-Dawson, the Methodist minister of three churches in the area. Luke has a shock of red hair just like his father. He had a younger sister once, but she died when Luke was just six years old. His mother, Alice, was the daughter of local counsellor, Tom Tewkes Maynard, who owned the local timberworks. She doted on young Luke and perhaps overprotected him after the tragic loss of little Maisie to meningitis at two years of age. She was devastated when the doctor eventually diagnosed meningitis and always wondered if Maisie could have been saved, had they diagnosed it earlier. However, she had bravely come to terms with her loss.

Luke was three quarters of the way through his paper round when he cycled past the local park and spotted a game of football in progress. He stopped to watch and learned from a bystander that the match was between local firemen and estate agents in a Business House League; the score was 1 – 1 with about ten minutes to go. Luke wanted the firemen to win and got excited whenever they launched an attack.

Luke was besotted with the game of football and was an excellent player himself; he was the star of the school team and the first name on the list when the team was selected. He played as striker and his goal-scoring was prolific but, if truth were told, he could play in almost any position, being taller than most lads of his age. He was also an excellent athlete and two years running he had won the schools cross-country run, beating boys of at least three years older than him.

If only his academic qualities could match his sporting prowess! Luke was not interested in lessons, as all he ever wanted to do was play football. He always did well in R.E. (Religious Education) though due to the influence, no doubt, of a father who was, after all, a minister of religion and a strict believer in Biblical teaching, particularly as far as Luke was concerned.

There must have been just minutes to go till the end of the match. Luke was watching when he heard the toot of a car horn; on turning around he saw his dad had pulled up in an old Ford Escort, which an old Parishioner had donated to him when she could no longer drive due to failing eyesight. Colin's car had given up the ghost and there had been no funds to replace it at the time. A car was essential for Colin who oversaw three churches, one of them fifteen miles away.

Luke went over to the car. 'Hi Dad, where are you going?'

'Home, Son. What are you doing? Have you finished your papers?' his dad asked.

'Nearly Dad, just a few more to do. I'll be finished in ten minutes. I just want to watch the end of this match; it's nearly finished.'

'No way, Son; get on and finish those papers. I suppose you have homework to do, have you?'

'Yes, but not much today, just Maths.'

'Come on, on your way!'

'Aw Dad, just a couple of minutes?'

'No, Luke, you have customers waiting for those papers. Off you go!'

Luke reluctantly got on his bike and rode off to finish his round, muttering about how unfair the world was. As his dad drove past with a toot of the horn, Luke did not even lift a hand to wave. His dad was not his favourite person at the time.

When Colin arrived home, he greeted Alice with a peck on the cheek, remarking, 'Something smells good, what's for dinner?'

'Beef stew,' she said. 'Mr Sands let me have a nice piece of brisket very cheap; he's a good man. I don't know how we would manage without the kindness of the parishioners.'

'God will provide,' Colin said. This was his reply whenever Alice brought up the subject of finance; the pay for a minister was certainly not an attraction for the ministry, even for a minister with the charge of three churches.

'Luke's late. He should have finished his papers ages ago. Do you think his bike has broken down again?' Alice asked.

'No,' Colin said. 'I saw him watching a game of football in the park. I moved him on so he should be here soon.'

'Honestly that boy and his football; that's all he ever thinks about. I wish he would put as much enthusiasm into his studies as his does his football. He asked me if he could have some new boots last week; one of his is starting to split, he said. There's no way we can afford a new pair of football boots. He really could do with some new shoes for school, but I can't afford them just yet. Maybe if I can increase my hours at the flower shop, but Sally says that business is slowing down since the supermarket started selling fresh flowers.'

'There's no way you are going to work extra hours so Luke can have new football boots,' Colin started to say, when Alice interrupted:

'No, it's not just football boots, it's for new shoes. And besides, his schoolbag is only just holding together; it can't take any more repairs. None of these are cheap and I know Luke is embarrassed by the look of his schoolbag; there's more sticky-tape visible than there is bag. I know the teachers understand our situation, but his friends don't, and children can be so cruel at times, taunting him. It's just as well that he has a calm nature and doesn't react; you have to give him credit for that.'

Luke arrived home and having put his bike in the shed, entered the kitchen asking, 'Can I have a sandwich Mum, I'm starving!'

'You're not starving Luke, you're hungry,' Colin said. 'You don't know what it means to be starving. If you were in some of the African countries, you'd know what it is to be starving.'

'Oh, Dad, I didn't ask for a lecture on the third world; I merely asked for a sandwich. Is that so bad?'

'Don't be insubordinate lad; I won't have you answering back. You are starting to get too big for your boots! And talking of boots, don't keep asking for new football boots. We can't afford them and that's that.'

'Sorry Dad, I didn't mean to be rude. It's just that it seems everything I do is wrong these days.'

'Look Luke, I'll make you a sandwich, but woe betide you if you don't eat your dinner. It's beef stew; I know it's not your favourite but there's lots of goodness in it—ideal for someone who will be a top England striker one day.'

'I will Mum, you wait and see. I'll win the World Cup for England one day and then I'll have lots of pairs of boots, with my own name on them too!'

'Scram! Get up there and get your homework done,' Alice said, giving him his sandwich and a kiss on the forehead at the same time.

'You spoil that boy,' Colin said. 'He can twist you around his little finger.'

'He's a good lad at heart, Colin; we have many reasons to be thankful to God. He doesn't get into the trouble some of the boys at school do in his class. The police were at school again yesterday over some vandalism overnight on Sunday in the school grounds, where damage was caused to the sports hut. They even tried to start a fire in it but were chased off by the groundsman. He apparently recognized one or two as being pupils from the school.'

'What are the parents thinking of, letting their kids out that late, not knowing where they are?' Colin said. 'I don't know what this world is coming to these days. God must be saddened by peoples' behaviour, especially when they have children so young. If only we could get those youngsters into church or the youth club, it may help to stabilize them a little and give them some sense of responsibility. Anyway, I'm going into my study; I've got some emails to answer. Please call me when dinner's ready,'

Luke had been sitting at his table near the window in his bedroom with his books in front of him. The window looked out onto the rolling countryside with majestic hills standing proud in the distance. Rural Hampshire was not the worst of places to live, not that Luke appreciated the views in any degree. He was staring at the green fields, picturing how one of them—which was flatter than the others—would make an ideal football pitch with huge stands around the four sides. The lanes would have to be widened, of course, to take the traffic on match days and a couple of other fields could be turned into car parks. And then there would have to be a training pitch and an indoor training area for bad weather, with gymnasium facilities and—at this point his daydreaming was interrupted by a tap on the door and his dad entering his room:

'Luke, I need to have a word with you. I did not mean to snap at you downstairs, but you need to understand that Mum and I are having some difficulty now trying to make ends meet moneywise. I know I always say, "God will provide," and I truly believe that, as far as essential needs are concerned, he has been good to this family. We have always had food on the table and clothes on our backs.

'The church congregation are fully aware that a minister's salary is not great and are very kind to us. We have a lot to be thankful for.

'All I ask of you is to be understanding when we have to turn down your requests for things like a new bike or new football boots. We just can't justify buying these things when we struggle to supply you with new shoes or uniform. My car has to have a service soon and that could work out to be expensive if repairs are needed.

'The only way you can have pocket money is because you are prepared to earn it with your paper round, and I am proud of you for that. Just be patient; my salary is up for review next month and God willing, things will improve.'

Luke stood up and gave his dad a hug and said, 'I understand Dad.'

'Thanks Son. How are you getting on with your homework? Can I help?'

"Nearly done thanks Dad, I can manage. Besides, it's maths and you often say that number-crunching is not your forte. Or, to put it another way, you can't count for toffee-apples.' Luke ducked just in time to avoid a playful clip around the ear.

'Cheeky young whipper snapper!' his dad said with a smile, leaving the room.

Luke called after him, 'Dad, can I use the phone please when I come down?'

'What for?' asked Colin.

'I want to ring the fire station.'

'Why on earth would you want to ring the fire station?' Colin enquired.

'The fire brigade was one of the teams playing in that match in the park; I just want to ask what the final score was.'

'I don't think so Luke. I'm sure the fire station has more important things to do than to answer the phone to give out football results. Finish your homework, dinner will be ready soon.'

At Alice's call, both Luke and his dad arrived in the kitchen for dinner—Luke from his room and Colin from the study. The kitchen was huge, with a relatively new cooker just about beating the solid pine kitchen table as the main centrepiece of the room. The Aga was Alice's pride and joy and was well used in the baking of fine cakes for the various stalls at church fetes and special occasions, as well as the family meals. It contributed too by heating the kitchen itself, along with one radiator that was totally inadequate for such a large room. But the kitchen was always warm and cosy despite its size and was the hub of the household during the major part of the day. When Mum was not working three-days-a-week at Sally's Flowers, she would invariably be found in the kitchen.

After Luke had said grace at his dad's invitation, his mum removed a large ceramic pot from the Aga and placed in on the table. Removing the lid caused the aroma of a wonderful beef stew to permeate the kitchen; nestling on the top were three of the largest dumplings you have ever seen. Alice served stew onto three plates with a dumpling on each and they all ate with relish, even Luke— who didn't particularly like stew. However, he cleaned his plate and thanked his mum for his meal saying, 'That'll rest nicely on the sandwich,' with a large grin on his face. They all laughed at Luke's cheeky retort.

Mealtimes were always good times in this household. It was usually the only time all three members of the family were together for any length of time in a busy week and was usually the time when problems and concerns were discussed. Alice and Colin considered Luke mature enough (even at only fourteen) to take part in these discussions and was often able to contribute some fresh train of thought; despite his academic problems at school, he often spoke a lot of common sense. The meal was just about finished and, after Luke had obtained permission to leave the table, he announced that he was going into the garden for a 'bit of a kick about'.

'Put your trainers on then,' his mum called.

'I have,' Luke said. He just loved being in the back garden with his beloved old football. His favourite game was to throw the ball against the uneven granite wall of the house—missing the windows by inches sometimes—and then controlling the ball in an instant, regardless of what angle the ball bounced back at him. As he was leaving the room, his dad called after him, 'Oh Luke.'

'Yes?' he replied.

'The fire brigade won, 2–1.'

'How did you know that?' Luke asked.

'They told me on the phone,' Colin replied.

'Yes!' Luke shouted, punching the air.

'What was that about?' enquired Alice.

'It's a long story,' Colin said, as he collected the dishes for washing in the kitchen sink.

'I'll do those. Go and finish your emails. I'll bring you a coffee in a minute.'

So, Colin adjourned to the study with a full stomach and a feeling of contentment, which he had felt all too infrequently of late with one thing and another.

Dishes done, Alice made sandwiches for Luke's lunch the next day, together with his favourite fruit yoghurt and an apple, placed them in a lunchbox, and put it in the fridge. Then, after making a batter for tomorrow's pancakes, which she also placed in the fridge, Alice took a mug of coffee into Colin on her way to the lounge to watch her favourite soap on the old television—the first time that day she had been able to sit with her feet up and relax.

She could not help her thoughts drifting to the earlier conversations with Colin about the house bills etc. and wondered if there was some way they could increase their income. She knew they were managing the bare essentials, but it was a struggle and Luke was growing so fast. He would be busting out of his uniform in no time at all and his feet seemed to be growing in leaps and bounds. The cost of petrol was going up all the time and Colin hated to curtail his visiting of 'his people', as he called them.

Colin was reluctant to pray for material things, in the firm belief that 'God will provide'; Alice could not argue with that sentiment because in truth she believed it herself. It never ceased to amaze her how Colin was so laid back about those things and did not seem to worry about it. She knew he had a caring nature and, in his own way, he too was concerned over the financial situation. But she believed he was deliberately dismissing it so as not to be diverted in his thoughts and become obsessed by the situation, which was by no means dire. She concluded that she was perhaps a worrier by nature and things would work out.

She was abruptly awakened from her thoughts by the closing music of her programme, having watched it all the way through without hearing a word that was said. She called for Luke to come in to get washed for bed, reminding him he needed to clean his shoes for tomorrow first.

On entering Colin's study, Alice saw him at his desk with his head resting on his folded arms, fast asleep. She saw that his coffee mug was untouched and the coffee was stone cold. She called him gently and he awoke, apparently unaware of the time of day or where he was; he had simply crashed out at his desk into a deep sleep.

'Are you alright?' Alice asked.

'Yes, I'm fine,' he said. 'I must have been more tired than I thought and dropped off.' He had finished his emails, four of them, and they had all been sent.

Alice said, 'Luke is getting ready for bed; we'll be ready for evening prayers in about ten minutes.'

'OK,' he said. 'I'll be right there; I'll just finish my coffee.'

'It's stone cold,' Alice said. 'I'll make you another.'

'Waste not, want not,' Colin replied and downed the coffee almost in one swig.

Colin then joined Luke and Alice in the lounge and, after reading several verses of the Bible, they took it in turns to pray—Colin finishing off with a prayer particularly for those in poor countries who have so little of life's necessities. Luke wondered just for a fleeting moment if his dad was deliberately making a point for his sake, then quickly dismissed it out of hand, remembering that this was often part of his dad's prayers in or out of church. Luke was able to say an enthusiastic and heartfelt, 'Amen!' to his dad's prayer.

After getting his mum's agreement to be able to read for a while, Luke retired with his copy of *Football Greats of the Past*. What else?

CHAPTER 2

The next morning was no different to most mornings in the house—Luke's mum up at the crack of dawn preparing breakfast and eating her toast as she flitted around the kitchen. Luke and his dad ate together at the table, Colin with his bran flakes and Luke with his cornflakes, followed by toast and marmite. Luke won the race for the bathroom, so Colin adjourned to his study for his quiet time of reading and prayer.

Alice had already vacated the bathroom ages ago, having to get ready for her day at the flower shop, which she always looked forward to. She loved meeting people and, perhaps at times, was a bit too chatty with customers, who all knew her. She was a popular person in the shop and well-liked by all. She was also very good at her job and loved flowers. As Alice was a member of the local flower arranging society, the owner, Sally, left the displays to her on the days she was due in; they always looked so much better when Alice did them.

During the day, her mind kept wandering back to the emails she had seen Colin sending last night. Over his shoulder she had noticed one in particular addressed to the supervisor of their Methodist Circuit. She must remember to ask Colin about that one later on and, to remind herself to do that, she drew a cross with ballpoint pen on her wrist near her wristwatch; it always worked for her when she wanted to remember something.

She had said her goodbyes that morning to Colin and Luke on leaving the house, reminding Luke to thank his dad for fixing his bike and to leave in plenty of time to get to school. Colin had wished her a good day as he gave her a peck on the cheek.

'You too,' she said. 'What are you doing today, by the way?'

'Later on, this morning, I must visit Ernie at the Home for Aged Pilgrims. He is apparently getting over his bout of the flu and may be well enough to attend worship on Sunday; I'll offer to pick him up if he feels well enough to come.'

'Give him my love,' Alice said.

'I will,' replied Colin.

When Colin took his coffee mug into the kitchen, Luke had just removed his lunchbox from the fridge and was placing it in his bag. 'I'm off Dad, see you later.'

'Ride carefully, Son. You know what the traffic's like around school.'

'I will. Oh, by the way, thanks for fixing the bike, its brill; you're in the wrong job Dad!' When Colin raised his eyebrows at that remark, Luke said, 'Sorry Dad, you know what I mean.'

'Lucky for you I do, young man, or you might be going to school with a slightly reddened ear.'

'You'd have to catch me first,' Luke said, as he dashed out of the door.

Colin just shook his head and, grinning, said to himself, 'I don't know. Kids these days.'

Colin and Luke had a wonderful rapport with each other and were very close. He could not help thinking on what Luke had said though. Oh, he knew his ministry was a calling and he felt that the Lord was using him in the situation he was in, but he did wonder sometimes if his calling was an imposition on his family, causing them to make sacrifices so they could make ends meet. He could not help but recall the state of Luke's schoolbag as he was putting his lunchbox in it in the kitchen this morning.

Then, with a quick shake of the head, he dismissed those negative thoughts from his mind and said to himself, for the umpteenth time that week, 'The Lord will provide.'

Luke arrived at school in good time along with Jason, whom he met along the way. Jason was the school goalkeeper and almost as tall as Luke. He lived on the council estate, which did not have a very good reputation in the area. The police always seemed to be calling at one house or another, but these were in the minority. Most of the residents were good, law-abiding citizens but people seemed to tar them all with the same brush.

Jason's mother had never married and had three other children— two boys younger than Jason and a two-year-old daughter. Jason always seemed to have the best of everything; his bike was a top of the range model and a Christmas present from his mum. There was no sticky tape on his schoolbag or on his football boots, but this never bothered Luke. He probably did not even consider Jason's apparel, but he did admire his football boots that were the best money could buy.

They entered the school gates, alighting from their bikes in accordance with school rules, especially as Mr Gibbs, the deputy head, was standing in the playground with two smartly dressed men and the groundsman/caretaker. Luke saw the groundsman, Mr Tombs, point at him and say something to Mr Gibbs. He, in turn, spoke to one of the strangers, who wrote something down in a notebook. Luke dismissed it from his mind concluding it was nothing to do with him, but he said to Jason, 'Who's that with Mr Gibbs?'

'The cops,' Jason said. 'They are C.I.D. (Criminal Investigation Department); I've seen them on the estate when they nicked Tommy Box for breaking into the timber yard and stealing some wood.'

'That would be "box-wood" then,' Luke said. They burst out laughing, parked their bikes and made off towards classes. On the way, Jason remarked, 'Big match, tomorrow. We play Old Vics College; got to beat 'em this year.'

'Yeah! Hope I'm picked,' Luke said.

'Course you'll be picked, our star striker you are. Who else is going to bang in our five goals?'

'That would be good, but Old Vics are a tough team to beat, and they've got a better goalkeeper than us,' Luke said, as he ran off before Jason could react.

Luke had handed in his maths homework before going off to the gym for assembly, which this day was taken by the Roman Catholic Priest, Cannon Rawlingston. Luke sat with Jason and could not make head or tail what the Priest was talking about. At the end Jason said, 'What a load of mumbo jumbo. Is that what your father does in his church on Sundays?'

'Absolutely not!' Luke said. 'My dad says it as it is; he talks a lot of sense and takes his sermons from the Bible.'

Jason dismissed Luke's retort saying, 'Yeah, well, each to his own, eh?'

'You should come one Sunday Jason and see for yourself; you might even enjoy it and learn something.'

'I do enough learning in this place thank you very much,' Jason replied.

As they were leaving assembly, they walked past their form teacher, Mr Ward. He said to Luke, 'Well done with homework, Luke; keep up the good work.' Well! You could have knocked Luke over with a feather; he could not ever remember getting a 'well done' from Mr Ward before. Jason said, 'Oh yeah, teacher's pet, eh?'

'No way,' said Luke. 'I don't think Wardy likes me very much actually, not since he had an argument with my dad over some doctrinal matter after church one Sunday morning; he hasn't been to church since.'

On their way to their classroom, they saw the two C.I.D. officers and Mr Tombs entering the headmaster's office. Jason said to Luke, 'Carry on, I'll be there in a minute. I just want to get something from my locker.'

Mr Ward was late coming into class and Jason had not returned yet. Before reaching his desk, Mr Ward said, 'Luke Tewkes-Dawson, headmaster's office straight away please.'

'Me?' Luke asked.

'Yes you; that's your name, isn't it?'

'Yes, sir,' Luke said.

'Well, go on then lad.'

With a dry mouth and legs like jelly, Luke made his way to the headmaster's office. He did not know why he had been summoned but he had it settled in his mind that rarely did a pupil have to go to the headmaster's office for a good reason. Yet, what on earth could it be for? His class work had not been that bad had it. Moreover, didn't he get a 'well done' from Wardy this morning? That must count for something surely!

He gingerly tapped on the office door. 'Wait!' came the shouted reply; he hung around waiting and spotted the notice board down the corridor. He strolled down and saw the team sheet for the match against Old Vics College tomorrow. There was his name on the top of the list of thirteen names with the letter 'C' in brackets after his name: team captain. Wow! He had never been named as team captain before.

He virtually skipped back to the headmaster's office but was quickly brought back down to earth when the door opened and he was ushered into the room by the headmaster, who stood Luke in front of his desk and then went to his seat behind it, flanked by two police officers. Mr Tombs was standing to the side with his cap clutched in his hands in front of him, almost standing to attention. Luke could not understand why but he wanted to cry there and then. He could not remember being so frightened since he accidently kicked a stone and cracked a church window one Sunday morning but he had done nothing wrong, despite the way that the headmaster glared at him.

'These two gentlemen are police officers, young Tewkes-Dawson. They are investigating a very serious crime: arson! Do you know what that is, lad?'

'Yes sir, it's fire I think.' Luke's voice was barely a whisper.

'What? Speak up boy?' the headmaster said.

'I think it's setting fire to things, sir.'

'You're so right, it is lad,' the headmaster growled at Luke.

The senior looking C.I.D officer then interrupted: 'Excuse me Headmaster, let me take it from here please.'

'Very well,' the headmaster agreed.

'I'm Detective Sergeant Belton from the Hampshire Constabulary and this is Detective Constable Pinns,' he said pointing to his colleague. 'What's your first name?'

'Luke,' Luke said.

'SIR!' the headmaster shouted.

'Luke, sir,' Luke answered.

'Alright Headmaster. Let's not get overheated about this. Let's take things nice and calmly, shall we?'

'Hmph,' the headmaster grunted and sat back with arms folded.

By this time Luke was close to tears and felt like turning around and running but instead he just stood there in a daze, not knowing if this scenario was for real or if he was dreaming.

'Now Luke, where were you at about 11 o'clock last Sunday evening?'

'I was at home in bed, sir. It was night-time.'

The headmaster piped up and said, 'Don't be insolent boy, we know 11 o'clock was night-time. Don't think being cheeky is going to get you out of this!'

'I wasn't being cheeky, sir; I haven't done anything.'

The headmaster had started to say, 'We'll be the judge of that,' when he was interrupted by the sergeant, who said firmly,

'Headmaster, I must ask you not to interrupt. You are merely here to ensure fair play for the boy's sake, not to take part in the interview.

Now, if you persist, I will have to ask you to leave the room or we will conduct this interview elsewhere. Do I make myself clear?'

'Go ahead,' the headmaster said. 'I was only trying to help.'

'I appreciate that, sir, but I would rather you left it to us,' the D.S. said.

'Now Luke, I ask again. Where were you at 11 o'clock on Sunday night?'

'I was in bed,' Luke said. 'I go to bed at 9:30pm when it's school the next day.'

'Are you sure, Luke?'

'Yes, absolutely sure. You can call my dad; he'll tell you.'

The headmaster was about to interrupt again when D.S. Belton held up his hand and glared at him. The headmaster thought better of it and resumed his defiant position in his chair with arms folded high across his chest.

'As you have probably guessed by now, Luke, we are investigating the break-in of the sports store and attempted arson on Sunday night.'

'Yes,' Luke said.

'Now Mr Tombs, will you tell us again what you saw on Sunday night?' D.S. Belton said to Mr Tombs.

Mr Tombs virtually clicked his heels together and relayed the fact that, on the night in question, he had heard noises from the sports hut and went to investigate. On his approach, he had seen three youngsters running away; one of them he recognized as a pupil from the school.

'And where were you just before 9 o'clock when children were arriving at school?'

'You know where I was, wiv' you two and Mr Gibbs in the playground.'

'Right, and who did you see arriving at the school?'

'I saw the same lad who was at the 'ut on Sunday night and I pointed him out to you.'

Pointing at Luke, the D.S. said, 'And this is the lad you saw on both occasions?'

'Yes, sir, I think so.'

'You think so?' the D.S. asked. 'Aren't you sure?'

'Yes, I am sure, sir. It was 'im.'

'OK, Mr Tombs, that will be all. You may go and thank you for your help; we may have to get in touch with you again.' Mr Tombs placed his cap on his head, virtually saluted and left the room.

By now, Luke was totally out of control. He was sobbing from deep down and saying, 'It wasn't me! Phone my dad, please phone my dad!'

'Alright, lad, calm down,' the younger officer said. 'Take a seat for a minute. Now, what's your dad's number? Is he at work?'

'He's the minister of Stanford Road Church. He might be at home, but I don't know.'

'Has he got a mobile phone?' the officer asked.

'No,' Luke said. 'They're too expensive, Dad says.'

'Yeah, I know where he's coming from,' the officer replied. 'Never mind. What's his home number?'

Luke told him, and then was told to leave the room and wait outside.

Once out in the corridor, Luke let it all out and cried his eyes out, rubbing them until they were red raw almost. He felt like he was having a nightmare and was so confused he felt the whole world was against him. Yet, the day had started so well.

After a few deep breaths and a good blow of the nose, Luke regained his senses somewhat and decided to do what his father would do in times of despair. He fell on his knees, put his hands together and prayed as he had never prayed before, asking God to lift the situation from him and make people see the truth and correct their mistake.

Luke did not know how long he had been on his knees but when he opened his eyes, the younger detective was standing over him and said,

"Amen to that Luke, Amen. You are obviously aware of where our help comes from in time of trouble. I hope your prayers are answered and the truth will come out. If it's any consolation at this stage, I believe you, but we desperately need to confirm your story. We can't get hold of your father; is your mother contactable?'

'She works at the flower shop in town, but I don't know the number,' Luke replied.

'What's the name of the shop?'

'I don't know,' Luke said. 'It's the one just past the post office.'

'Well, let's hope it says that in the phone book, eh!' the detective joked.

Luke managed a sort of smile; he liked this man. He seemed kindlier and more sympathetic than the other; 'besides he believes me,' Luke thought to himself. Things will turn out alright after all. Mum can confirm my whereabouts last Sunday, no problem.

After a couple of minutes waiting, Luke was invited back into the headmaster's office but not before he had re-checked the notice board and looked at the team selection for tomorrow. 'All the usuals,' he thought to himself, 'including Jason in goal—Jason!!' He did not come into class after going to the cloakroom. That was strange! 'I wonder what happened to him,' Luke thought. However, his thoughts had been interrupted by the invitation to re-enter the headmaster's office.

'Right, Luke,' D.S. Belton said. 'We've contacted *Sally's Flowers* where your mother works, but she is out buying stock apparently and they don't know how long she is going to be. Rather than prolong things, I've decided to leave it there for now and we'll make contact with your parents later. You are free to go back to your class now, but I must ask you not to discuss this with any of your friends. Do you understand?'

'Yes, sir,' Luke replied.

At this point, the headmaster stood up and said, 'Whoa, whoa, wait a minute. 'There's no way he can go back to his class in these circumstances.' He turned to Luke and said, 'You are suspended from school until further notice in accordance with school policy. I'll formulate a letter and get it to your parents later on today. Now, wait outside and I'll arrange for your belongings to be collected from your form; then you may go, and straight home mind, do you hear?'

'That's not fair, sir. I haven't done anything wrong. It wasn't me!'

'That remains to be seen lad. I know who I believe; Mr Tombs is not a liar.'

Luke waited outside the office and eventually Mr Ward, no less, arrived with Luke's pencil case and books from his desk. He couldn't hide the shock on his face when he saw Luke and the obvious distress he was in.

'Luke, whatever's the matter. Is there anything I can do? Have you had some bad news or what?'

'I have been suspended from school, sir. They think I tried to burn down the sports shed on Sunday night, but I didn't. It's all so unfair! I hate this school, hate it!'

'There must be some mistake, Luke. You wouldn't do anything like that; it's not in your nature. I'm sure it will all turn out alright. How are you getting home?'

'I've got my bike, sir. I'll ride home.'

'Are you sure, Luke?'

'Yes, sir, I'll be fine. Thank you, sir.'

'OK then, off you go. Now take it easy, and don't worry.'

Luke collected his bag from the cloakroom, noticing Jason's empty peg and the empty space where his bike had been in the morning. On his way home, he put two and two together. He remembered that Jason had known who the two strangers were in the playground with Mr Tombs and Mr Gibbs. He knew they were police and why they were at school. Had Jason something to do with the sports-shed incident on Sunday night? Was it him? Is that why he did a runner from school. 'Thanks pal, good friend you are! If I'd sussed that out at school I wouldn't be in this predicament. I would have told them, I think, or would I? What would have been the right thing to do? Dad will know.'

Luke was only on the road for about five minutes when he heard his name: 'Luke, Luke, wait for me.' Luke turned around and saw Jason pedalling furiously to catch him. Luke slowed and, when Jason was alongside, he said to Luke, 'Where are you going? Why aren't you at school?'

'I might ask you the same question,' Luke replied. 'Where did you get to this morning? You didn't come into class.'

'I know,' Jason said. 'I saw those coppers and I panicked. I think they were there about the sports shed.'

'You think they were? I know they were!' Luke replied. 'They interviewed me. They think I did it. I've been suspended from school. My dad's going to have a blue fit! As for my Mum, well, I don't know what she'll do.'

Jason fell silent for a while as they continued riding. Luke broke the silence saying, 'It was you, wasn't it Jason? You did the shed Sunday night; that's why you ran away.'

'Look, it's not what it seems. Yes, I was there, but I didn't have anything to do with breaking into the shed, or lighting the fire,' Jason replied. I told the others they were crazy and would be in big trouble, but they wouldn't listen.'

'You could have walked away,' Luke said.

'I did,' Jason replied, 'but I went back for my jacket. That's when old Tombs appeared, and we just ran for it.'

'So, what are you going to do now?' Luke asked.

'That depends on you; are you going to turn me in?'

'It would get me off the hook,' Luke said. 'I'm going to have to tell my father that I know who it is. Who are the others?'

'I can't tell you that. I can't grass on the others; my life wouldn't be worth living on the estate. It's no one from school, I can tell you that much. What will your dad do?'

'Well, I hope the first thing he'll do is tell school that I wasn't out on Sunday night. They'll believe him because of who he is; they know him at school from the assemblies he's taken, so I'll be in the clear.'

'Yeah, but you don't have to tell your dad that I was there, do you?'

'If he asks me if I know anything about it, I can't lie to him Jason. He'll know I'm lying. Anyway, I wouldn't lie to my dad, I respect him too much and what he stands for. Lying is a sin; my dad has said it many times in church. God doesn't like lies and punishes people who lie.'

'I thought you were intelligent Luke; how can you believe all that stuff?' Jason said. 'You need to get a life.'

'I know it's all true. I believe it, but I can't explain it to you,' Luke said.

'Fat lot of good it's done you, Luke. I'm not suspended from school,' Jason said.

'You've got a check,' Luke said. 'It's thanks to you that I'm in trouble and I haven't even done anything.'

Jason turned off at this point, making his way home to his estate with a 'See you around Luke, all the best for the match tomorrow.'

Luke rode the rest of the way home, parked his bike and went inside, knowing no one was home. His dad's car was not there, and his mum was at work. He went up to his room and flopped on his bed; his head was in a spin and his mind was racing through the events of the morning. He was almost dozing off when he suddenly sat up with a start: 'THE MATCH!', he said out loudly. 'I'm suspended; I won't be able to play in the big match tomorrow.' Tears ran down his cheeks and he cried audibly with loud sobs, his body jerking violently with each sob. 'Come home Dad,' he thought to himself. 'Help me; you can clear my name.'

He quickly got off the bed, ran downstairs and went out the front gate, looking up and down the road, no sign of his dad. Then he remembered his dad had said he was going to the retirement home this morning. He ran inside and picked up the telephone directory, thinking hard to remember the name of the place. Then he spotted the list of telephone numbers pinned on the little notice board on the wall, but there was no retirement home there. *Sally's Flowers* was there though—that will do.

He had just picked up the handset and was about to punch in the numbers when he heard his dad's car reversing into the driveway. He could not get out to the car quick enough. 'Dad, come quick, you've got to help me!' he said as his dad was getting out of the car and tried to hurry him, saying, 'Come on Dad quick, you've gotta phone school and tell Mr O'Donnell that I was at home Sunday night so I can play tomorrow.'

'Whoa, whoa, slow down and calm down. What on earth are you taking about and why are you here and not at school?'

'It's a long story Dad, but I'm suspended from school for something I didn't do; it's not fair. I'm being punished for something I had no part in.'

'*Suspended*!' Dad yelled. 'I think we'd better go inside and sit down. Then, perhaps *calmly* you can tell me what's going on.'

Luke sat at the kitchen table and waited while Dad took off his jacket in the hall and hung it up. When he entered the kitchen, he asked Luke who had telephoned, as the handset was resting in the table and the directory was on the floor. 'I was going to phone Mum, but you came home. I was desperate to contact you but I couldn't find the number of the retirement home.'

'OK Luke, just settle down. I'll make a cup of tea and then you can tell me all about it.'

They sat opposite each other with steaming mugs of tea in front of them and, after taking a deep breath, Luke related the whole story, starting with the fact that the school sports hut had been broken into on Sunday night, through to his summons to Mr O'Donnell's office and the conversation therein. He continued through the whole story uninterrupted by his father, apart from the occasions when his dad told him to slow down. He did not, however, relate the conversation with Jason on the way home.

At the end of his relating of the whole incident, he said, 'Mr O'Donnell was really horrible to me. He believes I'm guilty. You must ring him Dad and tell him I was home on Sunday night so that I can play against old Vics College tomorrow.'

Colin replied, 'OK Son, I'll do that in due course, but I have to ask you a question for my own peace of mind, although I know you well enough to know what your answer will be. Did you sneak out of your room on Sunday night and go to the school fields?'

'No Dad, I didn't. I wouldn't do that.'

'I know, I believe you, Son, but I had to ask. Now, the first thing we must do is contact the police, never mind the school for a moment. We need to clear your name as far as the investigating officers are concerned. Once we get that clearance, we'll contact school and get you re-instated.'

'No Dad, phone Mr O'Donnell now and tell him I was at home. I need to get back to school to play tomorrow.'

'Sorry Luke, my priority is to clear your name with the police. There's plenty of time to contact school afterwards. Do you know the name of the policemen in the case?'

'No,' Luke said. 'I can't remember but they weren't in uniform; one of them was very nice—I think he is a Christian. He heard me praying outside the head's office and he said, 'Amen,' when I had finished. I didn't know he was there, but he let me finish my prayer before he said anything.'

'Well done, Luke, I'm proud of you that you took it to the Lord in prayer. God will do his bit, now let's do ours. I'll phone the police station right away.'

They both went out into the hallway, Luke taking his mug of tea with him. He picked up the telephone directory to hand it to his dad, who said, 'I don't need that, I've got the number here.' Checking the list of numbers on the board, he got through to the station and asked for C.I.D., then asked for the officer who was dealing with the school sports-shed case. He was put on hold for a minute or two (seemed like ages to Luke), then was told that the officers were out and to leave his name and they would call him back when they came in. When this was relayed to Luke, he said, 'Aww Dad, that could take ages. Can we phone the school now?' Luke was hopping from one foot to the other as he spoke, spilling drops of tea on to the floor as he did so.

'For goodness' sake Luke, calm down will you. That won't help the situation.'

Colin started to make for the kitchen when Luke asked, 'Aren't you going to phone the school?'

'Yes, in a minute. I'm just going to get a cloth to wipe up your mess.'

'I'll do that,' Luke said. 'You phone the school.'

Luke almost ran to the kitchen, emptied the rest of his tea down the sink and grabbed a piece of kitchen roll. Dad was punching in the numbers when Luke returned and mopped up the drops of tea on the floor. When he had finished dialling, Colin pointed to the piece of kitchen roll in Luke's hand and mouthed,

'Bin,' and then pointed to the kitchen.

Luke ran to the kitchen, threw the piece of kitchen roll at the bin and missed it by a mile. It struck a cupboard door and fell to the floor leaving a mark on the door. Luke retrieved it and placed it in the bin. He tore off another piece of the roll, wiped the door and put that in the bin too. When he returned to the hallway, his dad was already in conversation and asked for an appointment with Mr O'Donnell. Luke tapped him on the shoulder and shaking his head whispered loudly:

'No, Dad, tell him on the phone, tell him.' Colin held up his hand to silence Luke and said:

'I need to see Mr O'Donnell urgently, straight away please; I can be there in ten minutes.'

Luke waited while his dad listened to the reply and, before putting the handset down, said, 'Thank you very much. I appreciate that, goodbye.'

'What did he say?' Luke asked.

'We have an appointment with Mr O'Donnell at 1 o'clock; he's taking a class at the moment.'

'Why can't you just phone him and tell him over the phone?' Luke said.

'I think it's best if we see him in person Luke, although he and I don't seem to get on very well since our conversation after the last time I did an assembly at school. He objected quite strongly to the Christian ethic of my speech and accused me of evangelizing to his pupils for my church. He didn't like it very much when I denied it and said I was evangelizing his pupils for God's Church, which was my job. Anyway, that's all water under the bridge.'

'Can you try the police station again as 1 o'clock is an hour away?' Luke asked.

'No, they will contact me when they are back in the office.'

'But what if they don't? What if they ring while we're at school?" Luke said.

'They'll leave a message on the answerphone Luke, don't worry so much,' Colin said. Placing his hands on Luke's shoulders, he turned him around and pointed him towards the kitchen saying, 'Come on; let's have a bit of lunch.'

'I'm not hungry,' Luke replied.

'You'd be better having something to eat; it'll take your mind off things for a while. Have you still got your lunch in your school lunchbox?'

'Yes,' Luke said.

'Well, eat it now and I'll make myself a toasted sandwich. Do you want one?' Colin asked.

'No thanks,' Luke said. 'I'll make us a cup of tea.'

They eventually settled to eat their lunch, with little conversation between them, Colin broke the silence by saying to Luke, 'Remind me on Sunday to collect Ernie from the retirement home for church. He's much better and one of the other residents wants to come too, so that's good.'

'It'll be a tight squeeze in the car,' Luke replied.

'You can always go on your bike if the weather's fine or you can sit on Mum's lap like you used to,' he said, laughing.

'No way,' Luke replied. 'She can sit on mine now.'

Luke nearly jumped out of his skin when the telephone rang, saying, 'Quick Dad, that'll be the Police.'

'Calm down Luke, for goodness' sake,' Colin replied, getting up from the table, and said to Luke, 'Stay there and finish your lunch.' He left the room, closing the kitchen door behind him.

'Reverend Tewkes-Dawson,' Colin said into the handset. 'Can I help you?'

'Hello darling,' Alice said. 'Sally told me the police tried to ring me this morning. When I rang them back, they said it was alright, you were dealing with it. What's happened?'

'It's a long story, love,' Colin replied. 'There's nothing to worry about. I'll fill you in when you get home. Everything's alright, don't worry. What time are you finishing work today?'

'About 4 o'clock. Sally said she can manage after that.'

'Do you want me to pick you up?'

Sally replied, 'No it's a nice day, I'll walk; I'll have plenty of time to get dinner. Will you just peel some potatoes please?'

'Yes, I'll do that, love. See you later then?'

'Oh, by the way,' said Alice, 'how's Ernie?'

'Much better,' Colin said. 'He's coming on Sunday.'

'Good,' Alice said. 'OK love, bye for now.'

'Bye,' Colin said and replaced the handset. He was hardly at the kitchen door before Luke said, 'What did they say?'

'It wasn't the police, it was Mum—she's worried. The police tried to get hold of her earlier today and she didn't know why. I told her not to worry, everything was alright,' Colin said.

'I wish it was, "alright" I mean,' Luke said. 'This whole thing is a nightmare. I'm the one who's suffering, and I've done nothing wrong.'

'Remind you of someone, Luke?' Colin said questioningly. 'It puts things in perspective doesn't it, when you consider what our Lord went through, having done nothing wrong.'

'Yeah, I know,' Luke said, 'but it still hurts.'

'Right, Luke, go up and give your face a bit of a rinse, get rid of those tear stains and we'll go off and see your Mr O'Donnell.'

'He's not my Mr O'Donnell,' Luke said as he left the kitchen.

Colin washed up the few dishes from their lunch and noticed that Luke had hardly touched his lunchbox; he replaced the lid and placed it in the fridge, expecting Luke to be starving hungry when they got back with everything sorted out. When Luke reappeared, they went out to the car and headed off to school. On the way, Colin said to Luke, 'Let me do the talking Luke. You're too emotional to get involved. Despite Mr O'Donnell's animosity towards me, I think he'll be more disposed to reason if I speak to him.'

'Suits me,' Luke said. 'I would probably get into more trouble if I spoke to him. Besides, he doesn't like me either; he's made up his mind that I'm guilty.'

'That's why we're going to see him Luke, to put that right,' Colin said, patting Luke on the knee.

CHAPTER 3

Alice was in her element this morning. She enjoyed nothing better than shopping for supplies for the flower shop, despite having to drive Sally's bright pink van with numerous pictures of various flowers emblazoned all over it. The van was well known in the area and caused much amusement when it first appeared. After calling at several growers and suppliers, Alice was driving past her father's timberworks when she decided to pop in to see him.

Tom Maynard had undergone a triple by-pass operation a year ago and had only recently returned to the timberworks on a regular basis, against the advice of Alice and the rest of the family. The yard had run perfectly well in his absence, but Tom was not the sort of person who would sit back and feel sorry for himself. He had built up the business from scratch by sheer hard work and the business was his baby; he enjoyed being involved in it.

Tom greeted Alice with a hug and obvious delight to see her. 'What brings you here today?' Tom asked.

'I was out and about getting stuff for the shop and I was nearby, so I thought I'd pop in hoping the kettle was on in the office,' Alice replied.

'Good idea,' Tom said. 'It must be a good thirty minutes since I've had a cuppa.'

As they entered the office, Alice said:

'You know, I think the lovely smell of wood in this place almost pleases me as much as the scents in the flower shop.'

The office was a typical industrial office: the untidiest desk you could imagine; two chairs with threadbare seats; bits of timber samples all over the place; and a mucky shelf under the window with half a dozen unwashed mugs, an opened packet of teabags, and a half jar of instant coffee. At the far end of the office was a washbasin with hot and cold-water taps, but both taps only produced cold water. The kettle was on the floor because the lead would not allow it to reach any shelf or elevated position from the one electric socket in the office. To use the kettle, you had to first unplug the electric heater.

Alice filled the kettle and put it on, chose two mugs but washed them first, deciding against drying them with the grubby tea towel.

'Honestly Dad, you're asking for trouble with this germ-ridden towel and these mugs. Why don't you replace the towel with one from home, even once a week?'

'I keep meaning to,' he said, 'but I don't wash the mugs anyway, and the boys haven't complained.'

'Oh Dad, what are you like?'

'I've survived so far,' he said. 'Apart from my old ticker, I've never had a day off for as long as I can remember.'

'That may well be,' Alice said, 'but you're not getting any younger. Your immune system won't be as strong as it was you know, especially after your op. It will take time for your body to recover.'

'Will you stop fussing girl. I'm as fit as a fiddle now, never felt better,' Tom said.

Alice poured boiling water into the two mugs with a tea bag in each, put two sweeteners in her dad's mug and then asked where the milk was.

'I finished a carton earlier; I've got one in the car I picked up this morning. I'll go and get it.'

While her dad was out of the office, Alice poured the rest of the water from the kettle into the remaining mugs in the sink and then, after adding some cold water, she washed the mugs using her hands. She was in the process of placing them upside down on the shelf when her father re-entered the office empty handed.

'Where's the milk?' Alice asked.

'Whoops, sorry, I forgot. I was talking to the men, and I forgot what I went out for.'

Alice just shook her head and said, 'Men!'

They settled down at last at the desk and Tom said, 'So, how are things? Colin ok is he and that young whippersnapper of yours?'

'Yes, they're fine,' Alice replied. 'I just wish Luke would pay as much attention to his schoolwork as he does to his football, although to be fair he does try.'

'I wouldn't worry about it, Alice. I left school without any qualifications and look at me now. I've got a thriving business, I employ five men, I want for nothing and I owe nothing to no one. Education is not the be all and end all you know,' Tom said.

'He'll have more options in life with a good education Dad; things have changed since your days,' Alice replied.

'Luke will do alright, don't you worry; he's got a couple of good parents in his corner,' Tom said.

'Actually Dad, while I'm here there's something I want your advice on.'

'Shoot!' Tom said.

'When I arrived at the shop this morning, before we opened up, Sally said that she wanted a word with me. As you probably know, she is six months pregnant and has been feeling tired by the end of the day. After the trauma of her miscarriage last year, she does not want to jeopardise this pregnancy. She asked me if I was prepared to do full-time, instead of the three days I do now. That would be virtually managing the shop while she takes a step back; she said she would do the paperwork if I would run the shop. She would employ a junior to help me and if I needed time off for any reason, she would still fill in on the odd occasion. She has given me until the end of the week to think about it.'

'How long would it be for?' Tom asked.

'Six months,' Alice replied.

'You want to do it, don't you love?'

'Yes, I would love it,' Alice said, 'but I don't know if it would be fair to Colin and Luke. I like to be home for Luke when he gets home from school and, most days, I'm virtually Colin's secretary, fielding his phone calls and the like.'

'They manage perfectly well three days a week; what difference would an extra few days make?' Tom said.

'I must say, the extra money would be very useful these days; there seems to be no end to the increasing prices.'

'Alice, you know you only have to ask if you need anything. Don't struggle because you're too proud to ask.'

'I know Dad, but things aren't as bad as that. I probably worry too much.'

'What do Colin and Luke think about it?' Tom said.

'I haven't had the chance to tell them yet; this only came up this morning. We'll discuss it later.'

'Well, if you want my advice, go for it. You love the work; Sally has faith in you; and you say the extra cash is not to be sniffed at. It's a win-win situation as far as I can see.'

Alice stood, picked up the now empty mugs off the desk and, walking over to the sink said, 'I must be on my way. Sally will be wondering where I've got to.'

'Leave those mugs, I'll wash them later,' Tom said.

'Yes, of course you will, Dad,' Alice said washing them anyway. She gave her dad a peck on the cheek and said goodbye, taking the grubby tea towel with her.

'I'm going to put this on your car seat to remind you to bring in a new one tomorrow,'

'Get out of here,' Tom said, laughing.

CHAPTER 4

C olin was about to turn into the school gates, when he had to give way to a car emerging from the school. As the car drove off, Luke said excitingly, 'Dad, that's one of the policemen who were at school earlier this morning, the nice one. We've just missed him.'

'Never mind,' said Colin. We'll learn more perhaps when we see Mr O'Donnell.' Colin parked up and then they both went into school. On the way, some of the other pupils acknowledged Luke with a 'Hello Lim', 'Good to see you', 'Are you back?' etc.

'Hello what?' Colin said. 'What did they call you?'

'Lim,' Luke said. 'It's just a nickname, short for "limited".'

'That's a bit unkind,' Colin said.

'No, it's because of my initials Dad, L.T.D.'

'Oh, I see,' Colin said. 'That's very ingenious of them. Who thought that one out?'

'I don't know, it started ages ago,' Luke said.

As they approached the headmaster's office, Mr O'Donnell was hurrying down the corridor towards them. He greeted Colin with a handshake and said, 'Hello Mr Tewkes-Dawson, please come in.' He ignored Luke, but Luke followed his dad into the office and Mr O'Donnell followed on, closing the door behind him. He pointed to a chair, invited Colin to take a seat, and walked around the desk to sit in his chair. Luke stood alongside his father.

Mr O'Donnell placed the large pile of books he had been carrying on the desk in front of him and remarked, 'A bad business this, Mr Tewkes-Dawson, a bad business! I'm sorry I couldn't see you earlier but I had to take a class today; one of our teachers called in sick so couldn't come. You must be devastated over this affair; you have my sympathy. You do your best for your children and this is how they repay you, eh.' He went on to say, although not very convincingly, how shocked he was to learn that Luke had got involved in this sort of behaviour.

Colin jumped in straight away and said, 'But the point is, Mr O'Donnell, Luke had nothing to do with this incident in any way. He was at home all evening after church and was, in fact, probably fast asleep when this whole thing happened. That's why I am here now, to confirm this with you.'

'How can you be sure that's the case? Could Luke have left the house without your knowledge?' Mr O'Donnell replied.

'He would not do such a thing,' Colin said. 'Besides, he assures me that he did not, and I believe him implicitly; it's just not in his nature. He is the victim of a huge mistake somewhere along the line and I ask that he be reinstated at school immediately.'

'I'm sorry Mr Tewkes-Dawson, I'm not at liberty to do that. I have taken advice from the Education Authorities, and they have backed my decision fully. It is the policy of the Authority that, while a pupil is the subject of a police investigation, he shall be suspended from school until such time as the investigation is completed. Luke was positively identified as being present at the scene; I therefore have no choice but to continue his suspension.'

'How can I be identified as being there, when I wasn't?' Luke interjected.

Colin placed his hand on Luke's arm in a comforting manner and said, 'Alright Luke, alright. Let me deal with this please. We don't want anybody to get overheated and say things we might regret later.'

'But it's so unfair!' Luke said.

Colin turned to Mr O'Donnell and said, 'Who identified Luke as being present at the scene?'

'I'm sorry, Mr Tewkes-Dawson, it's not for me to divulge information which is subject to a police enquiry; it's out of my hands. You will have to contact the police on that score. In fact, I'm surprised you're here. I would have thought you'd be better contacting the police.'

'It was Tombsy. I'm sorry, Mr Tombs I mean,' Luke said. 'He was here this morning in this office and confirmed that I was the one he had pointed out to the policemen in the playground this morning, but he was wrong.'

'Well alright, since you already know that much,' Mr O'Donnell said, 'I can confirm that it was Mr Tombs, our caretaker, who identified Luke, but I'm afraid that's as much as I can say about the incident. Now if you will excuse me, I have to try and fit in a spot of lunch before I take another class. I can only express how sorry I am over this whole unfortunate affair.'

'Do you believe that Luke is guilty, Mr O'Donnell?' Colin asked.

'It's immaterial what I think Mr Tewkes-Dawson, but I am very surprised at Luke,' Mr O'Donnell replied.

'So, you won't cancel his suspension?' Colin pleaded.

'No, I'm sorry; I can't do that—not until I hear from the police.'

Luke burst into tears and ran out of the room. Colin thanked Mr O'Donnell for his time and left too, deliberately avoiding shaking hands with Mr O'Donnell. He was not very happy with him.

When Colin entered the corridor, he saw Luke further along sitting on the floor, knees drawn up with his arms wrapped around them. He could hear Luke sobbing. Helping him to his feet, Colin tried to comfort him by saying:

'Don't worry Luke, the truth will come out; you'll be cleared of all blame. We know you're innocent and that's what matters most. We just have to convince the police that's all. That'll be easier than trying to convince Mr O'Donnell. He's certainly not fighting your corner, that's for sure.'

'Look!' Luke said, pointing at the notice board. 'They've crossed my name off the team sheet for tomorrow's match. I missed last year's match 'cos they said I was too young; now I've missed this one as well!'

'Oh Luke, it's only a football game for goodness' sake. There are more important issues at stake here; your whole future could be affected by this. There will be other matches,' Colin said, leading Luke out of the building with his arms across Luke's shoulders.

'You don't understand Dad,' Luke said. 'This is the big match of the season and the whole school will be there. Everyone wants to play in this one, and just because of ...' Luke hesitated, 'somebody, I can't play.'

'Because of whom, Luke?' Colin said. 'You know who it was, don't you Luke. Are you protecting somebody?'

'I don't know who did the damage, but I know someone who was there, but I can't split on him,' Luke said.

'But you must Luke; he can clear your name. If you have any information that will help the police enquiry then it is your duty to inform them. Why should you protect him? He's not doing you any favours, is he? If, as you say, he didn't do the damage then surely you wouldn't be getting him into trouble would you, so what's the problem?' Colin said.

'I don't want to be called a grass Dad,' Luke said.

'So, you'd rather be called a criminal, would you? Think about it, Luke. I know what you're saying, but this could be cleared up so easily.'

As they approached the car, they saw that the car they had seen earlier, leaving the school, was parked alongside and the young police officer was sitting in it. He got out of his car and extended a hand to Colin and said, 'I'm D.C. Pinns from Winchester C.I.D. Mr Tewkes-Dawson, is it?' he asked.

'Yes,' Colin said, 'and this is Luke, my son.'

'Yes, I know,' D.C. Pinns said. 'We've already met, haven't we Luke?'

'Yes,' Luke said.

The officer said, 'I thought I recognized Luke in your car as you drove in the gates, so I came back hoping to have a word with you. Come and sit in my car and we'll have a chat.'

Colin sat in the front passenger seat and Luke squeezed into the back seat with difficulty. His knees were pressing against the back of the driver's seat and D.C. Pinns said, 'Crumbs! You are a big lad aren't you, Luke? Just a minute.' He pulled his seat forward and said, 'That better?'

'Yes, thank you,' Luke said.

D.C. Pinns turned side on as best he could to face Colin and said, 'Look, sir, for what it's worth, I don't believe for one minute that Luke had any part in this incident. I have just been to the school to take a formal statement from both Mr Tombs and the Deputy Head. They were involved in the identifying of Luke in the playground this morning and that's where the mistake was made.' He said to Luke, 'Luke, when you arrived at school this morning, there was another lad with you, wasn't there?'

'Yes,' Luke replied.

The officer continued, 'Well, when Mr Tombs pointed across in your direction, Mr Gibbs passed on your name to us thinking he was pointing at you. He wasn't. He was in fact pointing at ...', he consulted his notebook and said, 'Jason Penney. That's why you were called into the office this morning Luke.'

'Yes, but even in the office he said it was me.'

'I know,' the officer said. 'I have questioned him about that and he said he was too scared to say that the Deputy Head had made a mistake. He now says he was sure it was the lad who was with you, Jason, who he saw on the night in question, I've now got a statement to that effect. Without meaning to be unkind, you have to realize that your Mr Tombs' lift doesn't go all the way to the top, if you know what I mean.'

'So, Luke is in the clear?' Colin asked.

'Well, as far as I'm concerned, he is, but it's not down to me. I have to contact my D.S. and he can make the decision.'

'Will you make sure he lets the school know?' Colin asked. 'And me, of course.'

'Yes, I'll do that as soon as I've had a word with my D.S.'

'Thank you,' Colin said, 'and thank you for being so understanding. Will you now go and see this Jason Penney?'

'D.S. Belton is looking for him as we speak. He did a runner from school, didn't he Luke?' the officer said.

'Yes, all of a sudden he disappeared after he'd seen you and the others in the playground. He knew who you were.'

'I'm sure he did. We've met before. Anyway, I'll be in touch,' the officer said as he got out of the car to let Luke out.

Before they left, Colin said to the officer, 'I know you from somewhere, I just can't place where I've seen you.'

'I've been in your congregation two or three times,' he said. 'I can't always get there due to duties but I come when I can. I appreciate your ministry; you tell it as it is and not enough churches do that these days. I hope to be with you on Sunday; all this will have hopefully blown over by then.' The officer shook hands with Colin and with Luke, and they said their goodbyes.

Once they got into their own car, Colin asked Luke, 'Is this Jason boy the one you knew was involved?'

'Yes, he met me on the way home this morning. He said he was there, but he didn't do anything, I believe him Dad. He had started to walk away but went back for something, and that's when he was seen by Tombsy.'

'OK Luke, the police will sort it. Things are looking better, aren't they?'

'Can we contact Mr Preece, the sports master, and ask if I can play tomorrow now? He would want me in the team.'

'No Luke, we have to wait for the police to do their bit first.'

The rest of the journey home continued in silence, Luke deep in thought wondering why his world had crashed all around him. What had he done to deserve this? Life was so unfair. Never before had he been so keen to get back to school. There had been times when he wished there had been reasons for him not to go, especially out of the football season. He was not too keen on cricket but was a reasonable bowler and could swing a bat.

CHAPTER 5

Alice arrived back at the shop and apologised to Sally for having been so long. She explained that she had popped in to see her father on the way and she had stayed for a cup of tea. Sally did not mind at all, saying that she had not been too busy to cope.

Alice started to unload the van and said to Sally, 'Come and see these. I got them for a bargain at the garden centre.'

Sally went out to the van and said, 'Oh my gosh! Alice, how many have you got there?'

There were several crates of little pots of Polyanthus in a profusion of colours.

'A hundred,' Alice replied. 'I knocked them down to 40p each and we can sell these easily for £1.50 each. I'll make a display on the shelves outside the shop. They'll go like hot cakes, you'll see.'

'I hope you're right,' Sally replied.

'Trust me, Sally.'

'You give me no choice,' Sally replied laughingly.

After unloading the van and refusing Sally's help to do so because of her condition, Alice dragged the four-tiered display shelves out to the front of the shop and placed nearly all the pots on the shelves. The wintery sun shone on them, highlighting the rich deep colours of the blooms. Alice then went to the back storeroom and, after several minutes, emerged with a large placard which read, £1.50 each.

'Four for £5.00,' she said to Sally. 'What do you think?' showing her the board.

'Yeah, that's good. Here's the staple gun. You can attach that onto the shelves.'

Alice completed the job and returned into the shop to help Sally complete some orders for bouquets and wreaths for the next day.

While working together at the workbench behind the counter, Alice told Sally that she had mentioned her proposition to her father over a cup of tea; he had said that she should go for it.

'You want to do it, don't you Alice? I want you to do it too,' Sally said. 'I ask you for purely selfish reasons as I don't want to do anything to jeopardize the safe arrival of this little bundle here,' she said, patting her tummy. 'I know the shop would be in safe hands with you, even though you have purchased enough pot plants to compete with the council's Gardens Department,' Sally said teasingly. They both laughed.

'You think they're not going to sell, don't you?' Alice said. 'Just you wait and see.'

No sooner had Alice finished speaking, than a customer came in and asked for four of the pot plants outside the shop. Alice served her from the ones in the shop and, before placing the £5 note in the till, waved it in front of Sally's face saying, 'four gone, just ninety-six to go, oh ye of little faith,' she mocked.

After completing the orders, Alice said, 'I'd better get ready. Colin will be here in a minute to pick me up and it's nearly four. Now listen

Sally, don't even think about bringing that display inside yourself. Your husband can do that when he comes home,' Alice said.

'Don't worry; I wouldn't even try,' Sally replied, 'although it might be empty by then, all sold out.'

'Bye Sal,' Alice said, laughing.

'See you,' Sally replied.

Alice walked a bit further down the road where Colin could more easily stop to pick her up—'a good day,' she thought to herself, 'a good day'. Colin had phoned Sally to tell Alice he would pick her up at 4 o'clock. When Alice got into the car she said, 'I told you I was happy to walk home; why did you decide to pick me up?'

'I wanted to speak to you about Luke in his absence,' Colin replied. He then related the whole story, after parking the car near the bus station, finishing with, 'It's going to be alright as soon as the police make contact but they hadn't phoned by the time I left. Maybe they'll be a message on the answerphone when we get home.'

'Where's Luke now?' Alice asked.

'He's on his paper round; I bet he'll do it in record time today.'

'If the Police haven't phoned when we get home, we'll have to ring them,' Alice said.

'Yes, I will,' replied Colin.

When Colin had arrived home earlier with Luke, after speaking to the officer, he had said to Luke, 'Why don't you change and then go off and get your papers done out the way?'

'Might as well,' Luke had replied and disappeared upstairs, but not before checking the answerphone first. As he left the house, he called out, 'See you later Dad.'

'OK, Son,' Colin replied, 'mind how you go.'

When Luke arrived at the paper shop, Mr Patel said chirpily, 'Hello Luke, you're early. Have you been at school this afternoon?' he continued.

'No, it's a long story Mr Patel, but I've been off school today.'

'Anyway, your papers are all ready for you. Oh, by the way, I've arranged cover for you tomorrow; you've got a football match, haven't you?' Luke did not answer but Mr Patel noticed that Luke was shedding tears as he picked up his bag of newspapers. 'Whatever is the matter, Luke? What have I said?'

'It's not you, Mr Patel, but I may not be playing tomorrow.' Luke went on to tell Mr Patel the whole sorry story.

'I'm so sorry Luke. I've never heard anything so ridiculous in all my life, but you mustn't worry so; don't let it upset you. The truth will come out and everything will be fine. You trust in your God, don't you?'

'Yes, I do Mr Patel, but I can't help feeling angry and upset and helpless all at the same time.'

'I know, Luke,' Mr Patel said sympathetically. He patted him on the back and said, 'Come on now, take a deep breath, blow your nose and off you go. Here, take this to help you on your way,' and he handed Luke a small bar of chocolate.

'Thanks so much,' Luke said and left the shop.

When Luke finished his round, he decided to ride past Jason's estate to see if he could find him and speak to him. He did not know which number Jason lived at, so just rode around the various streets hoping to see someone to ask. Eventually he saw a group of youths together, some on bikes, some just standing around smoking. Luke spotted Jason sitting on his bike with his back to him. Luke just stopped and was wondering what to do when he saw one of the youths point his way. Jason turned and, on seeing Luke, he called, 'Lim,' and started riding towards him. When some of the others started to follow, Jason said to them, 'Wait here,' and they stopped.

'Hello Lim,' Jason said, 'what are you doing here?'

'I came looking for you, Jason. Have the police seen you yet?'

'No,' Jason replied. 'They called home earlier when I was out. My mum agreed to take me to the police station tomorrow morning.'

Luke filled Jason in with the further developments since he saw him earlier in the day. Jason was genuinely sorry about the football match but said, 'You'll still be able to play tomorrow after I've been to the police in the morning. I'll tell them the truth Lim; I'll tell them that you were not there, so you will still be able to play after all.'

'I hope you're right, but can't you go to the police station this afternoon? Now even?'

'No, they made an appointment for 9 o'clock tomorrow morning. They'll be off duty now I s'pose! Look Lim, I'm sorry about all this; I didn't expect all this to happen. I didn't want you to get into trouble. Are we still friends?'

'Yes, of course,' Luke said. 'I know all of this is some stupid mistake and it's not really your fault. Well, it is partly, 'cos you shouldn't have been there Sunday night. What will happen to you do you think?'

'Nothing much. They're not going to hang me or anything,' Jason said.

'Aren't you scared?' Luke asked.

'I'm more scared of my mum than the police,' Jason replied. 'She's going to kill me.'

'When you see the police tomorrow, will you ask them to phone the school straight away?'

'Yes, I'll do that Lim.' Jason turned his bike around and, as he rode off, he said, 'See you around Lim; behave now, won't you.'

Luke didn't find the remark very funny but said, 'See you,' and rode off home, deep, deep in thought and with his fingers crossed as he gripped the handlebars.

When Luke arrived home, he told his father of the encounter with Jason. Colin said he has not heard from the police and said, 'I don't expect we'll hear anything till tomorrow now, after they've dealt with Jason.'

'Nobody seems to realize how urgent this is,' Luke said. 'The match is at 4 o'clock tomorrow and I need to be back at school again so I can play.'

'There's no guarantee that you'll be back tomorrow, Luke; these things take time. The police have to be totally sure that you're in the clear. I believe your young detective knows that now, after speaking again to the caretaker, but don't count on Mr O'Donnell being disposed to do you any favours.'

Colin then told Luke that he was going to fetch his mum from work and asked Luke to peel the potatoes he had left on the draining board. 'I won't be long,' he said as he left the room, coming back to get his car keys which he nearly forgot. 'I can't even think straight at the moment,' he said. 'With one thing and another it's no wonder I'm losing my hair!'

'Losing the plot more like,' Luke retorted.

'I'll sort you out when I get back, boy. Now, get those spuds done.'

'Bye,' Luke said with a big grin.

After peeling the potatoes and cutting them into chips, he pulled out the deep fat fryer from its cupboard and partially blanched the chips. He took three pieces of frozen cod in batter from the freezer and placed them on a tray in the oven and opened a tin of mushy peas—his favourite meal.

After ensuring everything was OK in the kitchen, Luke got his football boots out, went into the utility room and cleaned them as best he could with a stiff brush. Then he gave them a polish. He noticed that the split in his right boot had got worse since he had last used them. He searched the garage until he found the roll of black sticky tape. There was very little left, but he taped up his boot as best he could, using the rest of the roll.

Colin and Alice arrived home and found Luke sitting at the kitchen table looking sorry for himself. Alice immediately embraced him and said how sorry she was that she was not home for him this morning. She said that he should have gone to the shop. Luke replied that he had not wanted to disturb her at work; he also had not wanted to miss his dad, if he came home.

Colin said, 'Listen, there's nothing we can do more today, so let's not dwell on it. We'll put our trust in God. "God will provide," Colin said out of context. 'He has never let us down yet.'

'Let's think about dinner, shall we?' Alice asked.

Luke said, 'I've peeled some potatoes Mum, and I've taken some cod in batter out of the freezer and opened a tin of mushy peas. Can we have chips?'

'I s'pose we've no choice then,' Alice said. 'Fish, chips and mushy peas wouldn't happen to be your favourite, would it Luke?' she said.

'At least you haven't lost your appetite,' Colin said to Luke.

Colin adjourned to his study with the newspapers, while Alice laid the table. Luke went to his room and just laid on the bed until it was time for dinner. Nothing much was said during the meal. Each seemed to have their own thoughts: Luke about the match; Alice about the job offer; and Colin about the car's service and his request for an increase in his pay from the district.

At the end of the meal, Luke asked if he could go outside for a while for a kick about. Alice said, 'No, not tonight, Luke. I want to talk to you both about something which came up at work today.'

'What about?' Colin asked.

'Let's get these dishes done and go into the lounge and I'll tell you then. Don't worry, there's no trouble or anything.'

All three helped with the clearing of the table and the washing up and then adjourned to the lounge, Luke taking a chocolate bar from the fridge with him.

'You can't still be hungry, Luke,' Colin said. 'You must have eaten half a loaf with your dinner, for goodness' sake.'

All three settled in the lounge and then, in all its detail, Alice told them of the offer that Sally had made. She was unable to say what her wages would be increased to, but said it would be at least double, going from three to six days a week. She said that she had told Sally she would discuss it with them and let her know at the end of the week.

Colin was the first to speak and said, 'What do you want to do?'

'It's not for me to say one way or the other, it all depends how you two feel.'

Colin said, 'As far as I'm concerned, it would not affect me very much at all; the answerphone fields all my calls when no one is home anyway, and I can be at home most times when Luke comes home from school. I say if you want it, go for it; I've no objection at all.'

'How do you feel Luke?' Alice said.

'Would it mean I could have some new football boots?' he asked.

'Oh Luke, is that all you think about?' Alice said. 'I take it you wouldn't mind then, Luke?' she said.

'No, of course not; why would I mind?'

'Well,' Alice said, 'you would be coming home to an empty house a bit more often.'

'I don't mind that, I have my papers to do anyway so I wouldn't be home alone for very long. Besides I'm fourteen, not four.'

'I take it that's a "yes" then. I can tell Sally that you agree.'

Colin raised his arm and said, 'You've got my vote.'

Luke copied him and said, 'And mine. Now can I go outside?'

'In a minute, Luke. Let's have a word of prayer.' Colin prayed, mentioning Luke's predicament, Alice's job and the general financial situation of the household.

After the 'Amen', Luke went off to play outside and Alice and Colin continued the debate on Sally's offer, both agreeing that it was an answer to prayer, regardless of the outcome of the review of Colin's stipend. She told Colin that she had discussed it with her father, and he encouraged her to do it. Alice said she hoped she was not being selfish in wanting to do it; she just loved the idea of running the business, almost as her own boss.

'Not at all,' Colin said. 'It's good that you enjoy your job. It'll be good for all concerned; you have no reason to feel guilty about it. I just hope it doesn't become too much for you. You're not getting any younger you know.' Colin said the last remark as he left the room, laughing, but could not avoid the thrown cushion which hit him on the back of the head.

Luke was up early the next morning, in time to join his parents for breakfast all together, then the usual morning prayers. Alice had no work today but said that she had to pop into town for some food shopping later on. She said to Luke:

'You will have to stay in this morning Luke, as Dad will be out and about visiting today, Dad's going to drop me off in town and I'll bus back. I shouldn't be too long, but somebody should be here if your school should phone.'

'I hope they don't leave it too late,' Luke said.

Colin said, 'It won't be at least until late morning, Luke, if the police have the interview with Jason first. Then they may have to speak to others before they contact the school, so don't build up your hope too much.'

Just after 9 o'clock, Colin and Alice left the house and Alice told Luke to do nothing until one of them gets back, but just wait by the phone. Luke got out a piece of writing paper and a pen and tried to list the names of the players he had seen on the notice board at school. It was not too hard to do; the team consisted of regular players who played often. He left the position of goalkeeper blank, knowing Jason would not be there; his own name he penned in but with a question mark alongside it.

Just after 10 o'clock, the phone rang. Luke flew into the hallway and picked up the phone. 'Hello, the Manse,' he said. A male voice asked for Mr Tewkes-Dawson. 'He's out at the moment, can I take a message?' Luke said.

'Yes, would you ask him to ring the Circuit Superintendent please; he has my number.'

'Yes, I will,' Luke said, and they said their goodbyes. Luke's shoulders slumped as he returned to the kitchen. He rolled his team sheet into a ball and kicked it around the kitchen for a while, then dumped it in the bin. He sat staring out the window and watched birds feeding at the bird table. 'It's alright for you,' he told them, 'You have no worries: your food is readily available; you can just fly off and do your own thing; you don't have friends who drop you in it.'

Then the telephone rang again. Luke again said, 'Hello, the Manse.'

'Is that Mr Tewkes-Dawson?' the voice said.

'No, this is Luke. My father's out, I'm afraid.'

'Oh, hello Luke, this is Mr Gibbs. I have some good news for you. The police station has just rung the school to say that you are no longer part of their enquiry. Mr O'Donnell has agreed that you be re-instated.'

'So, I can come back to school today then?' Luke asked.

'Yes, of course,' Mr Gibbs replied. 'I suggest you come in for 1 o'clock Luke, and see Mr O'Donnell when you come in, will you?'

'Yes, I will,' Luke replied.

'By the way, Luke. I hope you don't blame me for the predicament you found yourself in. I was surprised as anybody when Mr Tombs identified you. I know you better than that.'

'No, I don't, sir, and thank you, sir,' Luke said.

'Alright, goodbye, Luke.'

'Goodbye, sir,' Luke replied. He put the phone down and danced a little jig down the hallway and around the kitchen table. Looking out of the window, he said to the birds, 'You don't know what you're missing birds; you've never kicked a football.' Luke sat at the kitchen table and said a little thank you prayer; he did wonder why he was put through that trauma though.

CHAPTER 6

It seemed an eternity before any of Luke's parents came home, but Alice arrived first with bundles of shopping which Luke helped her to carry inside. He had met her at the gate and spilled out the good news in a gush.

'Thank goodness for that,' she said. 'You've been like a cat on hot bricks for the last twenty-four hours. Now make sure you thank Mr O'Donnell when you see him, won't you?'

'What have I got to thank him for? He hasn't done me any favours,' Luke said.

'Well, he's cancelled your suspension straight away Luke,' Alice replied. 'He could easily have left it until tomorrow, and that would have been too late for you wouldn't it, Gary Lineker?' she joked.

'How do you know who Gary Lineker is?' Luke said.

'I'm not completely ignorant you know, young man,' Alice replied. 'Enough chat now, help me put these groceries away and then I'll get you some lunch before you go off to school.'

They were both sitting at the table eating some toasted sandwiches when Colin arrived home. He was relieved when he heard Luke's news. He made tea for all three of them but declined anything to eat, stating that he had eaten cake on two of his last pastoral visits. He said, 'I really must book the car in for a service. It didn't want to start when I left Rosy Simpson's house. Fortunately, I was able to roll it down the hill and bump start it.'

'Ring up now while it's on your mind. It may be ages before you can book it in,' Alice said.

'Good idea,' Colin replied as he left the room.

After making the call, Colin went into his study and noted the date on the desk calendar and in his diary. He then remembered that, as he came into the house, he had picked up the post from the mat and placed it on the hall table while he removed and hung up his coat. He went out and retrieved it and returned to the kitchen.

Alice said, 'Were you able to book the car in?'

'Yes, they can actually do it Monday would you believe, and they can let me have a loan car for the day too. Well, they call it a loan car but there's a ten-pound charge to cover insurance and fuel used, so it's worth it to me,' he said. He handed Alice her two letters and opened the remaining one.

Colin's letter was from the Circuit Superintendent thanking him for his letter and inviting him to a meeting to discuss the contents in two weeks' time, giving a time and date. He showed it to Alice who, after reading it said, 'What was your letter about?'

'I've asked the circuit to give consideration to increasing my stipend. I told them that my last increase was two years ago and the Retail Price Index has increased considerably in that time. I also told them that the mileage allowance for the car was totally inadequate now, due to the big increase in the price of petrol.'

'While you're there, you might tell him that the Manse is in need of redecorating and those gutters need replacing too,' Alice said.

'I'll mention it if the opportunity arises,' Colin replied, asking Alice what her post was.

'I can't believe it,' she said. 'I've been invited to be a judge at the flower show in April in the flower arranging section. I can't do that; I've never done anything like that before.'

'You must,' Colin said. 'They wouldn't have asked you if they thought you couldn't do it. You're good at it so you ought to be able to judge it. Besides, you probably won't be the only judge, and you'll most likely know everyone there anyway.'

'I'll have to think about it,' Alice said.

Luke arrived at school in good time and went directly to the headmaster's office. He was inviting in after knocking on the door.

'Ah, Tewkes-Dawson,' the headmaster said, 'take a seat will you,' pointing to a chair directly in front of his desk. Luke was surprised at this; pupils are hardly ever invited to sit in the headmaster's office.

'Now Luke,' he said. 'I wanted you to know that I never believed you were involved in this unfortunate incident right from the start. My hands were tied, and I had no choice but to take the action I did at the time. I can tell you that I was as pleased as anyone when I received the phone call from the police this morning absolving you from all blame.'

Luke couldn't believe his ears at the totally different attitude of the headmaster since he last spoke to him. He didn't know what to say except, 'Thank you, sir.'

The headmaster continued: 'Now Luke, let this be a lesson to you. You must be selective as to who you choose as friends in the future. Do you understand?'

'Yes, sir,' Luke replied, 'but Jason Penney is not a particular friend of mine—just another classmate that's all.'

'Well, he won't be any more I can assure you. I can tell you that he will be expelled from school; this will be announced to the school formally at the next assembly.'

Luke didn't know what to say except, 'Is that all, sir? May I return to my class?'

'Yes, Luke,' the headmaster replied. 'Run along now.'

Luke was about to leave the room when he turned and said, 'Just one more thing, sir. Now that I am back at school, am I eligible to play football for the school as well?'

'Of course you are. All the usual privileges are restored as they were before your suspension. Are you thinking about this afternoon's match?'

'Yes, sir,' Luke replied.

'Well, you'd better see Mr Preece.'

'Thank you, sir,' Luke said as he left the room, closing the door behind him. He checked the notice board for the team sheet, but it was no longer on the board.

After Luke had left for school, Colin asked Alice if she had anything planned particularly for that afternoon. 'No, nothing special, why?'

'I thought Luke might like us to be at the match to watch him play, that's all.'

'That's a good idea,' Alice said. 'We can get some fish and chips for dinner on the way back. Luke would like that!'

'It's a bit extravagant when we've food in the house,' Colin said, 'but I suppose he deserves a treat after what he's been through in the last twenty-four hours. We'll have to leave about 3 o'clock,' Colin said. 'The match is being played on the university pitch, kicking off at 3:30pm.'

'That gives me time to do a bit of housework,' Alice said. 'What are you going to do?'

'I'll just work on my sermons for Sunday for an hour,' Colin said. 'Call me at 2:45, I'll just forget the time otherwise.'

Colin adjourned to his study and sat at his desk. He had difficulty in focusing his thoughts on his sermon. He just stared into space with all sorts racing through his head: Luke's scare with the arson incident; Alice's offer of the new position at the flower shop; the forthcoming meeting with the Circuit Superintendent; the car's service and the possible cost of that. He just could not concentrate at all.

He had hardly written a word when Alice called out, 'Time to get ready love.'

He looked at his watch and could not believe it was 2:40pm.

'Coming,' he called and joined Alice in the kitchen. 'Better wrap up warm,' he said. 'It'll be a bit chilly.'

Luke was on his way to the gymnasium to see Mr Preece when his form teacher, Mr Ward, spotted him.

'Hello Luke, I was told that you were back. I must say I'm happy at the outcome, which must have been a frightening experience for you.'

'Yes, sir,' Luke replied.

'Come on then, just in time for class. Walk with me.'

Luke hesitated and said, 'But ...', then he stopped.

'But what?' Mr Ward said.

'Nothing,' Luke said.

'What's bothering you lad?' Mr Ward said.

'I just wanted to speak to Mr Preece about the match, sir; he may not know that I'm back at school.'

'I'm sure he'll know, Luke; you can see him in the break anyway.'

'Yes, sir,' Luke said reluctantly.

Luke was visibly embarrassed when he walked into the classroom and the whole class clapped and cheered him. He quickly made his way to his desk and sat down. looking around, he saw several of his classmates giving him the thumbs-up sign and he felt good. The lesson continued but Luke would not be able to remember the tiniest part of the lesson; English Literature was not his favourite lesson and he just did not get William Shakespeare at all. The break could not come quickly enough as far as he was concerned.

At the end of the lesson, Mr Ward reminded the class that there would be coaches in the playground from 2:30pm; this class has been allocated coach No.5. He reminded the class that the best of behaviour was expected from them, both on the coach and at the match. He also informed them that all the staff would be there and he hoped that this class will not let him down. He reminded those who did not need transport to report to him at the coach anyway, and only those who had previously notified him, through their parents, were allowed to make their own way; otherwise, everyone else would be on the bus. The class was then dismissed. Luke approached Mr Ward and said he would probably not be on the coach as he would be on the team's bus.

'OK Luke, I'll note that on my sheet.'

Luke then made his way to the gym area to look for Mr Preece, but he was nowhere to be found; he went outside to the playground but he was not there. He knocked on the door of the staff room and, when one of the other teachers approached the room, he asked Luke what he wanted. Luke replied, 'I need to speak to Mr Preece,' he said.

'You're too late, lad. Mr Preece left with the football team about ten minutes ago.'

'He can't have,' Luke said. 'I'm on the team.'

'I don't know anything about that,' the teacher said. 'The football match is more trouble than it's worth, disrupting the whole school it is. Happens every year; money could be better spent in the science room if you ask me.'

Luke turned away thinking to himself, 'Just as well nobody did.' Luke was beginning to panic. 'What was Mr Preece thinking about, going without him. Did he know I was back? If he did, why didn't he contact me? What shall I do?' he thought. Then he went to Mr Ward and confirmed he would not be on the coach. He did not say why and hoped Mr Ward would not ask him; he did not. Luke decided that if he rode his bike to the university ground he would be there before the coaches; his coach was fifth in line anyway.

Luke was about ten minutes away from the ground when the first coach passed him. It was now 3 o'clock. One of the other coaches overtook him, then stopped further up the road. Mr Ward got out and signalled to Luke to stop.

'Why aren't you on the bus Luke?' he said. 'You told me you would be on the team bus.'

'I know,' Luke replied, 'but it had already left without me. I didn't know what to do. I didn't want to be late, and I didn't know what time the coaches were leaving, so I rode instead.'

'Well, I hope your parents won't mind,' Mr Ward said. 'OK, Luke, off you go then. Be careful.' Luke rode off in even more of a hurry.

When Luke arrived at the ground, he immediately looked for Mr Preece and then spotted him out on the pitch with the team who were all kitted out and having a gentle kick about. His heart sank; he obviously was not part of the preparation. He could not believe what was happening. He walked around the pitch to the nearest point where Mr Preece was and called out to him. He walked onto the pitch and, as he approached Mr Preece, Mr Preece said in surprise, 'Luke, what are you doing here? Should you be here?'

'It's alright now, sir,' Luke said. 'It's all been cleared up and I'm back at school; I can play now,' he said hopefully.

'I'm sorry Luke, it's not as easy as that. It wouldn't be fair if I left your replacement out now at this late stage. Besides, you hadn't been told that you were playing, had you?' Mr Preece said.

'No, but my name was on the team sheet on the notice board, sir, so I knew I'd been picked,' Luke replied.

'Yes Luke, but I was instructed to take it off when you were suspended. Nobody told me that you were back. Why didn't you come to see me?'

'I tried,' Luke said, 'but you were already gone.'

'I'm really sorry Luke, there's nothing I can do now; we kick off in ten minutes and we've already had our team talk and instructions. Now you'll have to excuse me. I must have a final talk with the team.'

Mr Preece walked away leaving Luke absolutely devastated. With tears rolling down his cheeks, he slunk away and was walking off when he heard his name called: 'Luke, Luke, over here!' He looked up and saw his parents approaching. 'Whatever's the matter?' his dad said. Luke told him the whole sorry tale and his mother held him in her arms saying, 'I'm so sorry Luke, I know how much you wanted to play and that's why we came to watch.'

'There's no point now,' Luke said. 'Might as well go home.'

'That's not the right attitude Luke. We must stay and support the school. If you were playing, you would be grateful for the support from the rest of the school, wouldn't you?'

'I suppose so,' Luke agreed.

There was probably a crowd of three to four hundred around the pitch when the two teams appeared, and the noise was tremendous as each school cheered for their own team. The ache in Luke's stomach increased as the start of the match grew nearer; he watched as the two captains tossed up in the middle and couldn't help thinking he should be there.

The match kicked off amid much cheering and encouragement from the crowd. Old Victoria College was doing most of the pressing and the school's defence were performing heroics to keep a clean sheet. Mr Preece was walking up and down the touch line, occasionally calling instructions and encouragement. With just a few minutes to go before halftime, Old Victorians had a free kick some 20 yards from goal. The kicker struck it hard at the defensive wall where it was deflected into the goal, giving the goalkeeper no chance. The Old Vics were 1–0 up at halftime, much to the delight of the rest of the college pupils and the groans of the school.

Luke perked up a little once the match was underway. Colin nudged Alice on one occasion and nodded towards where Luke was standing. Luke got quite exciting on a couple of occasions. 'He's OK,' Colin mouthed to Alice and she nodded in agreement.

The second half started with the school putting all the pressure on Old Vics but coming up against a brick wall of defence. Mr Preece had obviously given them a 'pep talk' at halftime; they were trying so hard but getting nowhere it seemed. Halfway through the second half, Mr Preece came up to Luke and said to him, 'Have you got your boots with you, Luke?'

'Yes,' he said.

Mr Preece said, 'Not those old taped-up things, are they?'

'Yes,' replied Luke, 'but they're OK,' he said.

'What size boots do you take?' Mr Preece asked.

'Nine,' Luke replied.

'Come with me lad; you needn't bring your boots.'

He led Luke into the dressing room and said, 'There's some kit there; get it on. I'm putting you on, we're getting nowhere out there.' Mr Preece took off his own boots and said, 'Wear these. They are a nine, so should fit you.' He put on his own shoes and on leaving the dressing room said, 'Hurry now, and report to me when you're ready.'

Luke had never changed so fast in his life; it was all he could do to stop himself from dancing around the room. Within five minutes flat he was standing at Mr Preece's side ready to go. Mr Preece signalled to the referee that he wanted to make a substitution; the referee acknowledged him and, when play next stopped, he signalled to Luke. Mr Preece called and beckoned Tommy Price to come off and he sent Luke on to the field to play. There was less than fifteen minutes left to play.

As Luke ran onto the pitch, the whole school seemed to shout, 'Go Lim, go Lim, go Lim!'

Alice turned to Colin and asked, 'What are they calling out?' Colin told her of Luke's nickname. 'I didn't know they called him that,' Alice said.

'Neither did I until yesterday; he doesn't mind it,' Colin said.

The match progressed with the school still pressing the college defence and they eventually won a corner. The right winger took the corner—a high one. Luke had taken up a position by the near post. When the ball reached him, with just a flick of his head, he guided it into the goal: 1–1. Luke ran around like a banshee waving his arms in the air with several of his teammates trying to catch him to celebrate. He ran past his mum and dad with a huge grin on his face. He looked at Mr Preece and saw that he was clapping enthusiastically. The noise from the school supporters was unbelievable, still shouting, 'Go Lim, go Lim, Go Lim!'

The Old Vics made two substitutions and started to press strongly, putting the school defence under pressure again. Luke had dropped back to help but Mr Preece called out to him. When Luke looked across, Mr Preece was pointing forward, indicating for Luke to stay forward.

With just minutes to go the school's goalkeeper was in possession of the ball and took it to the edge of his area, where he gave it an almighty punt upfield towards Luke. Luke met it, controlled it on his chest and, before the ball reached the ground, Luke spun and hit it like a rocket. The ball hit the back of the net before Old Vic's keeper could move.

Luke fell on his knees with fists clenched and then was pounced on by his teammates. The school supporters went absolutely wild. Order was restored and the game restarted but within a minute the final whistle was blown. The school team were absolutely delighted, as was Mr Preece, who was almost the first to shake Luke's hand and say, 'Well done. Luke that last goal would have won any match!'

Luke eventually extricated himself from the melee and went across to his parents, where he got a handshake and a 'Well done!' from his dad and a big hug from his mum.

After the furore and excitement had died down, the two teams were asked to form a semi-circle at the side of the pitch, a few yards away from a small table. On the table stood a magnificent silver trophy. Crowds of onlookers stood behind the two teams to watch the presentation and listen to the short speech by the principal of Old Victoria College.

The principal thanked the two teams for a splendid afternoon's entertainment and said that he was sure the match was enjoyed by all. He paused to wait for the subsiding of applause and then went on to congratulate Manleigh Grammar School on their win. He then addressed Mr Preece and said, 'We ought to be grateful to you Mr Preece for not having this young man on the pitch at the start,' pointing at Luke, 'as we may have received a right drubbing.' Turning to Luke, he said, 'Well played young man,' amid loud applause from all present. Luke was visibly embarrassed but managed a faint 'Thank you.'

The principal then said, 'Now to present the trophy to the winning captain, but bear in mind it's only lent out until next year.' There were friendly jeers from the Manleigh pupils at this remark and smiles all round. The principal asked for their captain to come forward.

Manleigh's captain of the day left his place and walked over to

Luke and said, 'We've decided you should receive the trophy, Luke; you go and receive it.'

Luke looked at Mr Preece who just nodded his head and pointed to the table. Luke stepped forward amid loud applause and cheering. He shook hands with the principal and then accepted the trophy from him. He turned around and held it aloft, prompting even louder cheers. He spotted his mother and father in the crowd who both gave Luke the thumbs-up sign.

After the trophy had been passed from player-to-player, Mr Preece took charge of it and asked the boys to get changed as the bus was waiting; the crowd was also dispersing and the Manleigh pupils were making for their coaches for transport back to school. Colin waylaid Luke on his way to the dressing room to ask if he had his cycle lights with him; he did. Luke was told not to hang around as fish and chips were being collected on the way home: 'See you at home, Luke,' he said.

'Bye Dad,' Luke said. When he got into the dressing room, he took off Mr Preece's boots and said he would take them home to clean them.

Mr Preece said, 'You keep them, Luke. I've got a new pair I haven't worn yet. Just bin your old ones, will you?' he said.

'I will,' Luke said, 'thank you'.

Luke was floating on air on the way home. He was singing as he rode, causing not a little amusement to passers-by. Some looked at him a bit weirdly but Luke just waved at them with a big grin on his face. He had never felt better in his whole life. He didn't allow himself to think about the previous 24 hours or so. They were history as far as he was concerned, but he remembered to say a prayer of thanks as he rode along, thinking, 'You're right Dad, God does answer prayer.'

The family virtually arrived home at the same time. Luke was instructed to go and wash his hands while his mum got the table ready and plated the fish and chips. Colin buttered some bread and made a pot of tea. After Colin had said Grace, Luke tucked in. Never had fish and chips tasted so good. His mum had to tell him to stop wolfing down his food or he would end up with indigestion: 'Sorry Mum but this is so good,' he said with a big grin on his face.

Colin said, 'Luke, I'm happy that things turned out so well for you. You must remember to give thanks to God. You asked him to help you when you were in difficulties, so it's the least you can do.'

'Dad,' Luke interrupted, 'I have already done that. I thanked Him on my way home.'

'Good, well done,' Colin said. 'You see, the Lord will provide.'

Alice said, 'I wondered how long it would be before you came up with that!!' They all laughed.

'By the way, what football boots were you wearing today, Luke?' Colin asked.

'Mr Preece's. He gave them to me. After the game he said I could keep them as he had a new pair anyway. And before you say it Dad, yes, I did thank him.'

'That was kind of him,' Alice said. 'Where's your old ones?'

'In a skip at the university,' Luke said. 'I don't want to see those again.'

After dinner, Luke went into his room and laid on his bed. He replayed his part in the match over and over again. After a short while there was a knock on his door and his dad came in and said, 'Luke, do you have anything to tell me?'

'What about?' Luke asked.

'Well, have you taken a message for me from anybody? On the phone perhaps?'

'Oh Dad, I'm sorry, I forgot. The Superintendent rang yesterday; I completely forgot all about it.'

'I know, he just rang me. I'll forgive you this time as you had a lot on your mind, but I'll need to have a talk to you sometime soon. Come down for prayers now and then I suggest you go to bed; you've had a big day.'

Luke followed his dad downstairs and after evening prayers Luke suddenly felt really tired. He was asleep in minutes.

On the Saturday of that weekend, at breakfast, Colin announced that, on the next weekend, they were going to be favoured with a visit from the Circuit Superintendent, arriving on the Saturday morning and leaving on the Monday morning. He would be preaching at two of the churches on the Sunday and wanted to meet firstly with Colin on the Saturday and then, a joint meeting with all three congregations on the Saturday evening, where he would make an important announcement.

'Did he tell you what it was about?' Alice asked.

'No, but I think I have a good idea of what it might be, but I'll keep my thoughts to myself at the moment. Is it alright if we put him up for the weekend love? I told him it would be alright; I hope you don't mind?'

'No, not at all. He's good company, old Willsy,' Alice said.

'The Reverend Wills, I think you mean,' Colin said.

'Yes, that's right, old Willsy,' Alice said mischievously. Colin just shook his head.

Luke said, 'It wouldn't half be funny if you called him that to his face by accident.'

'That's not likely Luke, I can assure you. Just make sure you don't either,' she said.

Luke said, 'I'm going to get ready; we've got a match this morning.' (Luke played for a local junior club side on Saturday mornings.) 'It's a home match, so I can bike it, Dad. Don't want to overstrain the car before its service, do we?'

'Time you went I think, Luke,' Colin said. Luke left the room to get ready, firstly giving his 'new' boots a clean with a stiff brush. After he had left the kitchen, Colin said to Alice, 'I wouldn't be surprised if the Super is going to tell me that they're closing down Skipton and combining the congregations with either Manleigh or Rushton—probably Rushton as it's nearer to Skipton. That won't go down too well with Skipton; they are old stuck in the muds up there, but we'll see.'

'It seems the sensible thing to do doesn't it. There's not many at Skipton for such a large building,' Alice said.

'It would certainly make things a lot easier for me, that's for sure, but we're just speculating; it might be something completely different,' Colin said as he got up and left the room. On departing he said, 'Are you walking into the shop, or do you want me to drop you off?'

'I'll walk; it's a nice day,' she said. 'The walk will do me good, but you could pick me up at four please?'

'Will do,' Colin said. He kissed Alice and went to his study. 'See you later,' he said.

'Bye love,' Alice replied.

When Alice arrived at the shop, she noticed that the display with the pot plants was not outside the shop. After greeting Sally, she said, 'Where's the Polyanthus?'

Sally replied with a grin, 'What Polyanthus?'

'Are they all gone?' asked Alice.

'Every one of them; they went like hot cakes. You see Alice, you have a feel for this sort of thing. Have you spoke to Colin about my offer?'

'Yes, both Colin and Luke have no objections. If the offer is still there, I'd like to accept,' Alice said.

'That's wonderful news, thank you so much Alice! That's taken a load of my mind. Is Monday too soon to start or do you need more time?'

'No, Monday's fine,' Alice replied.

The conversation for the rest of the day sorted out all the details of opening and closing times, ordering, employing a junior and, of course, Alice's increase in salary, which was more than doubled to account for the extra hours and the responsibility. In fact, Alice even questioned if the sum offered was too much for the shop to absorb, what with employing a junior as well. Sally assured her that she had been through it thoroughly with her accountant and he saw no problems at all. Alice was inwardly thrilled to bits, and she knew Colin would be pleased too. Alice's only disappointment that day was that she was unable to obtain any more Polyanthus plants.

When Luke arrived at the pitch for the match, his team coach said to him, 'Well played yesterday, Luke; I saw the match. Same standard today please. I'm glad you didn't play the full match; you'll have plenty of running in you for today. I'm hoping for at least a hat-trick out of you. I was surprised you weren't on from the start?' Luke just shrugged his shoulders; he wasn't going into all that again. When Luke took his boots out of his bag, his coach said, 'Hey, what's this? New boots at last. That definitely means a hat-trick.'

'Mr Preece, our sports master, gave me these; they're good boots.'

'I can see that,' the coach replied. 'Five minutes,' he said, 'then out onto the pitch please, altogether—not dribs and drabs. Let's start as we mean to go on, as a team.'

Luke had his usual good game, although it was an under-16 side. Luke stood out among the rest, despite his age. He was unstoppable in possession of the ball and his speed was just too much for the opposition. Luke scored two goals in a 5-1 win and was disappointed he had not scored more. He was sorry when the final whistle went; he felt he could have played for ages yet.

He got a 'Well done!' from the coach and a joke saying, 'The boots were not as good as I thought—only two goals.'

'Yeah, but I made the others,' Luke replied, cheekily.

The coach smiled and said, 'Well done lads. Three good points today, well earned.'

On the way home, Luke popped into Mr Patel to collect his money as usual and treated himself to a bar of chocolate and a can of drink. Mr Patel remarked how good it was to see him back to his usual chirpy self.

'Have those on the house Luke,' he said, pointing to the chocolate and drink.

'Thanks Mr Patel, that's really kind of you,' Luke said.

'See you Monday, Luke,' Mr Patel said as Luke turned to leave.

'Sure thing, Mr Patel,' Luke replied.

CHAPTER 7

On the Sunday morning the family all went to church, collecting Ernie on the way from the retirement home. Ernie's friend had changed his mind at the last minute, so Luke need not have gone on his bike, but he didn't mind as it was a nice day. When Luke arrived at the church, he saw the young detective, D.C. Pinns, getting out of his car and went up and spoke to him. 'Hello Luke,' D.C. Pinns said, 'how are you?'

'Fine thanks,' Luke replied.

'I might as well tell you Luke that your friend, Jason Penney, and his mates are going to court—the Juvenile Court—in a couple of weeks' time. I don't know what the Court will do. They're all pleading guilty, but I think Jason is being hard done by. By all accounts, his part in the incident was minimal really, but we'll see. He'll have to hope that the Court realizes this and won't be too hard on him, eh?'

'He's not my friend really,' Luke said. 'He's just a schoolmate … well, was a schoolmate.'

'He needs a new set of friends,' D.C. Pinns said. 'They're a bad lot he mixes with.' They both went into church together and D.C. Pinns asked Luke if his father was preaching today; Luke replied that he was. 'Good,' D.C. Pinns said. 'I like his preaching.'

Luke met his mother in the church and sat by her. D.C. Pinns saw

Luke speak to her and she turned around. Luke pointed at him, then he got up and approached D.C. Pinns and said, 'Mum asked if you would like to come and sit with us?'

'Yes, thank you,' he said, walked forward and shook hands and introduced himself to Alice. She said she was pleased to meet him and thanked him for the kind way he had dealt with Luke. 'My pleasure,' he said. 'He's a good lad, Mrs Tewkes-Dawson.'

'Oh please, call me Alice,' she said.

'OK, I'm Roger,' he replied.

The service commenced and, as Colin arrived in the pulpit, he noticed Roger Pinns sitting with the family and Ernie and he nodded to them with a smile. There was a good congregation that morning, about sixty-five to seventy, including about twenty young people who went out into the rear hall with three teachers for the Sunday School. Luke asked Alice if he could stay in the church, and she agreed.

At the end of the service, Alice told Roger what a wonderful singing voice he had; this had been noticed by other members of the congregation too.

'Thank you,' Roger said. 'I used to sing in a choir.'

Colin greeted Roger at the door on the way out and remarked how good it was to see him. 'Day off today?' he asked.

'Yes, one of my few weekends off,' Roger replied. 'They seem few and far between these days. I don't like working weekends but it's the nature of the job, I'm afraid.'

'Same with me,' Colin said, with a grin and they all laughed and said their goodbyes.

'Nice chap,' Colin said to Alice.

'Yes, he is a lovely young man,' she replied.

Colin said, 'Why don't we invite him for lunch today? Would we have enough for another person?'

'Yes, of course, good idea. Luke, quick, run out and ask him.' Luke returned to say that he had said thank you, but his mother was expecting him, perhaps another time. 'OK Luke, thank you. Off you go, no dawdling. You can set the table if you're home before us, but don't forget to change first, will you.'

'Yes, OK,' Luke said. Roger waved at Luke as he drove out of the car park.

Before Colin was able to leave, he was approached by one of his stewards who asked him if it was true that they were going to close Skipton and merge their congregation with us. 'Where on earth did you hear that?' Colin said, shocked.

'Oh, I just heard it on the grapevine,' he said.

'Well don't you start putting that around because no such decision has been made. It would be most unfair to the folks at Skipton if they heard that. I'm preaching there this evening and I don't want to have to field that sort of question from them.'

'I won't,' the steward said, 'but the rumour is being floated around. They may have heard it, but not from me,' he said.

'Keep it that way,' Colin said. 'I've got a meeting with the Circuit Superintendent next Saturday, as you know, and he will be here next weekend.'

The following Monday was an eventful day for all three members of the family. For Alice, it was her first day in charge of the shop, so she got there early and learned from Sally that she could have full use of the shop's van; she could take it home at night and at weekends if she wished. She told Sally that it would be really handy and would save Colin having to pick her up or bring her in when it rained. She laughingly said Luke might feel a bit embarrassed to have such a gaudy-coloured van in the drive; he had always thought its décor was a bit over the top.

Sally introduced her to her new assistant. Christine was sixteen years old and a pretty, petite girl who lived with her mother not far from the shop. She was working for at least the next twelve months before going on to university and was desperate to save as much as she could to contribute towards her student fees. She told Alice that she loved flowers and wanted to learn as much as she could about their names etc., as it would be helpful to her for her course in Horticulture at university.

'Ideal,' thought Alice, a pleasant girl and keen to learn. Alice said she would also teach her how to make wreaths, bouquets etc. Christine was to work 9am–4pm, Mondays to Fridays and the Saturday girl would come in as usual. Alice would not have a set day-off but would take the odd half-day, when necessary. Sally would fill in, if and when necessary. A good arrangement all round as far as Sally was concerned.

Alice and Christine got cracking straight away making several wreaths for a forthcoming funeral. Alice was pleased how quickly Christine learned and, before the morning was out, she was making some almost unsupervised, just asking Alice for advice on occasions. It was immediately apparent to Alice that Christine enjoyed the job and would be a great help. She was also very good with customers too, very polite and pleasant. When Sally appeared later with tea and hot crumpets, Alice took the opportunity of telling her how good she thought Christine was going to be in the shop.

Sally said with a grin, 'She should be, she's my niece after all.'

'Really?' Alice said. 'Chip off the old block then, eh?'

'Almost,' Sally said. 'She's my husband's niece really. She's had a little bit of a rough time recently. Her dad left home for another woman, and she was close to her dad. Naturally the income has suffered so she really needs this job more than ever.'

'What a shame,' Alice said. 'She's such a nice girl.'

Luke was the centre of attention when he got to school. The news of the match had permeated among the pupils and staff. He was congratulated by many of his classmates and members of staff; even the headmaster, Mr O'Donnell, had said, 'Well done,' in passing. Luke felt on top of the world and just knew it was going to be a good day, until he was reminded that there was a double maths lesson that morning—not Luke's favourite subject by any means.

After Colin had spent a couple of hours in his study doing administrative stuff, he went out visiting. He decided that he would particularly visit the folk who attended at Skipton. Nothing had been said to him about the possible closure of those premises at the weekend but he wondered if they would be more likely to mention it on a one-to-one basis. Also, he thought that, because the congregation consisted of more elderly folk, they would be more likely to be in.

After the first three calls, he was pleased that the subject had not been raised. On his fourth call, however, old Mr Hickson jumped straight in with the question, 'Have you called to tell me Skipton is closing?'

'Not at all,' said Colin. 'It's just a social visit.'

'But is it closing?' Mr Hickson persisted. Colin had to convince him that no decision had been conveyed to him on that score and he did not know how all this conjecture started. Just because Revd Wills was visiting the circuit did not necessarily mean that there was a specific reason for his coming.

'We'll have to wait for the weekend and see. In the meantime, let's not speculate on what might or might not happen.'

'Well, I can tell you everybody at Skipton believes he is coming to announce our closure and, what's more, a lot of them have said they will not go anywhere else if we are closed down.'

'Do you say that too?' Colin asked.

'Well, I've been attending Skipton for over forty years,' Mr Hickson said. 'I can't envisage myself going anywhere else at my time at life. No disrespect to you, Reverend, but one gets attached to a place after so many years.'

Colin said, 'Well, perhaps it may not come to that, but you would be getting the same message whether you were at Skipton, Manleigh or Rushton—it's only a building after all. But let's drop the subject as we don't know what God has planned for any of us do we? He will provide.'

Colin said his goodbyes and left, having had confirmations of what he thought general thinking was in the congregation; he suspected deep down that they were right too.

It was approaching 11 o'clock when Colin suddenly remembered that his car had to go to the garage that morning for its service. He drove immediately to the garage and apologized for not taking it in first thing. They were understanding and agreed that they could still do it that day.

He drove away with the courtesy car, feeling good to be driving a decent car for a change. He called into the flower shop to see Alice on his way and enjoyed a cup of tea with her, learning that she had her own transport now on her working days. She told Colin that one of the customers had asked her if it was true that the church at Skipton was going to close and the congregation merge with Manleigh.

'Oh dear,' Colin said, 'I knew this would happen. The sooner the weekend is here the better. All this speculation is causing unnecessary fears and dread for the Skipton folk.' He told Alice of his conversation with Mr Hickson earlier that morning and said this was probably being repeated all over the county.

As he was leaving the shop, he met the postman and said, 'Anything for me?' The postman looked in his bag and pulled out a small bundle of mail and handed it to Colin. When he sat in his car he sifted through the bundle and saw that there was one addressed to Luke. He saw that the envelope was personalised in the top left-hand corner with a logo of some sort and the letters H.C.F.C. He dismissed it from his mind and drove home, remembering to park in such a way as to allow Alice to park the flower-shop van in the drive when she got home. Colin sorted out the letters in his study and went into the kitchen to start preparing dinner.

A short while later Luke arrived home, popped his head round the kitchen door and said, 'Hi Dad, just going up to change before I do my papers. A cup of tea would go down well before I go off.'

'You know where the kettle is,' Colin replied but a cuppa was ready by the time Luke came down again and he joined his dad at the kitchen table. 'Oh, by the way, a letter came for you today; it's on my desk in the study. Would you bring the others through as well please.'

Luke was already opening his letter when he returned. He sat down to read it then suddenly jumped up and, punching the air with his fist, he danced around the kitchen saying, 'Yes, yes, yes!'

Startled, Colin said, 'What on earth is all that about?'

Luke blurted out, 'I've been selected for trials for the County Youth Team.'

'Let's have a look,' Colin said and read the letter. He saw that Luke had indeed been invited to take part in an all-day trial's session on the 23rd of that month at the *Hampshire County Football Club*'s premises from 10am to 4:30pm and lunch would be provided. 'Well, congratulations,' Colin said. 'I guess for a fourteen-year-old that's quite an achievement, but remember Luke, it's only trials. Let's check the calendar.' When Colin returned to the table with the calendar, he pointed to the 23rd and said, 'Look Luke, it's a Sunday.' He looked Luke in the eyes and said, 'Sorry Luke, you know what that means don't you?'

'Oh Dad, it's the chance of a lifetime. Just this once wouldn't hurt surely?'

'Do you even have to ask Luke?'

'It's so unfair Dad. You know what this would mean to me, and I may never get another chance.'

'Yes, I do know what it means to you Luke, but I also know what the Lord's Day should mean to you too. I don't think you need me to tell you where your priorities ought to lie, do you?'

Luke knew in his heart of hearts that there was no way he was going to make those trials; he burst into tears. Colin placed his arms around Luke and tried to comfort him. He tried to reassure him, saying that he was still young and that there will be other opportunities, but Luke said, 'If you say once more "The Lord will provide", I'll scream.'

'Believe me Luke. If it's meant to be then it will be.' Colin passed the letter over to Luke and said, 'Now, pull yourself together and ring that number. The letter says you have to inform them if you can attend or otherwise; ring them now and get it over with.'

Luke took the letter and went into the hallway to phone. When the call was answered, Luke said who he was and explained that because of his church commitments he could not attend the trials on the 23rd but thanked them for the invitation anyway. The reply he got stunned him in his tracks and he asked the man on the other end to repeat what he had said.

He said, 'That's alright, come on the 22nd instead. We have trials on that day too. Can you make it then?'

'Yes, yes I most certainly can.'

'Good,' the man said. 'See you then.'

Luke bounced into the kitchen and blurted out the telephone conversation to his dad, who was delighted for him and was about to speak, but Luke said first, 'Yes, I know Dad, the Lord will provide.'

'Get on your bike and get those papers done,' Colin said.

'I'm on my way,' Luke replied as he left the kitchen.

'What about your cup of tea?' Colin said.

'You can have it,' Luke replied.

Colin just shook his head. 'Kids!' he said to himself. 'I dunno.'

Luke, in a cheerful state, collected his papers and went on his round. On the way he called in to the flower shop to tell his mother the good news.

'When is it?' Alice asked.

'On Saturday 22nd of this month. It's all day and they'll provide lunch as well.'

'Oh no! That's all my plans up the creek then,' said Alice.

'What plans?' Luke asked.

'Well, I was going to arrange a barbecue for you with some of your pals for your birthday.'

'Of course,' Luke said, 'it's my birthday. I'd forgotten about that; I thought the date rang a bell.'

'Oh Luke, you're hopeless. Fancy forgetting your own birthday. Maybe we can arrange something anyway.'

As they were talking Christine came out of the back room into the shop with a wreath for Alice to check out. Alice said, 'Christine, this is my son Luke. Luke, this is Christine, our new girl in the shop.'

'Hello,' Christine said. Luke just stared, his eyes nearly popping out of his head. He thought he had never seen such a beautiful girl in all his life.

'Luke,' Alice said. 'Christine says "Hello".'

Luke came to his senses and managed to mumble some sort of greeting to Christine but was otherwise dumbstruck. Alice just grinned at Luke's reaction to Christine; she was a pretty girl. 'You'd better be on your way to get those papers done,' Alice said.

'Yes, yes of course,' Luke stammered.

As he was leaving the shop, Christine called out, 'Congratulations Luke on your match the other day. You're quite the hero on the back page of the local paper, but I must say the photo doesn't do you justice.'

Luke blushed and said, 'Me? On the paper? I haven't seen that. I have been delivering them and I hadn't noticed. I must look and see it.'

When Luke got out to his bike, he sat on the saddle and took up a paper and read the back page, and then read it again. He winced when he saw the photograph; it was a school photo, probably a year old. He put the paper back in his bag and poked his head into the shop. Christine had returned to the back room. He said to Alice, 'Tell Christine that was an old photograph, Mum. It's awful.'

Christine reappeared and said, 'I can see that, Luke. You're much better looking than that photo.'

Luke just blushed and said, 'Bye, see you!' He left waving as he rode off and thinking he must pop in and see his mum more often. He was totally smitten with Christine, and he could not get her out of his head. Even his forthcoming trials were pushed to the back of his mind, well temporarily anyway.

When Luke arrived home just before dinnertime, he saw a strange car in the driveway and his curiosity was aroused. When he met his dad in the kitchen, he asked about the car and his father told him it was his loan car from the garage. Apparently, they had found a serious fault in his car which they could not fix until the next day.

'That sounds a bit expensive,' Luke said.

'I know, I'm dreading the final bill,' Colin said. 'Set the table please, Luke. Mum will be here from work soon.'

'How is she getting home?' Luke asked.

'She's got the use of the shop van, so she's got her own transport. It's much more convenient for everybody.'

'Don't tell me it's going to be parked in the driveway,' Luke said. 'How embarrassing is that!'

'Where else would she park it?' Colin said. 'You may knock it, but you'd be grateful for a lift to school in it when it's pouring with rain.'

'I'd rather get wet,' Luke said.

'I'll remind you that you said that one day,' Colin said laughingly.

'By the way Dad, have you seen the local paper today?'

'Yes, Son, I have. Now don't you go and get all above yourself. It's only a football match; you haven't saved the world from destruction you know. But congratulations, well done. You did play very well.'

'Thanks,' Luke said. 'I'm going to start a scrapbook for all my press cuttings,' he said.

'That's a bit presumptuous, Luke. Who says they'll be any more?'

'There will Dad, you'll see. And one day, I will be in the national papers too and when I score the winning goal for England, it will be on the front page.' They heard Alice reversing the van into the driveway and Luke just groaned and, looking out the window, said, 'Just look at that monstrosity. It's going to be the talk of the neighbourhood.'

'That's just what Sally wants,' Colin said. 'It's good for her business, clever advertising, I think. It will stick in people's minds and, when they need flowers, where will they go? That shop with the van.'

'Whatever,' Luke said resignedly. 'I just wish it could be anywhere else other than on our driveway.'

Once they had settled down for dinner together, there were many topics of conversation discussed. Colin mentioned his concern over the cost of the car and said how grateful he was that at least the garage was waving the £10 fee for the courtesy car for the second day's use and added that it may help to soften the blow when the final amount was submitted.

'You have to have a car love,' Alice said, 'so whatever it costs it's a necessary expense and you need it to be reliable. You can't afford to breakdown when you're out Skipton way or somewhere remote on your travels, but perhaps you won't be going out Skipton way for much longer. Everybody knows Skipton's going to close. It's all around the town.'

'Yes, I know, but until it's official we can't go around saying that.'

'So, you think it's going to be official then do you?' Alice said.

'I'm pretty sure it is,' Colin replied, 'and that's why I think the Superintendent of the circuit is coming at the weekend. I know the Skipton folk will be upset but they'll see the logic of it in due course. It's the only way to go; the upkeep of the building is costing a fortune and the sale of the building would provide much needed cash, which, I am led to believe, must stay in the circuit and cannot be directed elsewhere.'

'That means we may get the work done on this place then and your stipend increase could be looked on more favourably,' Alice remarked.

'Don't jump the gun,' Colin said. 'We shouldn't speculate on what's going to happen. Just satisfy yourself with the fact that God will provide.' Alice and Luke just looked at each other and grinned.

Alice remarked on how busy the shop was these days and said that it must be the time of the year when there were so many funerals. They had a job to keep up with the wreath orders.

'How's the new girl doing?' Colin asked.

'She's doing very well; she loves making the wreaths and I can almost leave that side of the business to her already. I have no fears leaving her alone in the shop when I have to go out on deliveries. Anyway, Sally is just upstairs if needed, so it's all working out very well really.'

'You're very quiet, Luke,' Colin said. 'I suppose you've got those football trials on your mind—you and your football.'

'I think he's thinking of something else right now, aren't you Luke?' said Alice, teasingly.

'I don't know what you mean,' said Luke, but he blushed visibly on answering.

'I think you do Luke, but I'll say no more. I don't want to embarrass you.'

'Aw Mum, be quiet. Anyway, I'm going upstairs to do my homework.' Luke left the table and playfully slapped his mum's arm as he passed her.

'What have I been missing?' Colin asked.

Alice explained how Luke was absolutely dumbstruck when he saw Christine in the shop this afternoon. 'I've never known Luke take an interest in girls before, but I think that may all have changed. He was totally smitten; he was so taken aback that he could hardly speak. It was so funny.'

'She must be quite something,' Colin said.

'She is a very attractive young lady and has a lovely personality, but she may already have a boyfriend for all I know. She may not be even interested in boys yet, she's only sixteen.'

'Don't you go matchmaking; Luke's got enough on his plate at the moment, what with the exams coming up, his paper round and his beloved football.'

'Oh, I'm not matchmaking at all,' Alice said, 'but watch this space, as they say.' They were interrupted by the telephone ringing. Colin answered, and it was the garage to say that the car was finished, and could he bring the other car back early as it was needed for another customer. Colin agreed to do so. When he told Alice she remarked, 'That's a good sign that they finished it earlier than expected; it may be a smaller bill.'

'Don't hold your breath,' Colin said as he started clearing the table.

'I'll do this,' Alice said. 'You go and do what you have to in your study.'

'No,' Colin said, 'you've been busy all day. I can do this; go and put your feet up.' They agreed to do the dishes together and, while doing them, Colin said, 'I should have a word with Luke, I suppose, if he has started to take an interest in girls, especially ones older than himself.'

'Who's matchmaking now?' Alice said. 'They've only just seen each other in the shop for a few seconds.'

'Yes, I know, but now is as good a time as any. He'll be fifteen soon.'

'Rather you than me,' Alice said. 'He'll be very embarrassed you know.'

'Yes, he probably will. He'll convince me that he knows it all and I'm wasting my time; we'll see.'

Alice said, as she dried her hands, 'I'm just going into the lounge to read the paper about my famous son; I haven't had a chance today. See you later.'

Colin entered Luke's room and asked if he could spare a few minutes, as he wanted to speak to him. 'Yes, sure,' Luke said. 'What about?'

Colin said, 'You know Mum was teasing you about Christine from the shop? Well, now that you're getting further into your teens—you'll be fifteen soon—it's time I had a talk with you about the things of life, 'when boy meets girl' sort of thing. Do you get sex education at school?'

'Oh, come on Dad, I'm not ignorant you know. I know all about the birds and the bees.'

'Yes, I guess you do,' Colin said, 'but there is much more to it than that you know. As a Christian in particular, you must have certain standards which youngsters of today have no respect for.'

'Dad, I know all the things you are going to say. I don't intend having sex before marriage and, when I choose a partner, I realize it will be for life. But, as you said, I'm only going to be fifteen next birthday, so that sort of thing is a long way off. However, I appreciate what you are doing, and thanks. You've done your duty, now enough said?'

'OK, Son, we'll leave it there. I trust you to use your common sense and apply the Christian principles you have heard in church. Now Luke, there is another thing which is causing me concern.'

'What's that?' Luke asked.

'Well, I know you have a remarkable talent for football and how keen you are. Your love of the game is not wrong in itself, but it seems to be the be all and end all of your life. I'm just worried about what happens if things don't work out the way that you want, for any reason—you could get an injury for example or others will not appreciate your talent or may not have the same expectations that you have for yourself. I just feel that you will be totally devastated if things didn't work out and, if you put all your energies into your football, you would have nothing to fall back on.'

'I know what you are saying, Dad,' Luke replied. 'My heart is set on a career in football; it's about the only thing I'm any good at. God has given me this talent for a reason. As you have said so many hundreds of times, 'God will provide.' If it is meant to be, he will open the right doors.'

'Well, I can't deny saying that, Luke. I just hope, if things go pear-shaped, you will be able to cope, that's all.'

'I don't believe that's going to happen, Dad. You just wait and see. You'll have a famous son, one day. I'll be a household name across the country.'

'Yes, well don't give up your paper round yet,' Colin said, laughingly, as he left the room.

Luke pondered on his dad's words for a few minutes and in prayer asked God to lead him in the way he should go. He asked God to indeed open the right doors to enable him to achieve his ambitions, if that was His will. His thoughts then turned to Christine; I hope she likes football, he thought.

The next morning, Colin collected his car from the garage and the mechanic explained all the things they had done. It all went completely over his head; he was just thinking how costly it all sounded and, when he asked what the bill came to, they were unable to tell him there and then as they had not worked it all out yet. They would send the account on at the end of the week properly. Colin read into that, and was worried it would mean heavy costs, and feared the worst.

As he drove away, his spirits were lifted by how well the car felt. He realized that they had done an excellent job and the car felt as new, especially as the car had been valeted too and was sparkling clean inside and out. He had no more worries about breakdowns and the start of his day felt good.

That changed when he called in at the retirement home to learn that Ernie had been taken into hospital overnight by ambulance, suffering from a serious bout of pneumonia. When he called in at the hospital, he learned that Ernie had died just in the last hour. This upset Colin; he had become quite close to Ernie in the past couple of years and regarded him as a good friend. Colin called into the flower shop to inform Alice, who was quite shocked to hear the news. He was introduced to Christine who appeared somewhat puzzled, for reasons unknown to Alice or Colin. After Colin had left Christine said to Alice, 'I didn't know your husband was a vicar.'

'Well, he's not a vicar, he's a Methodist minister. I'm sorry Christine, I suppose I should have mentioned it, I just never thought to.'

Christine said, 'That's alright. There's no reason why you should have. I was surprised to see his dog collar, that's all. Oh, I'm sorry, I suppose I shouldn't call it that, should I?'

Alice laughed and said, 'Don't worry, we do as well, but the correct term is clerical collar. He doesn't always wear it; it just depends on what he's doing in the day, like visiting members of the church or hospitals or stuff like that, and on Sundays and church events of course. I suppose it's his sort of uniform and clearly shows to whoever he meets what he does for a living.'

CHAPTER 8

On the Saturday morning, as Colin was about to leave to collect the Superintendent from the station, the mail arrived and included an envelope, which he suspected was from the garage. It was and Colin whistled when he saw that the account amounted to nearly £400. He was not totally shocked at the amount, but it was a little more than he expected. He showed it to Alice who had taken the day off to receive Revd Wills. She did not think it was too bad considering it would mean that the car was still good for hopefully another year.

Luke had left early in the morning to attend the football trials at the university pitch. On his arrival, he sought out the person in charge and was directed to the changing rooms, told to change and report back on the pitch. There were plenty of other lads in the changing rooms and he was pleased to see two or three familiar faces, which put him at ease.

When all the players had assembled on the pitch, the head coach introduced himself as Mr Batson. He told them all that they were here because they had been recommended by their sports masters or coaches of the teams that they played for. Some had been seen by Mr Batson himself, or perhaps one of his colleagues, while watching various games in the county. They were told this was the first series of trials and the number would be whittled down from forty to a finishing number of sixteen in the next few weeks. They were also told that, at the end of the day, they would learn if they would be required to attend further trials; they were warned that some will be disappointed but not to take it to heart as there would be opportunities in the future.

The rest of the morning was taken up with warm-up exercises, skills tests and competitive tests. A good element of fun was introduced, and Luke thoroughly enjoyed the morning and was pleased with himself after having received a few 'well- done' comments from the coaches. He was looking forward to actually playing in the match that would be organized for the afternoon. The buffet lunch was eaten with enthusiasm by all the lads and was also a good opportunity to get to know some of them.

About half an hour after lunch was over, the head coach appeared with his assistants, who were carrying either red or yellow training bibs. Mr Batson asked the lads to step forward and claim their bibs as their names were called out. Luke's was the very first name and he was given a yellow bib. Nine others were given yellow bibs and then the rest were told to collect a red bib each and go out to the pitch.

There were twenty-one players in all, only one of which was a goalkeeper. One of the lads had not turned up and he was a goalkeeper, so one of the coaching assistants would play in goal for the reds. Mr Batson would referee the match, which would be of thirty-five minutes each half.

As the game proceeded, Luke became the target for the red's defence. They obviously recognized him as a threat and also knew he was the youngest on the pitch. Despite many efforts to rough him up, Luke ably coped with all their tactics and scored one of the yellow's two goals in the first half with a rocket of a shot from about 20 yards out.

During the changeover at halftime, Mr Batson asked Luke if he was alright; he knew that Luke had taken one or two knocks. 'Yes thanks, I'm fine,' Luke said. 'I'm having fun out there; I'll get some more goals in the second half.'

Mr Batson laughed and said, 'Well there's nothing wrong with your confidence, that's for sure.'

As the game proceeded, Luke shone out as a very talented player. His speed and talent were exceptional and he certainly was not out of his depth among older boys. He had scored two more goals early on in the second half, when the yellows were awarded a free kick out on the right wing. Luke positioned himself in the penalty area and signalled with his arms for the taker to float the ball right to him. As the ball came in high into the area, Luke leapt up to head it and at the same time the goalkeeper (the assistant coach) rushed out to punch it. Luke got to it first and powered a header into the net. The keeper collided with Luke heavily and, although Luke was knocked down, he sprung up immediately to celebrate his goal. The goalkeeper was not so lucky; he stayed down winded and shocked. When Mr Batson asked his colleague if he was alright, he said, 'Yes, I'm OK. That was like hitting a brick wall; how old did you say that nipper is?'

'He's just fifteen,' Mr Batson replied. 'A big lad, eh?'

'Yeah, you can say that again.'

At the end of the game, Mr Batson thanked everybody for coming and said that they would hear by letter in the next week whether they would be invited back for further trials. When Luke had showered and changed and went out to his bike, he was met by Mr Batson who said, 'Luke, a quick word please?'

'Sure,' Luke said.

Mr Batson said, 'Luke, I've been involved in football nearly all my life and I've not met any youngster with the talent that you have at your age. I believe you could make a career as a professional footballer. Would you be interested?'

'I most certainly would; it's all I ever wanted to do,' Luke replied.

'OK, leave it to me, Luke. I've got some contacts in the game. I'll be in touch with you. We'll see you in two weeks anyway. You'll be called for the next stage of trials, that's guaranteed.'

'Thank you, sir,' Luke said, and he practically leapt onto his bike and pedalled off with a wave … or was it a fist punching the air?

Luke arrived home still in a state of elation and, as he entered the house, he called out, 'Dad, Dad, I've got some great news.' As he dashed into the kitchen, he stopped dead in his tracks when he was confronted by his parents and Revd Wills seated around the kitchen table. He had forgotten about the visit of the Circuit Superintendent that weekend.

'Luke, for goodness' sake, settle down will you. Say "hello" to Revd Wills.'

Luke dropped his sports bag on the floor and said, 'Sorry Dad.' He walked around the table and shook hands with Revd. Wills and said, 'Pleased to meet you, sir.'

Reverend Wills replied, 'And pleased to meet you too, young man. You are a big lad aren't you; you were only so high the last time I saw you. [He extended his hand to about four feet off the ground as he made the remark.] I don't know what your mother's been feeding you, but it has certainly worked for you.'

'Mum's a good cook, sir,' Luke said.

'I'm glad to hear it. I'll be able to judge that for myself this weekend and I look forward to it. Now, what's your good news that you were going to announce, before I put the dampers on it by my presence?'

'Oh, it's nothing really,' Luke said.

'Nonsense my lad, if it's good news we all want to share it.'

'Well, I've been attending football trials today and the head coach told me that I have the potential to be a professional footballer and he is going to pursue it for me and will be in touch; he says that he has some contacts in the game.'

'Wonderful!! If that's what you want?' Then, Revd Wills looked at Colin and said, 'And is father happy about that?'

Colin said, 'Well, naturally I am pleased for Luke, but I have reservations about a career in football for Luke. He is still very young and there are many options open to him, but we'll have a talk about it soon. It's early days yet.'

'Yes, of course,' Revd Wills said, winking at Luke.

'Right,' said Alice, 'time to eat. Luke, go and change. We're having a barbecue, as promised.'

'Oh yes, of course. Happy birthday, Luke,' Revd Wills said. Luke looked at Revd Wills in shock when his mum mentioned barbecues. Revd Wills laughed and said, 'Don't worry, Luke. I absolutely love barbecues, especially when I don't have to cook.' They all laughed as they left the kitchen. Luke took an immediate liking to Revd Wills, after expecting the Circuit Superintendent to be an old stuffed shirt. Revd Wills made his love of barbecues apparent by his vivacious appetite and was excellent company; a good meal was enjoyed by all. After they had eaten, Colin and Revd Wills adjourned to the study for a private talk.

Reverend Wills first addressed the question of the closure of the church at Skipton. He explained that it would be indeed closing down and merging with Rushton. The building would eventually be sold, and half of the proceeds would go into a building maintenance fund and the other half into the general accounts of the circuit. This would be announced at the public joint meeting that evening. He said that it was inevitable that some of the Skipton congregation would not move to Rushton but he hoped to persuade them otherwise at the meeting. He told Colin that having one church less under his charge would not affect his stipend as (in theory) the congregation numbers should not alter after a merger.

With regards to his stipend, Colin was told that there would be no increase on this occasion but, instead of a transport allowance, he would be provided with a car and the circuit would pay all the expenses of it, i.e. insurance, tax, servicing and fuel bills. This would come out of the proceeds from the sale of the Skipton building. At this point Colin showed Revd Wills the bill from recent car repairs and service. 'I'll have that,' Revd Wills said. 'The circuit will take care of that.' Colin agreed to sign over his present car to the circuit and was told it would be replaced with a new one in a year's time.

Arrangements were to be put in hand for the essential repairs to the Manse once Skipton's building had been sold.

Colin was inwardly thrilled to bits with all the news and secretly thought to himself, 'The Lord will provide.'

With the meeting over, Colin and Revd Wills joined Alice and Luke in the lounge for a general chat over cups of tea before leaving for the joint meeting at Manleigh's schoolroom at the rear of the church. Alice handed over a large, brightly wrapped package to Luke and wished him a happy birthday. Luke ripped open the parcel and pulled out a brand-new schoolbag with the England football badge clearly etched across it and his name, 'LIM', embroidered underneath it. Luke was clearly thrilled with it and gave his mum a hug and big kiss and also a hug for dad with a big thank you. He noticed there was a separate plastic lined pocket for football boots.

Revd Wills then said, 'Well, Luke, when I heard it was your birthday, I felt I couldn't come empty handed so I'd like to give you this little gift and wish you a happy birthday.' He handed Luke a gift-wrapped little box and, when he opened it, he saw that it was a wristwatch with a fine leather strap. Luke expressed his gratitude and he immediately placed it on his wrist. Reverend Wills said, 'It's an automatic; you don't have to wind it up. Mere movement of the wrist winds it up. Having met you now, I think the watch will remain permanently wound up.' They all laughed.

Alice said, 'Time we were on our way, I think. I'll just rinse these cups.'

Colin said, 'Before we go, let's just have a word of prayer and place this evening's meeting in the Lord's hands.'

Then, they all left the house to go to the church hall. When they got outside Revd Wills looked at the flower-shop's van and said, 'My goodness, other motorists should see that coming.'

Luke said, 'Yes, and then quickly turn the other way, I would think.'

'I take it you don't like it, Luke?' Revd Wills asked.

'I think it's hideous,' Luke replied.

'Perhaps you should decorate your bike in like manner to support your mum?' Revd. Wills said laughingly.

'I don't think so, sir,' Luke said. 'Mind you, I suppose it would never get stolen.'

Judging by the number of cars in the car park, there was obviously a big turnout for the meeting, with almost twenty minutes to go before the start.

As Colin and the Superintendent took to the platform, he noticed a large contingent of the members of Skipton Church sitting together in one area of the hall and feared the worst.

At 7:30pm sharp, Colin rose to his feet and the hall fell silent. He opened in prayer and then thanked everybody for coming. He explained to the meeting that this was a historic occasion and said that the purpose of the meeting is ('and I trust that this is why you are all here') to discuss the propagation of the gospel in this area in an acceptable and efficient way. He reminded everybody that it was their duty to support what was right and proper in that respect and not to let their feelings and prejudices influence their thoughts. He said that times change and while old values and traditions may be very precious to us, there are times when we have to cast them aside for the better.

Colin then said it was a pleasure to welcome and introduce the Very Reverend Richard Wills, the circuit superintendent, who will now address the meeting. Revd Wills stood to a round of applause and thanked Revd Tewkes-Dawson for his warm welcome and his wise words. He then addressed the meeting on the main reason for the meeting tonight:

'I am sure that much of what I am going to say to you this evening is superfluous, inasmuch as you have made up your minds about what I am going to say to you,' he began.

'The circuit has decided that it is no longer viable to keep the church at Skipton going. This is for several reasons:

(a) it was getting more and more costly to maintain the building in an acceptable state of repair. The cost of repairs over the last twelve months has far exceeded the income of the church.

(b) the congregation at Skipton is of the older generation and there are few young families in the Skipton catchment area:

(c) Revd Tewkes-Dawson, although extremely willing and able, is increasingly burdened by having a third church under his control and out in the sticks.'

He went on to say that because of the decreasing number of lay preachers available to the circuit, it was more and more difficult to fill the pulpits six times every Sunday and four times would be much more manageable. There were murmurings among the people in the hall but when Revd Wills asked if there were any questions thus far, no one spoke up. He continued:

'The idea is that all assets at Skipton would be transferred to Rushton. I would implore those of you currently attending at Skipton to join with Rushton with the loyalty and enthusiasm you have shown at Skipton for many years. You have embraced Colin in your community; please support him in the future, whichever building you choose to worship in.'

Again, he asked if there were any questions or comments from the floor and one person stood up and introduced himself as Mr Devonshire, a steward at Skipton for over thirty years. 'I have three comments to make,' he said. 'One, why were we at Skipton not consulted over this closure. Two, what will happen to the building, and three, what is the time scale in all this?'

Revd Wills answered by explaining that it was solely the responsibility of the Circuit Central Committee as to what happened to the churches in its area of responsibility and consultation would only have delayed matters and caused disruption and differences of opinion. The building would be sold at market value and the proceeds would be split in half: 50 per cent for general funds and 50 per cent would stay within the region for use of the two remaining churches. The time scale would be dictated by how soon Skipton's premises could be sold; we are probably looking at about six months from now.'

There being no further questions or comments, Revd Wills closed the meeting in prayer, after reminding all present that tea and biscuits were available after the meeting, when he would be pleased to meet them all individually.

Colin turned to Revd Wills and said, 'That went very well; I expected a few more comments than that, judging from the tittle tattle that's been around recently.'

'Yes, I did,' Revd Wills replied. 'I think your people can see the common sense in it all.' After a pleasant hour or so mingling with the people over tea and biscuits with no adverse comments at all, they drove home feeling very satisfied with the evening's outcome.

On arrival at home, Revd Wills excused himself and retired, saying he wanted to 'brush-up' on his two sermons for tomorrow.

After a relatively uneventful weekend, Revd Wills was duly conveyed to the train station on Monday and Colin took the opportunity to thank him for all his efforts regarding the financial aspects of the job. He said he now felt more secure financially and it would be so much less stressful for Alice trying to make ends meet.

'The Lord will provide,' Revd Wills replied. Colin took a quick glance at him to see if he was making fun of him, but he was deadly serious. Colin just grinned to himself and wished Alice and Luke were with them in the car.

CHAPTER 9

At the very first opportunity he had that day, Luke told Mr Preece, the sports master, of his experience at the County trials.

Mr Preece said, 'Yes, I know Luke. Donald Batson is a friend of mine and he phoned me at the weekend and said how impressed he was with your footballing skills. He wanted to know a little more about your character and general demeanour off the field.'

'Why would he ask that?' Luke said.

'Well, perhaps I shouldn't tell you this really but Mr Batson is going to recommend you to a professional football club for a place in their academy. But there's a long way to go before that, so don't build up your hopes too much. They will need to know that you are of good character before they would ever think of taking you on, so just keep your nose clean and train and practice hard and the world could be your oyster.'

'Thanks sir, I will,' Luke replied. He thought to himself, 'What is he talking about? I don't know if I even like oysters.

At every opportunity after that, Luke would be in the back garden with a football and the granite wall would take a pounding day after day. The next lot of County trials could not come quick enough for Luke. When they did, Luke noticed a stranger on the touch line in conversation with Mr Batson. When nothing was mentioned at the end of the day, Luke dismissed it from his mind but was pleased that he had been invited to the next lot of trials in one month's time.

On his way home, Luke popped into the flower shop to see his mum but, as he was talking to his mum, who was behind the counter, his eyes were constantly flicking to the rear of the shop where he could hear some activity. His face visibly showed disappointment when Sally emerged with a large bunch of flowers in her hands. It was obvious he thought Christine was there.

'Hello Luke,' Sally said. 'How are you?'

'Fine thanks,' he replied. 'I'd better be on my way. Bye Sally, bye Mum.'

As he turned to go, Alice said, 'She's just popped out to the shops, Luke. You might see her on your way.'

'Who?' Luke said with unconvincing innocence.

'Oh, come on Luke. I can read you like a book. You know who I mean,' Sally said teasingly. 'Would you like to buy a nice bunch of flowers in case you do see her on your way?'

'Don't you start as well,' Luke said with a blush all over his face. Luke left with Sally and Alice's laughter in his ears. He hoped he would meet her though.

The following week was not Luke's favourite time of that year. Nearly all the week had been taken up with exams and although Luke knew he would not set the world alight academically, he felt he had done as well as he could expect. They were all over now and he could concentrate his thoughts elsewhere.

He asked his parents if he could give up his paper round because it was so time consuming. He wanted to concentrate on football a bit more as he was now, more than ever, convinced that this was where his future lay. After little discussion, Colin and Alice agreed but insisted that he made sure Mr Patel had a replacement before he finally gave up.

When Luke told Mr Patel, he said he would be sorry to see Luke go, as he had been so reliable in the past two years or so. He said that he would have no trouble replacing Luke as he was constantly being asked if he had any jobs going. It was agreed that Luke would finish at the end of the current month, in two weeks' time, and in the last week he would show the new person the round.

At the end of that week, Colin took a telephone call from a firm of local builders to arrange a time for them to come and inspect the Manse and see what needed doing. He requested Colin's presence to explain any problems that they had been having, although he said he had been briefed by somebody from the circuit headquarters about the nature of the job.

This was duly arranged and when Colin told Alice, she immediately reeled off a whole list of things she felt needed doing. Colin reminded her that the circuit would have to approve the jobs and accept a tender, so they had to be sensible in what they pointed out to the builder. Alice reminded Colin that now the Skipton building was empty, it would soon be sold and there would be ample monies to do a good job on the Manse. Revd Wills has said that half of the proceeds of the sale of the Skipton building would remain in this circuit, so why not strike while the iron's hot; she said surely it would be a good investment for the future to do a proper job.

Colin had to agree that what Alice said made sense and added, 'As long as we don't push it, that's all.' Colin suggested that, when the builder arrives, Alice be present too.

The meeting had been arranged for the following Thursday at 2:00pm, so Alice arranged for Sally to cover her in the shop for an hour on that day. However, on the morning of that day, Alice phoned Colin to say she could not make it to the house at that time as Sally had gone into labour and was at the hospital, so she could not leave the shop. She asked Colin to write down the things that needed doing so he would not forget.

'I've already done that,' he said.

'Don't forget to ask when they would be doing the job and how long it will take.'

'Yes, yes, yes, don't fuss so,' Colin replied. 'I'll ring you once they've been and let you know what transpired, OK?'

'Yes, please,' Alice said. She then said her goodbyes and finished the call.

Colin just smiled to himself and shook his head saying, 'Women!', to no one in particular.

The builder duly arrived, with apologies for being twenty minutes late. He introduced himself as Ronnie James of James, Adcock and Co., handing Colin his business card. He told Colin that he had been briefed on what needed doing—the gutters, part of the kitchen roof etc.—and asked if there was anything else of an urgent nature that needed attention. Colin pointed out that the back door appeared to have warped and was difficult to close properly and one or two smaller problems, like a sticking sash window and a broken down-pipe from the kitchen sink. Mr James made a note of those and took a rough measurement of the guttering and also, by means of a ladder which Colin held for him, inspected the soffits and fascias.

He was there for just over an hour. He informed Colin that the rear door and frame would have to be completely replaced as rot had set in and that the fascias would have to be renewed for the same reason. The window could be eased with no problem, and everything seemed quite straight forward. In reply to Colin's questions, Mr James envisaged a couple of weeks work but could not say when that was likely to be until he heard back from the circuit headquarters. Colin thanked him for his time and shook hands. He said his goodbyes to Mr James and saw him out of the driveway as he drove away. Colin was just about to make himself a cup of tea when the phone rang; it was Alice, as Colin had guessed.

'I thought you were going to phone me,' she said.

'He only just left,' Colin replied. He told Alice of the meeting and she appeared happy enough.

She added, 'By the way, Sally had a little girl at 10 o'clock this morning: 8lb 2oz. She and the baby are fine. I'll be a little late for dinner, as I'll pop in to see her after work. I should be home by 6pm; do you mind?'

'Of course not,' Colin replied. 'Give her my love will you and, if you can find a decent flower shop, perhaps a bunch of flowers would be in order?'

Alice treated that remark with the contempt it deserved and merely said, 'Bye Colin, see you later!'

A few days later, Colin received a telephone call from Mr James informing him that his tender for the work on the Manse had been accepted and that the work would commence in a couple of weeks' time. He said he would ring and confirm which day they would be starting. Colin asked if there was anything he needed to do before their arrival. Mr James said that he would need space in the driveway for a rubbish skip and the truck. Colin thanked him for his call and said he would ensure that there was sufficient space, although he did not have a clue how they would manage with his car and the flower-shop van.

When he discussed it with Alice that evening, Alice merely telephoned a near neighbour, who was a good customer at the flower shop and a friend of Alice, and she agreed that the two vehicles could be left on their property for as long as it took.

'See,' Alice said, 'the Lord will provide, eh Colin!' Colin merely looked disdainfully over the rim of his glasses and said nothing.

'What?' Alice said grinning.

'You know what?' Colin said. 'You're making fun of me.'

'I'm not. It's what you would have said isn't it?'

'Yes, but I would have meant it; that's the difference.'

'I believe it too you know,' Alice replied. 'I just don't say it every other sentence, that's all.'

'Whatever!' Colin said, grinning.

When Alice opened her mail that evening, there was a letter asking her if she had made up her mind about whether to become a judge at the flower show, as the committee were keen to finalize the arrangements and appointments for the following month's show. Alice had forgotten all about it and had not contacted the secretary, as promised. She immediately phoned her and, after apologizing for the delay, she said she would be delighted to help in that way, but she stipulated that she would like it to be with an experienced judge, as it was her first time. She was assured that she would be and arrangements were made for her to meet her fellow judge beforehand.

'Good for you,' Colin said when she told him. 'You'll enjoy it, I'm sure. Besides, it will probably be good for the shop business to have an acknowledged expert on hand.'

'Who's making fun of who, now?' Alice said.

'No, I'm serious; it can only be good for the shop, surely.'

'I s'pose you're right,' Alice said. 'Sally will be pleased, I should think.'

'By the way, how is she and the baby?' Colin asked.

'She's fine and the baby really is a bonny little thing. Sally's husband, Rick, is over the moon. He's like a child with a new toy. I can see he's going to spoil her rotten. They come home tomorrow already; they don't keep them in long these days. I was in eight days for Maisie and Luke. I couldn't help thinking of our Maisie when I saw Sally's little one; it brought back many memories, I must say.'

'Where is Luke?' Colin said, deliberately changing the subject.

'He's in his room doing his homework, I hope,' Alice said. 'I'll leave him till dinnertime; he'll be down when he smells food,' she said.

And Luke did just that, saying, 'I'm starving.' Then, looking at his dad, he quickly corrected himself: 'I mean, I'm hungry.'

'When aren't you,' Colin said. 'I don't know where you put it all, I really don't.'

'Got to keep my strength up Dad, if I'm to play for England.'

CHAPTER 10

The builders duly arrived on the promised date and swiftly got into their stride with the work. After the first two or three days, Colin felt comforted by the fact that they were not shirkers and seemed competent in their work, disruption of the household was minimal, and the car-parking arrangement was working well.

When Colin arrived home late afternoon one day, one of the workmen approached him and said, 'Excuse me sir, but I think I know your son. Luke, isn't it?'

'Yes, that's right. How do you know him?' Colin asked.

'Well, my boy is involved in the County Trials and I went to watch him a couple of weeks ago. Luke was playing as well. He's quite a footballer isn't he! While I'm no expert, I have been involved in football all my life and I've never seen such a young player with so much talent. You must be proud of him.'

'Well, yes, I am proud of him,' Colin said, 'but not just for his footballing ability. He's a good all-round lad really. He embraces my belief in the faith and tries to live a good Christian life; that's what makes me proud of him more than any football ability he might have.'

'Well, I can understand that,' the workman replied, 'but it would be a shame if that talent went to waste; he could really go a long way in football.'

'That's what he wants,' Colin said. 'We'll see. God will provide,' Colin said.

'What does that mean?' the workman asked.

'We believe that we are all part of God's eternal plan, and what he wills for each one of us will come to pass,' Colin said. 'So, if Luke is meant to be a footballer, God will provide the way for him and the right doors will open up for him.'

'Well, I hope God knows football talent when he sees it, for Luke's sake,' the workman replied.

The very next day, among the mail was a letter addressed to Luke which Colin placed on the mantelpiece for him; the letters H.C.F.C. and a logo were in the top left-hand corner of the envelope. Colin remembered that he had seen this once before and remembered it concerned football.

When Luke opened the envelope and read the contents, he gave a loud 'Yes!' and punched the air with joy. He announced that he had been selected to play for *Hampshire* in the County Championships in two weeks' time. The letter included instructions on how to get to the ground and times etc. It was signed by Donald Batson, the county coach. When Colin read the letter, he noticed that the competition was for under 21's and he questioned the wisdom of a fifteen-year-old playing with much older boys.

'That doesn't worry me,' Luke said. 'I play against men sometimes on Saturdays for Hamleigh Town in the local League, so it's no different really.'

'If you say so,' Colin said.

'Would you be free on the 12th to take me, Dad? It's a big game for me and I'd like you to be there, and you, Mum, if you can?'

Alice said, 'I don't think I'll be able to make it, love, with Sally and the new baby and all; Saturday is usually a busy day in the shop. But I'm sure Dad will be able to juggle any appointments and come along, won't you Colin?'

'I'll check my diary, but I should be able to manage that.'

'Thanks Dad. Can I phone Mr Batson now and confirm my acceptance?'

'Yes, do it now while it's fresh on your mind, though I can't see you forgetting,' Colin said.

Luke spoke to Mr Batson, and he could hardly contain his excitement on the phone. Mr Batson told Luke he wanted a quick word with him before the match, as he had a bit of possible good news for him. He declined to elaborate on that but said he would see him on the 12th and congratulated him on his selection. Luke thanked him and said his goodbyes. He wondered what Mr Batson meant by 'possible good news' but couldn't think of what it might be. When he mentioned this to his dad, Colin said, 'Well don't try to guess what it is, in case you're disappointed when you learn what he meant—best not to speculate.'

'I can't think of anything anyway,' Luke said.

Alice said, 'You'd better go up and do your homework, if you can concentrate, that is?'

'I don't have any,' Luke said. 'I might just go kick about in the garden for half an hour; that'll be my homework for today.'

'Sorry,' Colin said, 'you can't. There's the builder's gear out there; there's no room.'

'Oh, that's annoying,' Luke said. 'I'll go up and read then.'

Luke left the room and Alice said to Colin, 'A happy young man I think, don't you?'

'Yes, I suppose I'm going to have to come to terms with the fact that he has just one ambition in life: to play football. I won't try to put him off, I just hope he doesn't get an almighty let down one day; he would be devastated.'

Alice just held her tongue and grinned to herself, resisting the temptation to say God will provide. When Alice went up to say goodnight to Luke, he was fast asleep; she didn't disturb him. She went downstairs and said to Colin, 'Luke won't be down for evening prayers. He's in dreamland, probably at Wembley Stadium.'

The big day came, and Colin got Luke to the grounds in plenty of time and then found a comfortable, sheltered seat in the stand. Luke sought out Mr Batson who directed him to the home dressing room where he would find his kit: 'the No. 9 shirt,' he told Luke.

'You wanted a word with me, you said, sir?'

'Ah! Yes Luke, but I've got to confirm something first. I'll speak to you shortly.'

There were several of the team in the dressing room when Luke entered. He was well known to several of them and there was much good banter going on. Luke felt well at ease and proceeded to get changed. He liked the kit: royal blue shorts, blue and white horizontal striped shirts with a large black number on the back, and white socks with a blue top. He felt really good and proceeded to do a few warm-up exercises. He couldn't wait to get out on the pitch but there was still almost half an hour to kick off.

Mr Batson popped in and signalled Luke to come outside the room. When they were in the corridor, he drew Luke aside and said:

'Now Luke, listen carefully. I don't want to put extra pressure on you today; that's why I haven't given you the captaincy. But there is a scout from a Premiership team here today. Although he will be watching all the players naturally, he is here to particularly watch you, as his club might be interested in you. Just play your normal game and ensure that you keep your nose clean on the pitch. In other words, behave yourself and don't do anything silly. The other team know you well and you could well be targeted by their defence, but I have every confidence in you. I'm sure you can handle it with a cool head; don't prove me wrong!'

'I won't,' Luke replied. 'Which team is it?' Luke asked.

'*Southtown Rovers*,' he said.

'Wow! My favourite team,' Luke remarked.

'Now call the rest of the lads out onto the pitch for a warm-up, will you? I'll meet you out on the pitch. Don't mention to the others what I've told you; I don't want to influence the way they treat you on the field, one way or the other.'

'OK,' Luke said.

After about ten to fifteen minutes of stretching and sprints and jumps, they were ordered back into the dressing room for a team talk, given by Mr Batson. He gave them a general pep-talk, told them how good they were and was expecting a good win. He informed them that Luke would take all free kicks within 25 yards or so of the goal and penalty kicks. 'Good luck,' he said and sent them out onto the pitch.

Luke was surprised to see quite a good crowd, about 1,200 in the ground. He gave his dad a quick wave and received a thumbs-up sign in return. The opposition, *Kent*, were in red and white and looked a good outfit. They all seemed to be bigger lads than the *Hampshire* boys, but maybe that was just an illusion. The weather and pitch were perfect for football and Luke was chomping at the bit. He felt so up for it and determined to do well; he had almost dismissed from his mind that the scout would be watching him. As far as he was concerned, he was doing the thing he most loved doing in the whole world—having a game of football—and this, as far as he was concerned, was just another game of football, regardless of who he was playing for or against.

Kent was doing all the pressing in the first fifteen minutes or so and *Hampshire*'s defence were doing all they could to withstand the pressure. Luke had very little involvement in the match at all. He had, without realizing it, started to fall back into the midfield area until he got a call from Mr Batson, waving him to go further upfield.

After a strong attack by *Kent* which ended up with the ball in the *Hampshire* goalkeeper's hands, he punted the ball hard upfield. Luke met it with his head and allowed the ball to skid off over the head of a challenging defender. He turned in a flash and chased after the ball. Running with it, he outstripped all defenders and, from just inside the opposition's penalty area, he let fly with a rocket of a shot at goal. *Kent*'s keeper made a brilliant save but only parried it out into the path of Luke's strike-partner, who side-footed the ball neatly past the stranded goalkeeper: 1–0 to *Hampshire*. The scorer ended up under a heap of congratulating team-mates, Luke being the first to get to him and knock him to the ground as he jumped on his back.

'Well done, Lim!' his captain said to him, as they reformed for the restart. Don Batson called out to Luke to stay up on their last man and not to wander back into midfield. He said, 'They are going to press hard now, don't be drawn.' Luke gave him the thumbs-up sign. Don Batson told Tommy to drop back for a few minutes to assist in midfield. The match swung to and fro, with *Kent* perhaps having a little more of the possession, but they were limited to two or three long-range shots, which were easily saved by the keeper or went high and wide.

With about five minutes to go to half-time, *Hampshire*'s midfield gained possession and, with a good passing movement, approached the opposing penalty area. The ball was slotted out to the right wing and then crossed beautifully into the box. Luke, running in at speed, leapt way above all defenders and thundered a header past the keeper before he even saw it: 2–0 *Hampshire*. Luke ran to the corner flag with arms raised to be given the same treatment as the previous scorer. The half-time whistle came without much further incident.

Once in the dressing room after the players had settled down, Mr Batson addressed them: 'Well done, you two,' he said to the two scorers. He then heaped loads of praise on the defence: 'They worked you hard and you did very well under the circumstances. Any questions?' he said.

Luke raised his hand and said, 'With a 2–0 lead, should we concentrate on holding them now? The defence must be tiring after that first-half battering and they'll be coming at us with all guns blazing. Tommy or I could drop back more into midfield to help out?'

Don Batson was amazed at Luke's tactics acumen for one so young.

He replied, 'They'll be expecting that, but I want you to stay up on their defence. They can't afford to give you too much freedom. They'll know that and the chances are they'll man-mark you, Luke; you'll be a target in their next half. That may give Tommy a bit more freedom so, midfield, look for Tommy when you get possession. Tommy, make sure you find space for yourself to be available. Now, any lumps or pains anybody?'

After receiving no reply, he said, 'Good. Just relax for five minutes, take deep breaths and then go out there and finish them off. We've got the beating of them; just keep focused and concentrate and the match is yours.'

One of the defenders said to Luke, 'Is it true you're only fifteen?'

'Yes,' Luke replied, 'why?'

'You just seem older, that's all,' he said.

The second half commenced and, as Mr Batson had predicted, one of *Kent*'s defenders latched onto Luke straight away. He called to Tommy and, grinning, he pointed at the defender and said, 'He drew the short straw.'

Tommy smiled and said, 'I'll have to get the goals, then.'

'Hope you do!' Luke said.

After about fifteen minutes, *Kent* won a corner on the right. The kick was taken well and *Kent* scored after a scramble in the six-yard box. Appeals for a foul on the keeper fell on deaf ears and the referee awarded a goal. The *Hampshire* boys were furious, and this obviously goaded them into raising their game. As time passed, they had more possession of the ball and mounted more attacks on *Kent*'s goal.

Within five or six minutes, a pass reached Tommy, who beat one player and slotted the ball past a defender into Luke's path. He muscled his marker off the ball and he fell, leaving Luke a clear run into the area for a one-on-one with the advancing keeper. He neatly poked the ball wide of the keeper's left, ran around him on the right and, after re-possessing the ball, he hammered it into the net with glee from 4 yards out.

The supporters were up on their feet, cheering and clapping. Luke ran to the touchline with a high five for Don Baston, who was applauding furiously. After extricating himself from the melee of congratulating colleagues, Luke looked up to his dad, who was also proudly applauding enthusiastically. The referee came over to Luke and said, 'Try to kerb your celebrations a bit, son!'

'Sure, ref,' Luke replied, but thinking to himself, 'You must be joking!'

Hampshire seemed to have knocked the stuffing out of *Kent* and had most of the possession now. *Kent* hardly mounted any threat at all. Luke played a big part in the game without having much of an opportunity to score, until the last five minutes or so, when flicked on a lovely pass to Tommy into the area. He was upended with a late tackle which brought a penalty decision from the referee.

Tommy quickly grabbed the ball and made for the penalty spot, but was interrupted by the captain, who took the ball off him and gave it to Luke, saying, 'Here Lim, it's yours; get your hat-trick.' Luke looked across to Mr Baston who just nodded and pointed at the goal.

Luke placed the ball on the spot, took several strides back, took a deep breath and waited. The whistle blew. Luke hesitated, then jogged up and lashed the ball with all his might into the bottom right-hand corner; the keeper had dived the other way. Tommy was the first to congratulate Luke and just said, 'Brilliant, great penalty!'

The match played out without much further incident; *Kent* was a beaten side and they knew it. When the final whistle went, there were handshakes all round and the player who had been detailed to mark Luke, on shaking hands, said, 'Well played, Luke. By the way, I heard what you said to your mate about the short straw; you were right, I did.'

'Thanks,' Luke said, thinking what a good sportsman!

In the dressing room, Don Batson said he was proud of them all. They well deserved their win, even after the slow start. He expressed his thanks that they had played to the agreed plan, saying, 'That's all a coach can ask. I go home a happy man today and you ought to too. You have every reason to feel proud of yourselves. I must commend you all on your discipline too,' he said, looking mainly at Luke.

When he had changed and was leaving the dressing room, Luke was approached by a man unknown to him. He introduced himself as a reporter from the *Southern Echo* and asked if he could have a few words with him. Luke agreed but said he would have to ask Mr Batson if it was alright. The man said he had permission from Mr Batson.

'Are you fifteen?' he asked.

'Yes, just,' Luke replied.

'Have you played with older players before?'

'Yes,' Luke said. 'I play for Manleigh Town regularly and they are a senior team in the county, so I'm used to playing with older players.'

'What is your ambition as far as football is concerned?' the man asked.

'I'm going to play for England one day,' Luke replied.

'Judging from today's game, I think you might just do that,' he said. 'Thanks for the interview,' the man said. Then, just as he was turning away, he said, 'By the way, why do they call you Lim?'

'It's short for *Limited*,' Luke said. 'My initials are LTD.'

'Oh, nice one,' the man said, laughing as he left.

On the drive home, Colin had to listen to Luke describe nearly every phase of the match. He merely grinned and bore it, deciding not to remind him that he had been there watching it.

Colin, not a great football lover himself, that day came to realize just how good Luke was, and he felt proud of him and was delighted to see Luke so happy. When they arrived home, Colin said to Luke, 'What did the coach want to speak to you about before the match?'

'O my gosh!!' Luke exclaimed. 'I forgot to ask him about it after the match.' He told Colin what Mr Batson had said to him about the scout from *Southtown Rovers*. 'I'll have to ring Mr Batson and ask if he spoke to the scout afterwards.'

When Luke spoke to Mr Batson on the phone, he told Luke that he had not seen the chap after the match; he must have left the ground immediately after the end of the game. He told Luke that the scout must have been impressed:

'You had a good game, Luke. I'm proud of you. Don't forget to buy a copy of the *Southern Echo* on Monday; there was one of their reporters at the match.'

'Yeah, I'll do that,' Luke said. 'Goodbye.'

When Alice arrived home from work, Luke couldn't wait to tell her about the match but, before he got very far, she held up her hand and said:

'Stop! I know all about it. Somebody you know well popped into the shop and told me about the win, and your hat-trick.'

'Who?' Luke asked.

'Christine was at the match; I knew she was going but I didn't want to tell you before the game in case it would put you off.'

'It wouldn't have put me off; why would it do that?' Luke said.

'Well, you might have tried too hard to impress her or something.'

'Why would I want to impress Christine? She's not a team selector or football scout, is she?'

'You know what I'm getting at Luke; do you want me to spell it out for you?'

'I'm sure I don't know what you're talking about. Anyway, when's dinner? I'm starving.'

'Don't let Dad hear you say that.'

'Hungry, then,' Luke replied.

'So, what's different?' Alice said. 'You're always hungry, but I suppose you have to keep your strength up as a football star.'

'Now you're making fun of me again,' Luke feigned anger and stormed out of the kitchen. Alice shouted after him that if he wanted an early dinner, he could come and help in the kitchen. 'Only if I can do it in silence,' he said.

'I promise, I won't say another word,' Alice said, and asked Luke to lay the table for four.

'Why four?' Luke said.

'I've invited Christine for dinner. Then I thought you might like to take her to the youth club tonight. I think she'd enjoy that. I told her you wouldn't mind, is that OK?'

'Of course it is, but you might have told me,' Luke said.

'I just did. I couldn't tell you before, I only asked her this afternoon in the shop. She'll be here soon.'

'I'd better go up and change then,' Luke said. 'Is there a clean shirt for me and where are my chinos? Have I got time for a quick shower?'

'For goodness' sake, Luke. Didn't you have a shower after the match? What you're wearing now you would normally wear to youth club, but perhaps you do want to impress Christine after all?'

'Don't start that again,' Luke said as he left the room. He was spick and span when he came down and the smell of deodorant was quite overpowering. Alice smiled but said nothing. Colin answered the doorbell and introduced himself as he welcomed Christine. He directed her into the kitchen, and she entered in time to see Luke finishing off the laying of the table.

After greeting Alice with a cheerful, 'Hello,' she said, 'Hi Lim, glad to see you're well trained.'

'Just be thankful I haven't cooked the meal. Who told you I was called Lim?' he said.

'I heard it at the match this afternoon and I asked your mum about it. Do you mind being called that?'

'No, not at all; I'm used to it now.'

Colin entered the room saying, 'When you lot have finished chatting, perhaps we could feed this young lady!'

'Anything I can do to help?' Christine asked.

'You can slice some bread if you like. The breadknife is in the drawer there; eight slices will be enough to start with.'

Alice was impressed when Christine went to the sink and washed her hands first. Luke got a large plate out of the cupboard and placed it by the loaf for her. He was grateful to find something to do rather than just stand around.

'Is football talk taboo at the moment?' Christine said.

'Why would that be?' Colin said.

'Well, I suspected that's all you've heard since the match this afternoon. I thought perhaps you've heard enough by now.'

Alice said, 'Christine, football is all we've heard about in the last ten years, a few more minutes won't make any difference.' They laughed.

Christine said, 'I just wanted to say 'well done' to Luke. I'm no expert but I know Luke did well today.'

'Just my usual game,' Luke said, shrugging his shoulders, grinning, 'but thanks anyway.'

There was a good atmosphere at the meal with lots of conversation about many subjects: very little football; lots on Christine's course at college and her ambitions; Alice's forthcoming debut as a judge at the flower show; the building works; and Luke's opinion on the flower-shop van—he hoped the building works would last forever so the van could be permanently parked elsewhere.

'Then where would you practice your kickabouts?' Colin said. 'We've no back garden at the moment.'

'Hadn't thought of that,' Luke said.

After the meal Alice told Luke and Christine to go in the lounge. 'Dad and I will do the washing up,' she said.

'This way' Luke said and led Christine through to the lounge.

After being seated Luke said, 'Do you mind coming to youth club? Mum didn't cajole you into it did she?'

'No, not at all. She mentioned that you usually go on Saturday evenings, and I said I wouldn't mind going along. I'm looking forward to it. I gather there's lots to do.'

'Plenty,' Luke said, 'if you like games and stuff, but many just hang around and chat. There's a TV lounge and games console and stuff and a little tuck shop type thing. We always close with a short epilogue and a prayer; it is a church youth club run by some members of the church.'

They walked to the club which took about fifteen minutes. They weren't hurrying and were full of chat along the way. On entering the hall, Luke was greeted with a round of applause and high fives and congratulations for his role in the afternoon match. He was most embarrassed and quickly changed the subject by introducing Christine to his closer friends.

Within a very short time, he and Christine had made up a foursome with two of his mates in a game of pool. It was obvious Christine had not played before and there were lots of laughs when she missed silly shots. She thoroughly enjoyed herself anyway and probably laughed loudest of all. Luke felt really good to see Christine having fun. He had been a bit apprehensive as to whether the club would be her cup of tea, but she had fitted in very well and had embraced the atmosphere almost immediately, not showing any semblance of shyness or reticence to take part in the activities. After they had assembled for a very short epilogue, which included a short Bible reading and prayer, Luke said he would walk Christine home.

'You don't have to,' Christine said. 'It's just around the corner really. I'll be home in five minutes. Besides Suzie lives my way and I can walk home with her.'

'I'd like to walk you home anyway, if that's alright with you.'

'Course it is, you're welcome,' she said.

The three of them walked together until Suzie turned into her gateway; Christine lived just a few doors away.

'This is my house,' Christine said. 'Thank you for this evening and for walking me home. I'd like to come next week as well, if that's OK? Night Luke,' she said and then leaned forward and gave Luke a peck on the cheek. She turned and walked to her door, giving Luke a little wave before closing the door behind her.

Luke stood rooted to the spot for several seconds, then said to himself, 'Wow, I think she likes me.' He skipped home, walking on air; he couldn't remember having a better day in his whole life, ever!

'Hi Mum. Hi Dad,' he said as he walked in. He answered their questions by saying they both had a whale of a time and Christine wanted to go again next week. He said he had walked Christine home, with Suzie, he quickly added, but did not mention the parting peck.

'Good,' said Alice. 'Off to bed then; you've had a busy day, and you've church in the morning.'

'Don't forget your prayers,' Colin said.

'I won't. I've got a lot to thank God for tonight.' As tired as he was, it was a long time before his thoughts (and not all football) let him get to sleep.

CHAPTER 11

The building works were completed on time and the site was left clean and tidy, which impressed Colin very much. The new back door had been installed, the gutters done, a small section of roof renewed and a window had been eased. Colin was happy to sign Mr James' form as 'job completed'. The builders thanked him for the endless supply of teas and coffees and cake. The family were happy to have their driveway back again, and Luke, his training ground at the rear of the house.

Alice began to suffer with nerves as the time of the flower show drew near. Colin could not understand why she was so nervous, as she was so knowledgeable about flowers. He reminded her that she was not the sole judge and Mrs Williams had been doing it for years and was well known to Alice. Colin was convinced that Alice would enjoy it; she would be in her element among the flowers; Alice was not convinced and was almost regretting agreeing to do it.

The day duly arrived. Alice turned up at the town hall at 8:00am, as requested. She was met by Mrs Williams, another Alice, and was shown into a small committee room to meet the other two judges.

'First things first,' Alice Williams said, 'a nice cup of tea. Best way to start the day, don't you think?'

Alice agreed and was introduced to the other two judges. One of them was a man, the proprietor of the local garden centre. He remembered Alice from the flower shop and remembered her buying his whole stock of Polyanthus plants. They had a good old chat and Alice was told that she would be paired up with Mrs Williams and would judge the arrangements; the other two would be judging the cut flowers.

Alice felt more at ease and as they entered the main hall, Alice was astonished at the sight which greeted her, and the smells. She had been given a clipboard which listed the categories the two Alices were to judge. Mrs Williams asked her to mark each arrangement out of a maximum of twenty; she would do the same and they would compare notes afterwards. She told Alice that the first impressions were usually the right ones and to mark the exhibit straightaway. She told her she could always deduct marks after a closer inspection for poor quality of bloom or any defects. She emphasized that they had to be reasonably quick as the hall opened to the public at 10:00am and the secretary and her assistant had to place the prize cards before that.

Alice walked down the rows and duly made her marks on the clipboard. She was amazed at the ingenuity of some of the arrangements and the variety of flora used, logging some of the ideas at the back of her mind for the flower-shop displays. When she had finished, they adjourned to the committee room to compare notes. She was agreeably surprised to see how close her comments were to the other Alice's judgements and, within a very short time of comparing marks and notes, they decided first, second and third in the two different categories, and were able to pass on the notes to the secretary by 9.20am.

'There, easy, isn't it?' Alice Williams said to Alice.

'Well, I wouldn't say easy,' Alice said, 'but I must say I really, really enjoyed it. I hope you will ask me again because I would love to do it.'

'You're on,' Mrs Williams said. 'Consider yourself invited for the autumn show.'

Alice asked if it was alright to go back into the hall once it was open to the public, as she wanted to look at the other section as well. She was told that it would be in order but was advised not to tell too many people that she had been one of the judges, as not all the exhibitors would agree with the results.

The public flooded in once the doors were opened, and Alice witnessed the squeals of delight when the winners saw the results with cards placed at their exhibits. She was very impressed with the quality of flowers in the cut-flower section and with the corporate displays who were advertising their businesses. She had to eventually tear herself away and said her goodbyes to Alice Williams and the other judges.

She called into the shop and relieved Sally, who had stood in for her that morning. She told Sally and Christine all about the show and how she had met many of their customers and suppliers too. Her enthusiasm was evident to both Sally and Christine, who had big grins on their faces as Alice described the occasion in great detail.

'I think you need a calming cuppa,' Sally said and duly made tea for all three of them, and biscuits.

On the following Monday morning, a letter arrived in the post addressed to Colin. He was intrigued by the envelope, which had a

Southtown Rovers Football Club logo in the top left-hand corner. The letter contained a request for one of the executive staff of the club to call on Colin and Luke at their convenience to put an offer to them on behalf of the club with regard to the possibility of Luke joining on a professional basis. Colin's heart skipped a beat when he read it, as he knew how much this would mean to Luke. The letter ended with a telephone number to call and ask for Mr Savilla or his secretary to arrange a time and date when he could call.

Later that day Colin called into the flower shop with the letter and showed it to Alice, who said, 'My, oh my. Will Luke be excited about this or what!'

They agreed that they should wait until after dinner to tell him, as he would not be able to contain his excitement. They briefly discussed whether this was something they would want Luke to do, as the football profession could be so fickle and wrought with all sorts of pitfalls. They decided to wait and see what sort of offer and arrangements would be made by the club before recommending a course of action to Luke. It was a foregone conclusion that Luke would snap up the offer, whatever it was, but Colin said level-headed thought was needed to make the right decision for Luke.

That evening, when dinner was ending, Luke asked if he could be excused; he wanted to go to his room to sort out his collection of football cards to paste in his new album.

Colin said, 'Oh by the way, you may want to read this.' He handed Luke the letter. The puzzled look on Luke's face quickly changed to one of pure ecstasy and shock. He stood bolt upright and said, 'Dad, have you seen this? Do you know what this means?'

'Of course, I've seen it,' Colin said. 'Do you want to meet this man or not bother?' Colin said teasingly.

'I think you know the answer to that,' Luke said. 'This is what I've been dreaming of all my life. This could be my first step to scoring the winning goal for England in the World Cup.'

'Whoa, steady up,' Colin said. 'You're getting a bit ahead of yourself, aren't you?'

'I've always told you both it will happen one day; I know it.'

'We'll see,' Colin said.

'Phone him now, Dad, please. Make the appointment.'

Colin said, 'I'll ring in the morning. He probably won't be in his office now. Go up and do whatever you were going to do and calm down. I'll see you after for evening prayers.' For no apparent reason, Luke gave his mum a big hug and a kiss and went to his room.

'One happy bunny!' Alice remarked. 'I hope he's not going to have a big let-down over this,' she said. 'He would be badly hurt if this didn't come off, you know.'

'Yes, I know,' Colin replied, 'but God will provide.' Alice just grinned. Colin said, 'You do realize that, if this all comes about, Luke will be leaving home, don't you? He won't be able to live here and fully commit to the club all that way. He would have to be living in close proximity to the football ground and training centre.'

'I hadn't thought of that,' Alice said. 'Do you think he's ready to leave home? He's only fifteen, after all.'

'We're jumping the gun. Let's wait and see what this Mr Savilla has to say,' Colin said.

They finished cleaning up and washing the dishes together without further discussion on the subject, but Colin could tell Alice was mulling things over in her mind, and he guessed she was particularly thinking about the 'leaving home' bit; her motherly protective instinct was kicking in, he guessed.

The next morning just before he went to school, Luke reminded his dad to make the phone call, which he duly did and arranged for Mr Savilla to call on Wednesday at 7pm. Mr Savilla remarked to Colin, 'You have a very talented son, you know. People in the game around here are very aware of his talents and our club would clearly love to have him on our books. I think you will be agreeably surprised at the set-up we have here for youngsters like Luke.'

At school that morning, Luke just couldn't wait to tell his mates about this new development and in particular Mr Preece, the sports master. He told Luke that he knew something was in the pipeline as he had been contacted by Mr Batson, the county coach, who had been in contact with *Southtown Rovers*. Luke phoned home at lunchtime to ask if his dad had made the phone call and Colin informed him of the appointment.

'Not till Wednesday?' Luke said. 'That's a long wait.'

'It'll come soon enough,' Colin said. 'Just be patient; see you later.'

'Bye Dad,' Luke replied and then punched the air with a mighty, '*Yes, bring it on!*'

'Happy are you, Luke?' Mr O'Donnell, the headmaster, said as he walked through the corridor.

'Yes, sir,' Luke replied sheepishly as he skipped off to class.

Luke had never done his paper round so quickly as he did on that Wednesday and was home in plenty of time to have dinner over before the arrival of Mr Savilla; not that Luke felt like eating much as he was so nervous.

Alice said, 'I'll adjourn to the lounge while you two have your meeting; this is a man thing, you won't want me around.'

'Not at all!' Colin said. 'This is Luke's future we will be discussing, and you should be in on it too; two heads are better than one.'

'Three you mean, Dad.'

'I meant two rational heads, Luke. You can't count one that is up in the clouds and not thinking straight. Your excitement won't allow you a rational judgement. You will have a one-track mind. I don't mean that as a criticism because I know how much this means to you. In normal circumstance you are very sensible in your thinking, but you may not see the possible pitfalls. We all want the right thing for you and will always support you—you know that—but this is a crossroads in your life. Turning the wrong way could be disastrous, that's all I'm saying.'

'Yeah, I know, thanks Dad,' Luke said, but his nerves were still on edge, and he kept looking at his watch and checking the wall clock. Alice and Colin looked at each other, hiding grins on their faces.

'You have half an hour yet,' Alice said. 'Why don't you go up and start your homework, if you have any?'

'I haven't any,' Luke said.

Luke nearly jumped out of his skin when the doorbell rang at 6:45pm. Colin went to the door and, after a few minutes, he entered the kitchen saying it was Mr Hambard, who wanted to borrow the key to the hall to set up the tables for Saturday's jumble sale. He had no sooner sat down when a posh looking car drove into the drive. The two front doors opened and two smartly dressed men emerged from the car and approached the front door. Colin met them at the door and introduced himself as Colin Tewkes-Dawson, Luke's father.

'I'm Joel Savilla and this is Mr Simms, the lawyer for *Southtown Rovers Football Club*.'

After handshakes, Colin invited them into the kitchen and introduced Alice and Luke with further handshakes all round. The two visitors declined tea or coffee, stating that they had stopped for refreshments on the drive up. All were seated around the table when Mr Savilla opened the conversation.

'What I have to say to you, sir, is this,' he began.

Colin interrupted and said, 'Please call me Colin.'

'Right Colin. Several weeks ago, Donald Batson, the county's football coach, contacted us and said he had seen Luke play and thought he had the potential to be a professional footballer. We followed this up by sending a scout to watch him play on two separate occasions; he then contacted our first-team coach and excitedly told him that he had seen someone special. Sorry to embarrass you, Luke,' he said. 'Our first-team coach, or manager, as he is known in most circles, unusually watched him for himself and was so impressed that he recommended to our board that we attempt to sign Luke on in our youth programme; this is why we are here today.

'We want to make Luke an offer. We know he is only fifteen and still in education, but we have a scheme which takes that all into account. Before we go any further in outlining our proposal, I have to ask two questions: A) Is Luke interested in joining a professional football club, and B) Would you both be happy for him to do so, if the conditions are right?'

Luke jumped in with, 'Yes, I am very interested.' Colin and Alice said that they would not stand in his way, if the conditions were right.

Mr Simms then took over and said, 'This is the offer we would make to Luke. We will sign him on in our youth programme for a period of three years—that is, until his eighteenth birthday. He will receive fitness training and coaching with the club as well as playing for our reserves and youth team. He will need to be living in close proximity to the club—we'll discuss this in a moment.

'He will initially be paid £150 per week, £100 of which will be paid into an account weekly which he cannot touch until he is eighteen years of age, or if he leaves the club for any reason. The other £50 will be paid weekly into a current account for his use. His accommodation and board will be provided by the club as well as all the kit he will need for training and playing. He will have two days off per week, one of which we would like him to enrol in the local college of further education on a course of his choice and this will include two evenings per week. This is done so that Luke would have something to fall back on should anything happen to end his football career: perhaps an injury or illness or something like that, or perhaps he might change his mind in a couple of years' time and want to leave.'

Luke was shaking his head at this, and Mr Simms said, 'It has happened before; this is why we make this arrangement at the college.'

He went on to say, 'We would also ask Luke to sign an agreement whereby he would promise not to do anything which may bring the club or the game of football in general into disrepute, I have to say we are quite strict on this. We are aware of how easy it is for youngsters to slip into bad habits in the present-day culture of young people. We want to protect our young people from that, for their own good as well as for the reputation of the football club.

'Well, that is the offer on the table. Naturally, you will need some time to consider it and I will leave a copy of this proposal with you and you can contact me personally, say next Friday? That will give you a week to think it over. My number is on that sheet; call me any time. Do you have any questions at all?'

Colin spoke first. He said, 'Yes, I have a couple: what happens out of the football season? And will Luke be expected to play or train on Sundays?'

Mr Simms replied, 'Oh yes, I should have mentioned it. Between the end of May and the beginning of August each year, Luke's time is his own, but occasionally within that period a squad of youngsters are taken on a tour to play some games in Europe or sometimes even further afield. However, that takes no more than a week or ten days of that period. During the summer months, Luke's payments drop by £50 to a total of £100: £50 still going into his current account but just £50 into the other.

'With regard to your second question, he would not be expected to train on Sundays, but we do have some games which are occasionally played on a Sunday. Would that be a problem for Luke?'

Colin replied, 'Well yes, it would. Luke is a Christian and a regular churchgoer and would not be able to play on Sundays."

Mr Simms said, 'I don't think that would be a problem. The

matches are always in the afternoon and would not clash with morning or evening church times.'

'No, you don't understand. Regardless of what times the matches are played, Luke would not play football on a Sunday, full stop. This is in accordance with biblical teaching which sets aside the Sabbath day for rest and worship and, as a Christian, Luke is committed to those beliefs and would not wish to compromise them. Is that right Luke?'

'Yes,' Luke said and lowered his head in dejection.

'OK,' Mr Simms said. 'Let me take this back to the club and I will be in touch with you again.'

'There is one other thing,' Alice said. 'What is the accommodation provided for these youngsters?'

'Ah yes,' Mr Simms said, 'he will live with a selected family near the ground—a family you would meet and approve of before a decision is made. We have several families who are great friends of the club and have been helping us in this way for many years. We are very careful who we use and can recommend any of them as suitable people to house our youngsters. I must say we have never had any trouble with any of our youth who have stayed in such accommodation.

'Finally, if this all comes to fruition, we would expect Luke to join us in early September this year. If there is nothing else, we'll take our leave of you. Thank you for your time and interest, which we hope will lead to the mutual benefit of us and yourselves, Luke.'

There were handshakes all round and Colin showed them to the door. On departing Mr Simms said, 'I'll come straight back to you on the Sunday question.'

When Colin returned to the kitchen, he noticed that Luke was nearly in tears and Alice was trying to comfort him. 'What's up?' he said.

Luke replied, 'It's not going to happen is it. Did you notice the look between them when you said I couldn't play on Sundays?'

'They had to be told, Luke. Would you rather they found out once everything was signed up. Think of the trouble that would cause. It would be a bigger let down for you then, wouldn't it?'

'I s'pose,' Luke agreed, reluctantly.

'My big question to you, Luke,' Colin said, 'is, do you agree with not playing on Sundays? Is it the right thing to do or do you think it doesn't matter?'

'No, I don't think it's right to play on Sundays and I wouldn't do it. I do respect the Sabbath day and would not want to compromise that; it was the right thing to do to tell them.'

'I'm so glad to hear you say that, Luke. I'm proud of you that you would make that stand,' Colin said. 'As Christians and followers of the Lord Jesus Christ, we have to make sacrifices sometimes but the Lord will honour that, just remember ...' and before Colin could finish his sentence, both Alice and Luke said in unison, 'THE LORD WILL PROVIDE!' They all laughed, then Colin said, 'We'll commit it to the Lord at prayers this evening; now off you go and do your homework, if you can.'

CHAPTER 12

At prayers that evening, Luke's predicament was duly mentioned and the whole matter was placed in the hands of the Lord, Colin eventually persuading Luke that God knows best and will honour those who are faithful and obedient to his precepts and commandments. Luke was in a better frame of mind when he went up to bed, but he still put his own requests to the Lord before he nodded off.

The next day, Luke once again rushed through his paper round after school in order to hurry home in case there was any news, but he still found time to pop into the flower shop to tell Christine of the latest development. She, of course, had been told by Alice of the previous day's meeting and said she was thrilled for him and hoped it would turn out as he would want. She assured him she would see him as usual on Friday for youth club and he was quite shocked when she gave him a peck on the cheek as she said goodbye.

Luke, blushing, looked straight at Alice who merely grinned and said, 'See you later, Luke. Mind how you go now; your eyes look a bit misty.'

'Yeah, right, thanks Mum,' he replied, giving a little wave as he left the shop. Turning right at first and then backtracking to where his bike actually was, he rode off, seeing Alice and Christine through the window both laughing their heads off. Luke was on a high all the way home until he remembered that there may be a message waiting for him. On arrival, he saw that his dad's car was not in the drive, so he was no wiser. He was on tenterhooks until his dad arrived, but Colin had not heard anything, stating that he had been out most of the day. There was nothing on the answerphone.

During dinner that evening, the phone rang and Colin said, 'You can answer it, Luke. It is most likely the call you have been waiting for.'

Luke picked the phone up and, on saying 'hello,' the caller said, 'Is that Colin?'

'No, it's Luke,' he said.

'Hello, Luke. It's Mr Savilla here; I'm ringing on behalf of Mr Simms, the club lawyer. We have had a discussion with the manager and spoke about your church commitments on Sundays. I have to say that the manager accepted it was not an ideal situation. However, based on all the recommendations he has received from people whom he regards as most reliable in the game, we have decided that the original offer should stand, as we feel you would be an asset to the club. We will merely add a clause to your contract that you will not play or train on a Sunday.' Before Luke could say anything, Mr Savilla added:

'You will have to be aware that, in team selections when you are not picked for Sunday games, there is always the possibility that the manager may not wish to change his selection for other games. You ought to be aware of this possibility when considering our offer.

'Anyway, discuss this with your parents and come back to us with your decision as soon as possible, so that we can get the ball rolling (excuse the pun) with accommodation and contracts etc., should you decide to except the offer.'

'Thank you very much,' Luke said. 'Will you thank the others for me too please?'

'I will. Bye Luke.'

'Bye,' Luke said.

Luke hesitated just a minute before re-entering the kitchen and then he put on a sad face and made out to be rubbing his eyes with his fists as he entered the room. Alice saw this and said, 'Oh no, what is it, Luke?' He maintained his play and just shook his head.

Colin asked, 'Have they withdrawn the offer then?'

Luke could not maintain his façade any longer and laughing, said, 'No, the offer is still on. They will include the non-Sunday playing in the contract, so it's in my court now whether to accept or not.'

'Wonderful news, Luke,' Colin said. 'I hope you thanked them.'

'Yes, I did,' Luke said. 'They want an early decision, Mr Savilla said, so they can set things in motion if I accept.'

'Congratulations, Luke,' Alice said, 'but let's not make a hasty decision before we have weighed up the pros and cons. We know what you want, Luke, but we have to see if there are any downsides to you taking this up. You're only fifteen, remember. It's a big step so early in your life.'

'As far as I'm concerned, I see no downside to it. It's what I have always wanted and it's something I know I can do,' Luke replied.

'OK,' Colin said, 'let's look at it rationally, Alice, what can you see as a downside?'

'Well, Luke will be away from home and his friends for long

periods. He has never been away from home before. Will he be homesick?'

'What do you think, Luke?' Colin said.

'Well, it's not as if I will be the other side of the world, is it?' he said.

'No, agreed,' Colin said. 'You'll only be an hour's drive away, but I have a concern that you will be away from Christian influences for long periods of your week. Your faith will be severely tested, and your digs will have to be right for you in that respect.'

Alice said, 'We will have a major say in that, as Mr Simms said. So, we can safeguard that aspect of your life, Luke.'

'Your education is another consideration too,' Colin said, 'but you will be nearly sixteen if you were to join the club in September, so I can't see any problems with the school as regards your leaving.'

'So,' Colin said, 'taking all things into consideration and subject to your accommodations meeting with our approval, Mum and I would be happy to support you, if you wish to accept the offer of *Southtown Rovers*. What do you say, Luke?'

'Yes, a million times!' Luke replied. 'And thank you both.'

Colin said, 'I'll ring Mr Simms tomorrow and ask about arrangements for viewing the available accommodation.' All three gathered together in a huddle and hugged one another. Colin said, 'God is good, isn't he?'

'Don't you dare!' Alice said, before Colin could say anything about God's provision.

'I wasn't going to say anything,' he said, but his fingers were crossed when he said it and they all laughed. Then they celebrated with a nice cup of tea.

That weekend was one of sheer elation for Luke. He told everybody he met of the fact that he was going to be a professional footballer: his friends from school; members of the youth club; his footballing mates he usually played with at weekends; and of course, Christine, who, while absolutely delighted for him, was mindful of the fact that she would be seeing much less of him once he moved to Southtown. She mentioned this to Luke.

He said, 'Yes, I know. I had thought of that, but I'll come up and see you at every opportunity and perhaps you may be able to come down sometimes? I would love to have you there when I'm playing.'

'We can keep in touch by phone too,' Christine said.

'I'm glad you want to,' Luke said.

'Of course, I want to Luke; you know how much I think of you.'

'Me too,' Luke replied. 'I'm so glad I met you; you're the best thing that has happened to me.'

'What, even after your news this weekend?' Christine said.

'Oh yes, over and above that,' he replied.

This brought a glassy appearance to Christine's eyes, and she was just in time applying a tissue to disguise a tear drop from falling. She said, 'Oh Luke, thank you. That's such a lovely thing for you to say. I know how much your football means to you.'

'You can love two things at the same time,' Luke said.

They kissed before Luke went on his way, reminding her he would see her at the youth club later. Christine pondered on their conversation and wondered if Luke knew what he was saying in mentioning the 'love' word and in what context he said it in relation to her.

At church on the Sunday morning, Luke spoke to Roger Pinns, the detective who regularly attended, and mentioned his good news. He also mentioned that next weekend he and his parents were going down to inspect the accommodation. Roger Pinns congratulated Luke and said he would come and watch him play whenever there was a home match, if he was not on duty at the time. He gave Luke his home telephone number and asked Luke if he would let him know when he was playing; Luke agreed.

The following evening Colin answered the telephone and Roger Pinns was on the line. After initial pleasantries, Roger mentioned the conversation with Luke on Sunday morning and remarked on the fact that they were due to go down to Southtown at the weekend to 'sus' out accommodation for Luke in the autumn. Roger said he had had a word with his mother, and she had agreed that, if he wanted to, and the club approved, Luke could lodge with them. She had accommodated university students for several years and would welcome someone like Luke. She had no students at present and would welcome the company, 'especially a good Christian boy,' as she put it.

Colin thanked him profusely for the offer and said he would speak to Luke and the football club but, as far as he was concerned, it would be an ideal situation for Luke. Luke readily agreed and, when Colin contacted the club, they said that if Colin was happy, they were. They asked for the name and address of Mrs Pinns, so they could contact her regarding payment for Luke's accommodation.

They also said they could all still come down at the weekend to see the facilities at the club and they would be shown around and lunched in one of the executive suites as guests of the club. Then, if they wished, they could watch the match against *Bolton Wanderers* that afternoon. Colin thanked him and said that they would be delighted to accept the invitation. Colin then arranged to call on Mrs Pinns after the match to introduce Luke to her. She invited them all to stay for dinner and looked forward to seeing them.

Colin, Alice, and Luke arrived at the club at about 10:00am on the Saturday morning and were met by the public relations (PR) man who was most welcoming and friendly. After declining any refreshments, they were shown around the whole complex, from the club shop to the dressing rooms and the medical centre, which greatly impressed Colin with the range of equipment available to the club doctor and physiotherapists. They were shown the gym and indoor training hall and then walked out onto the pitch itself and were in awe of the grandeur of it all. The roar of the crowd was played over the loudspeakers so Luke could savour the atmosphere of the first team players as they walk out onto the pitch. Luke had goosebumps as he imagined himself being one of those players one day.

The two-hour tour ended when they met in the hospitality suite which had huge windows overlooking the pitch. They were shown to a beautifully laid-out table and handed menus for lunch. Alice remarked that the menu choices were as good as any restaurant she had ever been to. They were joined at the table by another PR man, a former player with the club, who asked if they had enjoyed the tour of the complex. They praised the facilities highly and said they had no idea what a professional football ground consisted of. Luke said he was impressed with the dressing room to see all the kit ready for the team, later that day.

The PR man said, 'I bet you imagined your shirt hanging up on its hook one day, didn't you?'

'Yes, I did,' said Luke.

'Well, work hard, listen to the coaches and before you know it, you'll be hearing the roar of the crowd for real. I remember having the same aspirations as you and they came true for me and I didn't have the talent you've got, so they tell me.' They all laughed.

When Mr Savilla and Mr Simms joined them for lunch, the PR man excused himself, saying he had some more meeting and greeting to do. Mr Simms asked if they intended to stay and watch the match and, when they said they would, he said that after lunch they would adjourn to the office and go through the contract together. They could take a copy home and peruse it before signing. The three-course lunch was duly served and all remarked on the quality of the food and service. Colin thanked them for a lovely lunch.

They then went to the office and Mr Simms systematically went through the contract with them and asked if there were any questions or any additions they wished to make. Colin said, 'No, it all seems to be in order.'

'Well,' Mr Simms said, 'take this copy with you and peruse it at your leisure and, if you are happy with it, we'll meet again for signing.'

After a quick consultation with Alice and Luke, Colin said they would be happy to sign then and there, if that was OK?

'Of course, if you're sure,' Mr Simms replied.

So, all three Tewkes-Dawsons signed the contract, as did Mr Savilla and Mr Simms on behalf of the club. There were handshakes all round and Mr Savilla said, 'Luke, you are a professional footballer with *Southtown Rovers*. Welcome to the club; we hope you will have a long and happy association with the club.' Then, he added, '... And will score lots and lots of goals.' They laughed. Colin was given a copy of the contract which he pocketed.

They were shown to an executive box where they would be able to watch the match and were told that at halftime a steward would come and take any order for drinks which they might want. Just before the match was due to start, a steward came into the box and gave Luke a small parcel; this contained club memorabilia, badges, a small history of the club and the names of the behind-the-scenes staff, from the head caterer to the groundsman, from the manager to the physio and club doctor. Luke was completely overwhelmed by it all and was walking on air. The teams walked out onto the pitch, and they focused on that. Luke's eyes were on the back of the central strikers and the number 9 shirt; Alice and Colin looked at each other and grinned.

There was a crowd of over 22,000 and were noisy in the extreme. Colin remarked that he had never seen so many people in one place before. The first half was quite uneventful with both teams seeming to cancel each other out. There were no outstanding players and only half-chances for either side to score, although Luke insisted, along with another 19,000 or so supporters that *Southtown* should have been awarded a penalty.

At halftime, a steward arrived to take their orders for drinks. Colin asked for a pot of tea and Luke asked for a cola. This was duly delivered with the steward declining a tip offered by Colin. The plate of pastries, delivered with the drinks, was mostly devoured by Luke, while Alice and Colin were engrossed with the halftime entertainment: a formation, marching brass band which were excellent.

The second half commenced with *Southtown* in the ascendancy and, when they scored, Luke frightened the life out of his parents with an almighty shout of 'Yes!!' and jumped out of his chair; Alice, and Colin merely applauded. The game continued with *Southtown* scoring two further goals, none by the number 9, much to Luke's disappointment.

At the end of the game all three had thoroughly enjoyed their afternoon and said so to Mr Savilla as goodbyes and thanks were exchanged in the car park. Luke was told that he would receive joining instructions in due course.

It was a good twenty minutes before they could exit the car park to drive to the home of Mrs Pinns, who welcomed them at the door and showed them into the lounge. Introductions were duly made, and Mrs Pinns said that Roger would be joining them shortly, when they would have dinner in the dining room. Mrs Pinns offered to take them on a tour of the house and show Luke his room. Alice fell in love with the kitchen which was very modern; Mrs Pinns said she had it installed just last year.

Alice said to her, 'Roger tells us that you are an excellent cook, so I guess you spend a lot of time in here?'

'Not as much as I would like to,' she said. 'I have few to cook for now that my students have gone, and now with Roger not able to have regular meals due to his shift work, I spend less time in the kitchen. But now that I will have Luke to cater for, I can make good use of the kitchen again.'

Colin said, 'Luke could eat for England so you will have your work cut out keeping up with him.'

'On no, on the contrary,' she replied, 'when the club representative came to see me, he left me a diet sheet for Luke, although he said it was only a guideline and not a strict regime. He stressed how important it was for Luke to have a balanced diet, but that's no problem. I'm perfectly happy with it and the club has been very generous in the amount they are paying for Luke's board.' She said she would show them the diet sheet before they leave, and they then went to see Luke's appointed room upstairs.

The room was a large one with fitted wardrobes, a double bed, one large window overlooked the botanical gardens and another towards the city with *Southtown*'s ground clearly visible in the distance, about two miles away as the crow flies. The room was not en suite but there was a large bathroom with bath and shower immediately opposite Luke's door. Luke was pleased to see that there was a large modern TV in the room. To say that the accommodation met with the Tewkes-Dawson's approval was an understatement.

Following a call from Roger who announced his arrival home, they went downstairs to the dining room and sat at the table after Mrs Pinns had removed a white tablecloth which had been placed over the table. This exposed a wonderful array of neatly arranged sandwiches and homemade cakes, together with a pretty tea set of cups and saucers and plates. Colin was invited to say Grace; then they were invited to tuck in while Mrs Pinns made a pot of tea. Luke did not need a second invitation and duly 'tucked in' with enthusiasm.

Roger said, 'You must have guests more often Mum. We get to use the good crockery rather than the usual old, chipped mugs for tea, and we get nice cakes too.'

As Mrs Pinns placed the teapot on the trivet, she clipped Roger on the ear and called him a cheeky young pup. Roger winked at Luke, and they all laughed. Dinnertime lasted for ages and Colin remarked how time had flown and they must be getting on their way. Goodbyes were exchanged and an invite extended to Colin and Alice to visit again whenever they could, especially once Luke was in residence.

On the drive back, Luke was told how very lucky he was to have such a good and homely place to lodge when he moved down to Southtown in Autumn. They agreed that they had got on very well with Mrs Pinns and she had made it obvious that Luke would be very welcome. Roger and Luke seemed to get on very well, especially as Roger was a keen *Southtown Rovers'* supporter and Luke would be going into a Christian family atmosphere. Things could not have worked out better for Luke.

Luke said, 'God has provided, eh Dad?'

Colin said, 'You're lucky I'm driving, Luke.' He looked in the rear-view mirror and said, 'Just wait till I get you home, Son. I'll teach you not to make fun of your father.'

When Luke retired that night, he took ages before dropping off to sleep. The various events of the day were racing through his head, plus the fact that a letter, lying on the doorstep for him, was from the local newspaper asking for an interview for publication at the weekend.

The interview was duly arranged, and Luke was interviewed and photographed in football kit. The article appeared as a front-page headline in the local paper saying, 'LTD FUTURE UNLIMITED', and a sub headline saying, 'Local lad goes pro for *Southtown Rovers*'.

The article explained the significance of 'LTD' and went on to say how he was scouted by the club after playing at local and county level. It quoted the county coach, Donald Batson, as saying that there were no doubts in his mind Luke had the talent to one day become a national figure in football and that he was going to a club renowned for taking on youngsters with talent to achieve their full potential. Colin was pleased that the article had mentioned Luke's stand against playing on Sundays and the writer suggested that it was indicative of what the club thought of him to still sign him regardless of his unavailability to them on Sundays.

Overall, Luke was pleased with the article and was not misquoted at any point. He did remark that the photograph made him look terrified of the camera, but he stated that he hated being photographed anyway, adding, 'unless it was a good action shot of me scoring of course'.

That weekend, Luke was the talk of the town and received congratulations left, right and centre from school chums, youth-club members, churchgoers and an excited telephone call from his Grandpa Maynard, who was 'over the moon' and said he would be framing a copy of the paper and hanging it in his office for all to see. Christine, of course, was thrilled to bits and said she could boast now of going out with someone who was famous.

Luke knew she was teasing and said, 'In future you will have to make appointments to see me, I'll have such a full diary, but I'll try to fit you in as much as I can.'

'Will I have to curtsy in your presence?' she said, 'because I'd better start practising; I wouldn't want to get it wrong in front of someone who is so perfect.' They both laughed and Christine thought it was good that they could tease each other without either of them taking offence; it showed that they had a good relationship, which pleased her greatly.

Luke was no longer permitted to play for the county side as he had signed professional forms, but he resolved to keep himself fit throughout the off season. He regularly went for training runs in the neighbourhood and was recognized and waved to by passers-by. He continued to practise in the back garden too and went to the swimming pool regularly throughout the summer months. He was determined to be as fit as possible by the time he joined *Rovers* at the end of August.

He eventually received his joining instructions and the date and time he needed to report to the training ground. It was a Tuesday and arrangements were made for him to move into the Pinns' address on the Saturday before. He said goodbye to a tearful mum; then his dad drove him off that day. They stopped briefly on the way at the flower shop so Luke could say his goodbyes and promised to ring Christine in due course.

It was a pensive Luke who was driven the rest of the way with little conversation taking place on the journey. Luke's thoughts were all over the place: from Christine to the training ground; from the Pinns to his mum and home; then to next Wednesday when Christine would be coming down to help him celebrate his sixteenth birthday. Luke decided, 'Life is good. Thank you, Lord.'

He had not realized that he had spoken his thoughts out loud and Colin said,

'What was that, Luke?'

'Oh, nothing. Just thinking, that is all.'

'A bit nervous, are you?' Colin said.

'No, of course not.' He lied.

Luke settled in that night and had a long, friendly chat with Mrs Pinns that evening. He had agreed to attend the local methodist church with her on the Sunday morning.

Wearing his brand-new suit, bought for him by his mum and dad, he walked with her to church, just ten minutes away from the house. There was a congregation of about a hundred people and they all seemed to know who Luke was. Mrs Pinns felt quite proud to be a companion of someone who seemed to be the focus of attention. After the service many came up to meet him, including the minister who told Luke that he knew his father very well. Luke immediately felt at home there and determined that he would be quite happy to regularly attend that place of worship.

After lunch, Mrs Pinns took Luke for a drive to show him the area and places of interest. That evening, Luke went to church on his own; Mrs Pinns attended mornings only. At the end of the service, Luke stayed on in the rear hall where tea and cakes were served. He mixed in well with a group of teenagers and was questioned repeatedly about his forthcoming period of time with *Southtown Rovers*—something he was quite happy to do.

When he eventually got back to his digs, he declined any further refreshments and said he was going to have an early night. He would call on the College of Further Education in the morning to obtain a list of courses available and details of when they were held etc. Mrs Pinns offered to drive him there, but he said he would walk it and then stay in the town for a while to look around the shops and maybe get a bite to eat while he was there.

CHAPTER 13

After obtaining a load of paperwork from the college, he went into the town and bought a newspaper and entered a café, where he had tea and toasties while he read the report of Saturday's match. He strolled back home and entered the lounge, where he immediately smelt a most appetizing smell from the kitchen.

He called to Mrs Pinns. 'Something smells good.'

Mrs Pinns replied, 'It is Roger's favourite: homemade steak and kidney pie, mash and mushy peas. Hope you like it, Luke.'

'If it is food, I'll like it,' he said.

'Come through to the kitchen, Luke, and have a cup of tea with me. I like to have company.'

Luke told Mrs Pinns what he had done in the morning and for lunch. He showed her his purchases which included a mobile phone which also had a camera, mini- computer and played music. Mrs Pinns was most impressed but cautioned Luke to be sensible with his money now that he would be earning big wages. Luke appreciated her concern and said that he had already resolved to be careful. She asked him about the college and Luke told her he had a list of subjects, dates and costs and he would go through them with his dad when his parents came down on Wednesday for his birthday. He remarked how kind it was for her to arrange dinner for them all.

She replied, 'Don't mention it, Luke; I enjoy it. It's like I have a family again and I love it.'

Luke was due to report to the grounds at 10am on Tuesday and Mrs Pinns offered to drive him there as she had some shopping to do in the town. He said he would make his own way back as he did not know what time he would finish that day.

On arrival at the ground, he was instructed to attend in the dressing room, where he and the rest of the reserves and the youth squad would be addressed by the club manager, Mr Calluna. He was given a name badge and had to pin it to his top.

On entering the dressing room, he found a seat among about twenty other youngsters and boldly introduced himself to those near him. Some had been there last season and there were some new recruits as well as himself. After several minutes the hum of conversation died down and Mr Calluna entered the room. He wished everybody good morning and said who he was and that he wanted to be addressed as 'Boss':

'Because I am!' he said. 'Some of you know me already so are aware that I expect high standards from you all. You respect me and the club and I will show you respect in return. If you don't, I will come down on you like a ton of bricks!'

He went on to say, 'You are here because you have potential and, to realize that potential fully, it will require hard work. You may think you are fit now; you're not,' he said, 'but you will be. My assistant here, Mr Willis, will see to that. Above all of that we want you to enjoy your time here. How long you stay here is entirely up to you and your commitment to *Southtown Rovers*. Some of you will fall by the wayside; some of you will go on to Premiership Football that should be the aim of all of you. Good luck to you all. I leave you now in the hands of the reserve team coach, Mr Donald Batson, who some of you will know as the former county coach.'

Mr Calluna left the room with Mr Willis.

Mr Batson then took about half an hour to explain what their average week would consist of and the League programmes for which he was responsible for finding teams. He explained that they would have one day off in the week, as well as Sundays, unless they had a match. This would usually be a Wednesday, and there would also be some evening games.

He turned to Luke and said, 'I know your Sunday situation, Luke, so don't worry about it.'

'Thank you,' Luke said.

They were then all asked to change into kit and be on the training ground in exactly ten minutes; any late comers would incur a press-up penalty.

After warm-up, running around the pitch, Luke learnt his first lesson. The fitness coach asked them to run around the edge of the pitch for two circuits; he said he would lead them. After the first lap, Luke felt that it was all too slow, took the lead and stretched out in front of them all. When he got back to where they had started, he stopped and turned around to see the others; they had not yet rounded the last corner. On the coach's instruction, they sprinted the last 50 yards or so. Luke had a big grin on his face until the coach approached him and said,

'Do you remember what I said at the start of the run?'

'No,' Luke said.

'Well, let me remind you. I said I would lead, didn't I?'

'Yes,' Luke replied.

'Then why did you lead after the first lap?'

'I don't know. I just felt good and could go quicker.'

'And why didn't you sprint at the end?' the coach asked.

'I didn't know I had to,' Luke said.

'Exactly,' the coach replied. 'You were not with us when the instruction was given. So, jog up to the top of the pitch and sprint down to us then give me twenty press ups.'

When Luke had completed the task, the coach addressed them all and said,

'Let this be a lesson to all of you. You are not individuals; as footballers you are part of a team. Listen to your coaches and trainers. There is always a reason for a specific instruction. You are here to learn, and obedience is part of the learning process.'

They were then formed into two teams and finished off the training session with a friendly game between them, where they were only allowed one touch of the ball and were penalized if they needed a second touch or if the ball went over head height. Following this, they had an hours break for lunch, which was provided for them, and then were told to change out of their kit and into other gear for an hour's gym session.

When they were changing, Tommy Boyle, one of the other strikers who was alongside Luke, said to him,

'What did Batty mean [referring to Mr Batson] when he said about your Sunday situation?'

'Oh, just that I do not play on Sundays,' Luke replied.

'Why not?' Tommy Boyle asked.

'Because I'm a Christian,' Luke said.

'So, what has that got to do with anything?' Boyle continued.

Luke replied, 'The Bible says the Sabbath day is a day of rest and has been set aside for worship, so my Christian principles tell me that I should obey the teachings of the Lord as depicted in the Bible.'

Boyle replied, 'I've never heard such a load of rubbish. What harm can it do playing football on Sundays for goodness' sake?'

'I don't expect you to understand; you are not a Christian,' Luke responded.

'Oh, so you think you are better than us, do you? You need to get off your high horse around here mate, or you will find yourself out on a limb.'

'I don't think that at all,' Luke said close to tears. 'It is how I was brought up and something I happen to agree with. The club knows my feelings and they are prepared to make allowances for them. If you don't like it, take it up with "Batty" as you call him.'

There was silence in the dressing room as Luke left for lunch. At lunch, Luke was aware that there were murmurings among some of the players, but a couple had sat with him and told him to take no notice of Boyle.

They stated that 'if anyone thought himself better than others it was Boyle. He likes to be the centre of attention; he thinks he is the best footballer that ever walked this earth. Don't worry about him.'

'Thanks,' Luke replied. 'I can handle him.'

After a gentle series of exercises in the gym, they were dismissed and asked to report again at 9:30, the next morning.

Luke strolled back to his digs deep in thought and was mentally tired more than physically tired. He wandered how far the ribbing would go and if Boyle was going to make his life difficult. He resolved to ignore it, but knew it was not going to be easy and hoped he could handle it.

During the evening meal, Mrs Pinns asked how the first day had gone.

'Fine, thank you,' he said.

He did not want to burden Mrs Pinns with his problems already. After his meal, he excused himself and said he was going to his room to make some phone calls. He phoned home and spoke to his father and then his mother, who told him that they, along with Christine, were coming down tomorrow for his birthday. Mrs Pinns was arranging dinner for them all and they would be staying overnight. This cheered him up considerably and when he telephoned Christine he was in high spirits and had a long conversation with her, saying how much he was looking forward to seeing her tomorrow. He made no mention of the spat with Boyle, either to Christine or his parents.

He went downstairs and sought out Mrs Pinns who was in the kitchen, and said to her,

'Thank you for having Christine and Mum and Dad tomorrow. That is really kind of you.'

'My pleasure, Luke,' she said. 'I like company and I get on so well with your parents; they are nice people. I look forward to meeting Christine too. By the way, I find you calling me Mrs Pinns a bit formal. How about Auntie Ruth? That sounds a bit more friendly, don't you think?'

'Yes, of course, I will do that. Thank you,' Luke replied. 'Oh, and by the way, you can call me Luke,' he joked.

'Get away with you,' she laughed, flicking a tea towel at him. 'If you want to make yourself a drink just help yourself. There is tea and coffee in that cupboard and milk in the fridge.'

Luke decided to make a cup of tea and Mrs Pinns had one too. They sat and drank their tea together, until Mrs Pinns said,

'Right, now leave the kitchen or you will get no surprises tomorrow.'

Luke left, after saying goodnight, and adjourned to his room to watch TV for a while. He had not realized just how tired he was and was nodding off in his chair. He turned in for the night, after setting his alarm for the morning. Within a few minutes he was fast asleep.

He walked to the training ground the next morning and, on the way, wandered what the day would bring. Boyle was already in the changing rooms when Luke walked in and greeted him by saying, 'Here's Holy Joe! Careful what you say boys, he might put a curse on you or cause a lightning bolt to come down from heaven or something,' laughing loudly.

Luke ignored him and was pleased when one of the other lads said,

'Leave it, Boyle. What has he done to you? He's entitled to his beliefs.'

Luke responded, 'It's alright. I'm used to that sort of ignorance; it doesn't bother me.'

Boyle took exception to that remark and came across to Luke shouting,

'Did you call me ignorant?'

Luke was a bit taken aback by the vehemence in Boyle's voice, but he stood up and fronted him saying,

'No, I didn't, but you are showing that you know nothing of how a Christian thinks. However, if you want to learn, I am happy to teach you all that I know.'

Before the confrontation could continue, Mr Batson entered the room and invited everybody out on the pitch. After a series of warm up exercises, Mr Batson got them all to sit down and explained that they had an under 18s' League match on Saturday morning, so the first team reserve squad would be sent to one of the other trainers, while the remainder would stay with him.

They practised their set pieces for the next hour or so. Then Luke was separated off to practise taking penalties. At the end of the session, they were all reminded that Wednesday was a day off and that the selected team would be on the board Friday morning, when they came in for a light training session.

There was some gym work after lunch again and Luke ensured that he stayed clear of Boyle. Several more players sat with Luke at lunch, and he was pleased that he had not isolated himself by standing up for his Christianity. He was told that Boyle had been 'let go' by his previous club because he had caused trouble in the squad. Another boy asked him if he thought that he was putting his career in jeopardy by not playing on Sundays. 'After all,' he said, 'you might miss some important matches.'

'I know,' Luke said. 'I am aware of that, and I am prepared to risk that rather than compromise my faith. Besides, the club knows my position but still decided to take me on. I have to be happy with that.'

'You have to be admired for that, Luke,' commented one of the lads. 'We'll be behind you all the way. Don't worry about Boyle; he'll get little support from the rest of us. He's not the most popular card in the pack but the trouble is that he's a very good player and useful for the team.'

'Thanks for your support,' Luke replied. 'I really appreciate it.'

After the gym session and before he showered and changed, and in order to avoid Boyle, he asked if he could have a word with Mr Batson and was invited into his office and to take a seat.

'What can I do for you, Luke?' Mr Batson asked. 'Is everything OK? How do you like it here?'

'I like it fine, thanks,' Luke replied. 'I wanted to speak to you about attending the college. I've got a copy of the list of courses available and the one I would like to do would mean a day attendance every Wednesday and two evenings a week on Monday & Thursday. Would that be alright?'

'It sounds OK to me. You would normally have Wednesdays off anyway and rarely would there be a youth match on a Monday. It's possible on a Thursday but only a couple a season.'

He told Luke to leave it with him and he would check it out and come back to him.

'What have you chosen to do?' he asked Luke.

'Architectural Drawing, if I can,' Luke replied. 'I like graphic design and drawing and that sort of thing, so I think that course would suit me. And it is over a period of three years, so it is not too intensive.'

'Good for you,' Mr Batson responded. 'I'll get back to you on that as soon as possible.'

Just as he was about to go out of the door, Mr Batson called, 'Oh Luke!'

As Luke looked back, he said, 'Happy birthday.'

'Thank you, sir,' Luke replied, and walked off with a big smile on his face.

The changing room was deserted when he got there, so he quickly showered and changed but could not find his trainers anywhere. He checked under and on top of the lockers, but they were nowhere to be found. He checked the toilets and saw them lying in the pan in the first cubicle; he really felt choked up. He rinsed them under a tap and put them on and walked home with them sopping wet; he had no choice. He did not have to think too hard to work out how they got there.

However, he soon cheered up when he suddenly remembered Christine would be there when he got home. As he entered the driveway of the house, he saw a brand spanking new 98cc scooter with a tag hanging from the handlebars. He dropped his backpack on the ground and read the writing on the tag:

'Happy Birthday Luke, From Dad, Mum, and Gramps Maynard. *Drive carefully!*'

Luke was so taken aback he did not know what to do; he placed his hands on his head and said, 'WOW!' He looked around him but there was nobody to be seen. His dad's car was there, but no sign of life.

Then he spotted everyone at the window watching him. There was his mum, his dad, Christine, 'Auntie' Ruth and Roger all laughing their heads off. Luke just pointed at the scooter and then at himself and shook his head disbelievingly. They all came outside, where there were hugs and kisses all round and many, many 'thank-you's, expressed by Luke. His wet trainers were now completely forgotten.

When they eventually went inside, after fully inspecting the scooter, it was explained to Luke that motor Insurance had been arranged for him, but he would have to get his provisional licence by completing the forms they gave him and taking them to the appropriate office.

After he had opened several cards and Ruth had placed them on the mantel piece, Christine handed him a neatly wrapped package and with a kiss and wished him a happy birthday. In the package was a lovely gents watch with a fabric strap in the colours of *Southtown Rovers*. Luke thanked Christine once again with another kiss and put his watch on admiringly.

Then, Roger handed him a wrapped present with a tag on it saying, 'Happy Birthday from Auntie Ruth and Roger.'

As Luke took it, Roger said, 'You are not going to like this, Luke; in fact, you may grow to hate it, but I am sure you will find it useful.'

Luke was intrigued and very carefully unwrapped the package and found a box, which indicated the contents as a novelty alarm clock. This was in the form of a rocket and launch pad, about 12 inches high. Roger held out his hand and said,

'Here, I will show you how it works. You set the time like this,' and he pressed some buttons. 'Then you set the alarm like this,' and he pressed some more buttons. He then placed it on the table and said, 'Watch this.'

A voice came from the rocket saying, '5, 4, 3, 2, 1, lift off!' and the rocket flew about two feet into the air while the launch pad emitted a piercing persistent bleeping sound.

'The only way to stop the bleeping,' Roger said, 'is to replace the rocket on the launch pad.' And he did just that.

Luke said, 'Thank you very much, I think!!' and they all laughed.

Ruth said, 'I am going to remove the alarm clock that is in your room at the moment, so you will have to use this one. This means you will have to get out of bed to stop it. No extra five minutes snooze for you, I'm afraid.' They all laughed again.

Alice had noticed that, when Luke removed his trainers on entering the house, his socks were wet. During a lull in the conversation, she asked Luke why this was. Luke merely said,

'Oh, there was a bit of an accident in the dressing room, and they got wet.'

'So did you walk home like that then?'

'Yes, I had no others with me.'

'You should go and change into some dry ones, Luke. You will catch cold if you stay in those. Besides, if you leave wet footmarks on Mrs Pinns floor, she'll be kicking you out.'

'It would take more than that, Alice,' Ruth replied. 'I like his company, and he's such a credit to you—so polite and thoughtful.'

Luke stood up. 'I'm out of here. Too much praise in one go.' He said to Christine, 'Come up and I'll show you my room.'

He left with Christine carrying his new alarm clock.

'Dinner in ten minutes,' Ruth called after them.

'We'll be there,' Luke replied.

Christine was impressed with Luke's room and sat on the bed and asked Luke if he was really happy with things here. As Luke dried his feet with a towel and took some clean socks from the drawer, he replied that he was. He said 'Auntie' Ruth was brilliant, like a second mum, and he was enjoying his football.

'How did your trainers get so wet?' Christine asked questioningly. 'I thought your answer to your mum was a bit evasive. I can read you like a book, Luke. What is going on?'

'It's a long story,' Luke replied sighing. 'It wasn't the right time to say anything.'

'Tell me,' Christine said. 'I know there is something troubling you.'

Luke then related the whole story regarding Tommy Boyle and the hassle he was getting from him, but he told Christine he could handle it. She wasn't convinced but let it rest at that. Luke then mentioned that he was going to go to Architectural Drawing classes at the college, if the club approved the timings of the tutor periods.

'That's great,' Christine responded. 'Maybe you can design a house for us one day?'

Luke's shock at her remark showed on his face.

'I'm sorry, Luke,' Christine said. 'I didn't mean to say that. Forget I said it; that was very forward of me.'

'Not at all,' Luke replied. 'I'm glad you said it, if it means you see a future for us?'

'It is early days, isn't it Luke. Who knows what may happen in the future.'

At that point, Ruth called out, 'Dinner, you two.'

'Coming,' Luke replied, putting on his sock and shoes.

They had a sumptuous dinner, during which Roger said he would help Luke with his license application and point him in the right direction to get training on the scooter before taking to the roads.

His mum reminded Luke that he should ring Gramps Maynard to thank him for the present. Luke agreed he would do that.

Towards the end of the meal, Roger carried in from the kitchen a large birthday cake, decorated in the form of a football pitch with the four corner flags depicted by lit candles. They sang 'Happy Birthday' to Luke and then he blew out the four candles in two puffs. Alice remarked on how beautifully the cake was decorated and that it seemed a shame to cut it. She thanked Ruth for making it, saying she never would have had time or the talent herself.

Roger spoke up, 'Would you two ladies stop chatting and cut the cake. Luke is drooling over getting the first piece.'

'He can cut it then,' Ruth retorted, handing him a large knife, which Luke took and proceeded to cut a thin slice of cake.

'That's tiny,' Roger remarked.

'That is your piece, not mine,' Luke replied laughing and they all joined in.

Alice said to Ruth, 'That side of him is nothing to do with me.'

After dinner, they spent the evening relaxing in the lounge, once Roger and Luke had played around with the scooter outside. Space was restricted in the driveway, but Luke was able to start it and ride a few yards back and forth. It was arranged for Luke to keep it in the garage, as it was never used for either of the cars.

When Luke came in, he phoned Gramps Maynard and thanked him for the generous gift.

Gramps told Luke, 'You must promise me that you will be very careful on it. I'd never forgive myself if you got injured, or worse, in an accident.'

'I'll be careful, Gramps,' Luke promised. I do not intend breaking any speed records with it, but it will be very useful for getting to and from the football club and college. Also, Mrs Pinns will not feel obliged to take me here, there and everywhere, although she is more than willing to do so!'

Gramps said, 'When you have time, you must come up and see me some time; I haven't seen you for ages, and you've probably grown several inches since I last saw you. All I have is an old picture on my office wall.'

'I will Gramps. As soon as I get my license, I'll pop up and see you. Thanks again for the present; it was very kind of you.'

'Not at all. You're my only grandchild and where else would I spend my money, anyway? Enjoy the rest of your birthday and give my love to your mum and dad. Bye Luke.'

Luke said his goodbyes and joined the others in the lounge; he passed on the message to his mum and dad, who asked if Gramps was OK.

Luke replied, 'He sounded in good spirits.'

At the end of the evening, when they had all decided it was time for bed, Colin asked them if they would all like to join together in evening prayers. They all said it would be nice to do that. Colin read a few verses from the Bible and then prayed, thanking God for his goodness and asked a blessing on all present and for absent friends. He thanked God for his provision in arranging a loving family for Luke, and then asked for strength for Luke in overcoming any difficulties he may meet along the way.

As Luke was leaving the room, Colin asked if he might have a word with him.

Luke stopped and asked, 'What about?'

'Just a word,' Colin said. 'It won't take a minute.'

The others left the room, but not before Christine gave Luke a peck on the cheek and said she would see him in the morning. Colin asked Luke to sit down and then said,

'I have some bad news to tell you. I don't want to spoil the end of what has been a good day for you, but there is something you should know. Mum is quite ill. She has been diagnosed with some sort of growth on the brain and it is in such a position that it is inoperable. They are not sure what it is yet, but she has to have further tests. We will know more in a couple of weeks' time. Until then, we will have to take it to the Lord in prayer and place it in his hands. As yet, it has not changed her lifestyle. She still goes to work but on occasions has very painful headaches. Initially they were controlled with medication, but this no longer has any effect.'

'Is she going to die?' Luke asked, holding back the tears.

'We will be clearer on that when they get the results of the tests. In the meantime, we must remain hopeful. Your mum is a strong woman and otherwise healthy, which must go in her favour.'

Luke gave Colin a hug and replied, 'Dad, this is scary; I feel absolutely drained. What will I say to Mum in the morning?'

'Don't worry about speaking to your mum about it; she is quite philosophical and is at ease talking about it. It is everyone else who is worrying; she is taking it in her stride.'

They said their goodbyes and went to bed. Luke tossed and turned with a mixture of emotions going through his head: the pleasure of seeing Christine and his parents; the scooter; Tommy Boyle; and the awful news about his mum. It had been quite a day! He should have been totally exhausted and he was, but it was a long time until he could catch his sleep.

He was awakened in the morning with a tap on his door and his mum saying,

'Are you awake, Luke?'

'Come in,' Luke said.

Alice came in and sat on Luke's bed. He sat up and gave his mum a hug.

'Dad told me, Mum.'

'Yes, I know,' she said. 'Now, don't you worry yourself? It will be fine; you haven't noticed any difference in me, have you?'

'I haven't seen much of you lately, have I?' he replied.

'This has been going on long before you left home Luke. We just didn't think it was right to burden you with it in case it influenced your decision about coming down here. It wouldn't have been fair on you to put my health concerns into the equation when making your decision. Anyway, this may all be a fuss over nothing, so don't you go and fret over it.'

Luke was about to reply when they heard, '5, 4, 3, 2, 1, lift off'. Luke was reaching out for the alarm, when Alice grabbed his wrist and said, 'No, let it go off. I want to see it go.'

The rocket left the launch pad and the beeping started. Alice stood up and gently kicked the rocket to the far side of the room and laughing said, 'See you at breakfast Luke. Christine is downstairs.' Luke threw the pillow at her but merely hit the closing door. She partially opened the door and said, 'Missed,' then disappeared downstairs.

Everybody was down for breakfast, except Roger. Ruth said he has a day off, so she let him sleep in. He did not get many opportunities to do so, as he often has to work his days off because they are so busy.

They discussed how they were going to spend the day over breakfast. Colin said they would have to leave about lunchtime as he had some preparation still to do for Sunday. However, he agreed to take Luke and Christine to the college to formally enrol into his course and sort out fees etc. Christine said she would make enquiries at the same time about starting her course in horticulture, as the university offices were quite near to the college. Alice and Ruth would hit the shops in the meantime. They decided they would all meet for lunch at 12:30pm at Ruth's favourite café, where the pastries were to 'die for'.

'What, better than yours?' Luke exclaimed.

'I'll let you be the judge of that,' she replied. 'Besides, I'm not sure you are allowed pastries! I will have to check your diet sheet.'

'Well done, Ruth. We can't have a fat boy playing for England now, can we!' Alice interjected.

Luke found his mum to be in good spirits considering the circumstances and perhaps he was worrying unnecessarily, or was it just one of her better days? He was not sure.

Luke and Christine piled into Colin's car and Alice went off with Ruth, Colin called out, 'Don't spend all the money in one shop, will you?'

'Can't promise!' Alice replied, closing the car door.

When Colin had dropped Christine off at the university, he went on to the offices at the College of Further Education with Luke to formally enrol in his course. They were amazed to find that the football club had already been in touch with them to make arrangements about paying the fees. Apparently, they (Luke's club) would pay the sum due and would recover Luke's share of fifty per cent through his wages. Both Colin and Luke thought this to be a good arrangement.

Luke's first day would be the following Wednesday. He was provided with a list of requirements he would need initially and the name of the supplier where he could get discount for his purchases. They, then, collected Christine, who said she would be starting in January, next year.

They went on to meet Alice and Ruth for lunch and, after lunch, Colin, Alice, Christine, and Ruth said their goodbyes and left for their drive home. Luke went home in Ruth's car.

On the way home, Ruth commented to Luke how brave his mother was being and seemed to be taking this problem in her stride. Luke explained how he felt a bit guilty being away from home when his mother was so ill. Ruth reassured him he should not feel like that, as his mother told her that she took great comfort knowing he was well settled here, and she had no worries for his welfare.

To change the subject, Ruth asked, 'What would you like for dinner?'

'I don't mind,' Luke replied, 'as long as there is plenty of it; I am starving … hungry,' he corrected himself. 'Dad tells me off if I say I'm starving and quotes the third-world countries at me.'

'I'll check your diet sheet guidelines, then halve it I think!' Ruth said, jokingly.

'But I need the energy,' Luke said, 'or I will fade away.'

When they got home, Roger was washing his car and he greeted them on arrival. He told Luke that he could now use his scooter as the application form and fee for his provisional license was lodged at the office and would be sent to him in due course. Luke said he would have to get some 'L' plates first, but Roger had recovered some from the garage, which just needed a clean. Luke cleaned them up, put them on and said that he would go for a short spin on the bike. He rushed inside and got his helmet and jacket, then jumped on the scooter and started it up.

'You be careful,' Ruth said. 'And don't be late for dinner,' she added.

'As if!' Luke replied, as he rode off gingerly through the gate.

He returned half an hour later feeling very pleased with himself. He had enjoyed his ride and remarked how easy the scooter was to handle. Looking at Ruth, he added, 'even at ninety miles an hour!'

'I am not going to bite, Luke.' They laughed and went inside.

Ruth had made a lovely lasagne for dinner, which Luke devoured with relish; he declined dessert, surprisingly, but finished off a chocolate bar, claiming it was energy food.

Roger asked Luke what was on the cards for him tomorrow. Luke replied that he had to be in for 10 o'clock for a light training session as the youth team had a match on Saturday morning. He said he could not wait to get there, as the selected team would be posted up on the board when they got in.

'Do you think you have a chance of making the team?' Roger asked.

'Yes, I think so,' Luke replied. 'Mr Batson is the one who picks the team. He knows me well from the county youth team and training has gone well for me, I feel. So, I am hopeful, but there's lots of older under 18s, some of which are in their second season and have been regulars in the team.'

'Well good luck, Luke. I hope you make it,' Roger said.

'Thanks,' Luke replied.

'I'm probably working on Saturday, so I won't be able to come and watch you I'm afraid, if you get picked that is.' Roger added, 'Where is the match anyway?'

'I haven't a clue. I don't even know who we are playing against,' Luke replied. 'I guess I will find out in the morning.'

At bedtime that night, Luke prayed for his mum and asked the Lord to heal her and keep her free from pain. He asked a blessing for all who had been so kind to him on his birthday and prayed that he might be picked for the game on Saturday.

CHAPTER 14

Luke was in nice and early on the Friday morning and went straight to the notice board, where he learnt that it was a home game with the kick-off at 10:30am. The opposition was *Fulham F.C.*'s youth team in the South Home Counties League. A copy of the League table was on the board which showed both *Fulham* and *Southtown Rovers* had played two and won two, as had three other teams who had six points. The team sheet was also displayed and showed Luke to be in the starting eleven, as was Tommy Boyle. The instructions were for players to be at the ground no later than 9:30am or forfeit your place on the squad.

Luke was delighted and punched the air with a resounding, 'YES!' He determined there and then that there was no way he was going to be late in. Luke checked out the rest of the team and the reserves. He was surprised to see who was not in the starting line-up; one or two had looked so good in training.

Once they had all changed, the team and the reserves were separated off and the rest were sent out for training. On the notice board in the dressing room, Mr Batson went through the system that they would be playing and their individual positions. It would be a 4-4-2 formation, with Luke and Justin Campbell as the two strikers. Luke liked Justin; he had been one of those who supported him during the Tommy Boyle furore in the dressing room. Boyle was picked to play in a midfield role. Luke was told he would be the penalty taker were any awarded and he would be practising penalty-taking later that morning.

They were informed that *Fulham* were a very well-organized side, but Mr Batson did not know if they had any new players this season. He warned it would not be an easy match and they would need to play to their full potential. He ordered them outside to warm up and do some loosening-up exercises. Then, they would be separated into forward and defensive players and go through some set pieces. On the way-out, Luke asked Mr Batson if squad numbers had been allocated yet.

'Oh yes, I had forgotten about that. Thank you for reminding me. I'll announce them outside in a moment.'

When he came out after a few minutes, he called everyone together and said, 'Here are your shirt numbers which you will retain the whole season; they have to be registered with the Football Association. He started with numbers 1 and 2 for the goal keepers. Luke was allocated No. 9 and Justin, No. 10. Tommy Boyle was No. 6 and Colin Gilby, the No. 8, was captain. They continued with their warmup exercises and then the two squads were separated.

After they had been through a few set pieces, Luke was called aside by Mr Batson who instructed him to take five penalties. Luke scored with everyone, varying which side of the goalkeeper he placed the ball. He was told to continue for a further twenty penalties and only one of them was saved by the keeper; he was on target every time.

'I'm happy with that,' Mr Batson said.

He called all the squad together and said, 'Good luck tomorrow. Don't let yourselves down; I want good discipline at all times. Now, off you go and I'll see you in the morning.'

After Luke had changed and before he left the ground, he phoned home to tell his mum and dad the good news. He learned that his mum was fine. He then phoned Christine and had a long conversation with her, telling her how much he had enjoyed being with her yesterday; the feelings were mutual. She wished him all the best and asked him to let her know how he got on. He said he would.

When he approached his scooter, he noticed that the front tyre was flat. On closer inspection, he saw that the valve had been loosened; he concluded that this was a deliberate act, and he knew in his own mind who was responsible. One of the staff saw Luke at the scooter and asked if everything was OK. Luke explained what he had found.

'We can pump that up,' the chap said. 'I'll get a pump.'

He arrived with a pump that they used for footballs and a box of various attachments. Fortunately, one fitted, and the tyre was inflated sufficiently to be ridden. Luke said he would pop into the garage on the way home and get it inflated properly.

'I wonder how that happened?' the staff member asked.

'It must have worked loose, I suppose,' Luke replied (thinking to himself, 'with some help!').

Ruth was delighted for Luke when he told her his good news.

'You must let your parents know,' Ruth said.

'I have already done that, and Christine,' Luke replied. 'Auntie Ruth, will you make sure I am up in good time tomorrow morning? I have to be there without fail for 9:30am or I lose my place.'

'Yes, of course, but you will have no trouble in getting up, especially with your new alarm clock. Just make sure you set it tonight. I will give you a call anyway though, shall I?'

'Yes please,' Luke requested.

'You have to have special meals on match days too, don't you?' she asked.

'Yes, but I don't know if it says anything about breakfasts for morning matches,' he replied.

'I'll check,' Ruth said.

There was nothing special on the sheet, so it was decided he would just have his normal breakfast of cereal and toast. He was OK in training with that so it should not be any different.

Luke spent the afternoon helping Ruth in the kitchen making sandwiches for the Women's Institute (WI) meeting that evening, which Ruth was attending. After dinner, he relaxed in the lounge and watched television but he hardly heard or took in a word of what was being said; his mind had been transported to the football pitch of *Southtown Rovers* in Carrow Lane. The morning could not come quick enough for him. 'Must have an early night,' he thought to himself, 'and make sure I set my alarm properly too.' He went to bed at 10:10pm, when Ruth got home.

Luke arrived in good time at the ground in the morning. He was amazed to see all the kit had been laid out neatly in the dressing room; his No. 9 shirt was hanging up on its hook and his shorts, socks, and boots, all nice and clean, were on the bench underneath it. Luke immediately had butterflies in his stomach as the nerves kicked in. He took a good swig of water from the water cooler. Others started to arrive and the banter in the dressing room started, which made Luke forget his nerves. One of the players on entering said:

'The *Fulham* coach has arrived, and it looks like a coachload of fans has arrived as well.'

Luke said, 'Fancy fans following a youth team away.'

Justin replied, 'We get about a hundred who come to our away games, depending on how far they have to travel and who we are playing against.'

'So how many would we expect here today?' Luke asked.

'Well, for a morning match there will be a crowd of about three to four hundred,' Justin answered.

'I've never played in front of so many before,' Luke replied.

'Get used to it,' Justin said. 'You will be aware of the supporters rooting for you; let them lift you and enjoy the support.'

By 10 o'clock, all the team were ready and were addressed by Mr Batson:

'You've all received your instructions. Remember what we went through yesterday. You have the beating of this team if you focus on what your individual roles are, and you work for each other as a team. Now, let's go out for a gentle warm-up and stretching.'

They filed out onto the pitch in their tracksuit tops and were taken through various exercises and short sprints. Luke could not help but look around at the crowd of about three hundred or so. It felt more like three thousand to him; he just could not wait for the game to start. They were eventually called to the side of the pitch to deposit their tracksuits. *Southtown*'s captain, Colin Gilby, went to the middle for the toss up; it was *Southtown* to kick-off. The referee called them to take their positions and then, after getting the thumbs-up sign from his two linesmen, he blew his whistle to start the match.

The first half progressed with *Southtown* just about having the majority of the possession of the ball, but without any real goal scoring chances being created. Luke had plenty of involvement and did not let himself down. The game, however, changed completely just after half an hour of play when *Southtown* was awarded a free kick out on the right wing.

Luke and Justin took up their positions in the penalty area and immediately two of *Fulham*'s biggest defenders latched onto Luke. The ball floated in at a perfect height and Luke easily outjumped everybody in the area and powerfully headed the ball into the back of the net, giving the goalkeeper no chance at all. There was loud acclaim from the fans and his teammates mobbed him with 'high-fives' all round. Luke felt good.

He had plenty possession of the ball after that, and it clearly showed that he was in a class of his own. He outran, out tackled, and out dribbled his opponents; they could not get near him. He had one shot superbly saved by the goalkeeper and created at least two good, goal-scoring opportunities for his teammates which were off target.

His chance for a second goal came when, just a few minutes before the end of the half, Justin was blatantly tripped in the area, and they were awarded a penalty. Luke picked up the ball and placed it on the penalty spot. At the referee's whistle, Luke ran forward and smashed the ball in the top corner of the net, the goalkeeper not getting anywhere near it. The score was 2–0 at halftime.

They all made a fuss of Luke back in the dressing room; Luke calmly sat down and drank his tea, feeling pleased with himself.

Mr Batson said, 'Well done everybody. Now, be aware that in the second half they are going to come at you. So, discipline please; don't give up possession of the ball.'

He instructed the captain, Colin, to drop back a little in the first fifteen minutes or so, to support the defence.

Southtown did come under pressure in the first ten minutes or so but managed to hold *Fulham* at bay very well and no scoring chances were created. After fifteen minutes, *Southtown*'s goalkeeper punted the ball up the field and Luke latched onto it, cushioned it on his chest and then spun with the ball past the nearest opponent. He jinxed passed two more and then, just inside the area, he unleashed a mighty shot at goal which bent around the goalkeeper and inside the far post: 3–0.

Mr Batson remarked to his assistant, 'That kid's a genius.'

Southtown continued with most of the possession and were clearly out-playing *Fulham*. With five minutes to go, Luke gained possession of the ball and ran at the defence. As he was approaching the area, he became aware of Tommy Boyle running on his outside.

Boyle shouted, 'To me, to me, now!'

Luke slipped a perfect pass through the defence and Boyle scored the fourth goal. He was not mobbed by the other players but Luke high-fived him on the way back to the centre of the field. The match ended at 4–0.

Mr Batson shook hands with the opposing coach, who pointed at Luke and said:

'Where the heck did you get him from? I hear he is only sixteen, too?'

'That's right; he turned sixteen only a couple of days ago. Good, isn't he?'

'He sure is,' the other coach replied. 'And you'll have him for a couple of years too, I guess?'

'I doubt it,' Mr Batson replied. 'I think Pablo will be snapping him up before too long.'

'Pablo?' the coach said.

'Yes, Pablo Colluna,' Mr Batson expounded. 'He hasn't seen him play or train yet but, in fairness to the kid, I will have to recommend him for higher things.'

'Well, I hope that's the last we see of him. I wouldn't want my team to face him every week, that is for sure!'

When Mr Batson entered the dressing room, he said:

'Well done everybody. I have just been talking to their coach; he is still a bit shell shocked but accepts that they were beaten by a better team. I am proud of you all, well done.'

He deliberately did not single out Luke for special praise but said to him:

'Not a bad debut Luke: a hat trick. You've got to keep that up now, you know.'

Luke smiled.

'See you Monday, boys. Don't be late, 10 o'clock sharp,' and he left the room.

'Bye, Boss,' most of them replied.

'What happens about our dirty kit?' Luke asked Colin.

'Just leave it on the bench; the laundry lady will collect it. You just have to clean your own boots.'

'Thanks,' Luke replied.

The dressing room was almost empty when Tommy Boyle was about to leave. Luke called after him and said.

'Tom, can you hang on a minute. I need to speak to you?'

'What about?' Boyle asked.

'It's private,' Luke said. 'Wait till the others have gone.'

'Well hurry up, I haven't got all day!'

When the others had gone, Luke went over to Boyle who was sitting on the bench and stood in front of him and said:

'What have I done to upset you?'

'I don't know what you mean,' Boyle replied.

'You know exactly what I mean Tommy. You keep mocking me about my Christian faith; there were my trainers down the toilet; my bike tyre let down. What next? How far are you going to go with this?"'

'I've had enough of this,' Boyle said as he tried to stand up. But Luke merely put his hands on his shoulders and forced him back down on the bench saying, 'You are not going anywhere till we have sorted this out.'

Boyle tried to get up again but Luke, despite being two years his junior, was bigger and strong enough to prevent Boyle from standing.

'Look,' Luke said, 'I do not intend reporting these incidents to Mr Batson, but I want them to stop here and now. Your childishness is going to split the team. If Mr Batson finds out what has been happening, you would be out on your ear. I won't tell him but, if these things carry on, can you guarantee someone else won't tell him and, if he approaches me, I will not lie. Why are you doing this Tommy?' Luke ended.

'To bring you down to earth,' Tommy retorted. 'Your high and mighty, better than us attitude just got my back up, that is all. You are no better than any of us.'

'I don't think that at all, Tommy; honestly, I don't. In fact, like most Christians, I am the first to recognize how low I am. The Bible tells me I am a sinner; I'm no better than anybody else. If I've given you any other impression then, perhaps, I should apologize to you.'

Tommy was stunned by Luke's remarks and just sat there in silence for several seconds. Then, he extended his hand and said, 'Truce?'

'Sure,' Luke replied. And they shook hands.

As they walked out together, Boyle said to Luke:

'Good game today, Luke, well done. I am glad I am on your side. I wouldn't like to play against you. I realized how strong you are back there in the dressing room.'

'You wouldn't have to worry about that, Boylie,' Luke said. 'You wouldn't catch me!'

Then he ran off towards his scooter. He turned and saw Boyle shaking a fist at him but with a big grin on his face. Luke sat on his scooter, slammed his crash helmet on and said to himself, 'SORTED!' He rode off singing, much to the puzzled look of others in the car park.

When he got home, Ruth asked him how he had got on today.

'We won 4–0,' Luke replied.

'Oh well done, and how did you do?' Ruth asked.

'Fine. I was happy with my game.'

'Are you hungry,' Ruth continued.

'I could eat two horses,' Luke replied.

'What would you like?' Ruth asked.

'Could I have a full-English-breakfast-type meal?" Luke asked.

'You mean a mixed grill?' Ruth corrected.

'I suppose so, but can I cook it?' Luke requested.

'Why?' Ruth asked, surprised.

'No reason. I just like to do it, that's all, if it is OK with you?' Luke replied.

'Of course it is. I'll get the food and the pots and pans out for you,' Ruth offered.

Luke was in the middle of frying sausages and bacon when Ruth called him to say Christine was on the phone for him. He left the kitchen and spoke to Christine telling her all about the match and his part in it.

She said, 'Well done, I am proud of you.'

When Luke returned to the kitchen, he confessed that he had completely forgotten about the food he was cooking, and thanked Ruth for taking over.

'That's what happens when you get involved with us females,' Ruth teased.

Luke sat down and thoroughly enjoyed his meal and then spent the afternoon watching sport on TV. When Ruth came in with a cup of tea, Luke asked her if she minded if he went to see his parents for the day tomorrow.

'Of course not,' she replied. 'I am sure they would love to see you but maybe you should check with them first, in case they have something planned.'

'Yes, I will phone them, but Dad is probably preaching anyway, so I can attend church with him' Luke said.

Luke checked with his mum who said it would be good to see him. He learned that his dad would be preaching at his home church and that Christine would be there too, as usual. He asked his mum not to tell Christine; he wanted to surprise her. She agreed. She also said she would invite Christine back for lunch.

Luke decided he would ride up in the morning and go straight to church. Alice reminded him it was a long drive; he would have to leave early if he wanted to get to church on time. He told Ruth of the arrangements and that he would not want any meals tomorrow as he would stay for the evening service too.

'I've got the day off then!' Ruth stated.

'You have,' Luke replied, smiling.

Luke arrived in plenty of time for church and even enjoyed the ride up; he loved the freedom of the open road. He was welcomed at the door by one of the stewards and learned that his dad was in the vestry; his mother and Christine were in their usual pew. Christine was visibly shocked to see Luke coming into the pew and was delighted as he sat down alongside her. She gave him a quick peck on the cheek saying, 'What are you doing here?'

She turned to Alice and whispered, 'Did you know he was coming?'

'Yes,' she said. 'But I was sworn to secrecy.'

'No wonder you invited me to lunch,' Christine continued.

When Colin entered the pulpit and welcomed everybody, he asked forgiveness for giving a special welcome to Luke.

'Not quite the return of the prodigal son, but very welcome. It's good to see you, Luke.'

Luke raised a hand in acknowledgement. At the end of the service, Luke was the centre of attention. He was questioned repeatedly about how he was getting on; was he enjoying it; was he missing home etc. He was glad when it was time to leave; he was quite overwhelmed by all the attention. He proudly showed Christine his scooter, who suggested that he should put some flower stickers all over it to promote the flower shop.

'Like your Mum's van!' she suggested.

'You must be joking,' he replied.

'I'll tell you what; 'let me do some artwork on your helmet instead,' Christine suggested.

'The only thing going on my helmet is what is already on it: "No. 9",' Luke retorted.

'Why 9?' Christine asked.

'That's my squad shirt number at *Rovers*,' he replied.

After lunch, Luke and Christine went for a long walk and caught up with all the latest news.

'You seem taller,' Christine remarked.

'I don't think I have grown in a matter of days!' Luke said. 'But the training is really hard and the work in the gym is very intensive, and I've been eating good healthy food. Maybe that has had some effect. I have never felt fitter in my life.'

During tea and before the evening service, Luke asked his mum how she had been.

'I get my bad days occasionally, but I've been quite well. I have to go for another scan on Thursday to see if there has been any change, but I doubt if there has been as I don't feel any worse than before,' she answered reassuringly.

Luke left immediately after church to ride back down to Southtown. He said goodbye to his mum and dad. Christine saw him off in the car park; a hug and a kiss sent him on his way and removed any worries about his mum from his mind.

'Ride carefully,' was Christine's parting shot as he drove off. The ride was uneventful, and he made good time.

Over the next few weeks, Luke's training went very well. He was a regular in the team and was the team's top scorer with eleven goals over seven matches. He became the star player and was making a name for himself in the League and among the other teams. He had also settled in very well at the college and enjoyed the tutorials. He felt he had made the right choice when choosing Architectural Drawing.

Just a week before Christmas, Luke was called in to Mr Batson's Office. He was told to take a seat. Mr Simms, the club lawyer was also present. It was Mr Batson who opened the conversation by saying:

'Don't look so worried Luke. We have some good news and some bad news for you. First the bad news ... You were expecting to be back home for Christmas. I'm afraid that is not going to be possible. You see, Mr Colluna wants you for the first team squad over that period as they have three matches to play in eight days and, with the list of injuries they have, they need to supplement the squad. Mr Colluna has seen you play and heard good reports on you and, therefore, wants you to join the first team squad over that period. This does not guarantee that you will get a game in the first team, but Mr Colluna wants that option available to him. What do you say to that?'

Luke was shocked beyond belief and overjoyed at the same time at the opportunity. He accepted the offer without any hesitation whatsoever.

Mr Simms then said, 'What we have to do now Luke is review your contract and change it from a youth contract to a fully-fledged pro contract. This will mean a huge jump in salary but will preclude you from playing in the youth side anymore. So you have to weigh up the possibility of playing less football and take the chance of playing in the first team squad.'

Mr Batson jumped in and spoke, 'Luke, let me give you a bit of advice here. If I were you, I would take this opportunity. I believe you have the talent to play regularly in the first team and, even if you don't, there is always the reserves, so you will still get plenty of opportunity to play football.'

Mr Simms asked Luke if he wanted some time to think it over or speak to his parents first.

Luke said, 'No, they'll let me do what I want regarding football; I'd like to do it please.'

'Very well,' Mr Simms said. 'This is a temporary contract to cover for the next two weeks only; we will draw up a new contract in the meantime and sort it out after Christmas. You will be paid the sum of £5000 for the two weeks, regardless of how many games you play; your old contract will be null and void.'

Luke could not believe his ears and said, '*How much?*'

'£5000,' Mr Simms repeated and added, 'Luke, let me tell you now. If you make the first squad on a permanent basis, that is just chicken feed compared to what you will be paid then!'

When Luke left the room, he was walking on air. He telephoned his dad immediately and broke the news. Colin was delighted for him but thought the sum of money mentioned was ridiculous for a sixteen-year-old. He wanted assurance from Luke that he knew what he was doing. Luke assured his father that he was getting good advice from Mr Batson.

'In that case,' Colin said, 'congratulations Luke. We wish you all the very best, but we will miss you at Christmas. Just one thing Luke, I have to ask. This will not compromise your stand on playing on Sundays, will it?'

'No Dad, I just wouldn't do it,' Luke assured him. 'Nothing changes in that respect.'

'Good,' Colin said. 'Keep in touch, won't you?'

'I will,' Luke replied, and then said goodbye.

When he came off the phone, Luke started to worry whether or not Mr Colluna had remembered about Luke not playing on Sundays. The more he thought about it, the more he feared that he may not have taken it into consideration. When he arrived home, he quickly said hello to Ruth and then excused himself to make an important phone call. He got Mr Batson's office and spoke to his secretary, who told Luke that Mr Batson had gone home and, unfortunately, she could not give him his home number as it was against club rules. After much pleading, Luke persuaded her to ring Mr Batson and ask him to contact Luke urgently.

Luke was in the process of telling Ruth and Roger the latest development when the telephone rang. Roger answered it and he called for Luke, telling him Mr Batson was on the line.

When Luke said 'Hello,' Mr Batson said, 'Don't tell me you have changed your mind, Luke.'

'No, not at all,' Luke said. 'I'm just worried that Mr Colluna may have forgotten that I do not play on Sundays.'

'He is fully aware of that Luke, don't worry; he has taken that into consideration. He has said to me it may cause him a problem from time to time, but the pros outweigh the cons. Don't worry Luke. The club will honour their agreement on that score, whatever level you play at.'

'Phew, thank goodness for that,' Luke exclaimed. 'Thank you for ringing. I hope you did not mind me contacting you.'

'You're welcome,' Mr Batson said. 'I am here to help.'

Luke returned to Ruth and Roger and finished relating his news.

'They must rate you pretty highly?' Roger said. 'There can't be many sixteen-year-olds who have an opportunity to play premiership football. I hope it happens for you Luke. You have certainly worked hard to get there, plus your natural talent of course,' he added.

Luke checked him out to see if Roger was teasing him but realized that he was being perfectly serious.

Luke commented, 'It all seems to be coming together; I hope it continues.'

Luke was contacted to join the first team squad for training the following Friday at the club's training ground. There, he was spoken to by Mr Colluna, who told him he would be on the subs bench for the match the following day against *Arsenal*. He took part in the light training that day and almost had to pinch himself to make sure he was not dreaming, being on the same pitch as some of his heroes, especially as they treated him as an equal. The strange part, as far as Luke was concerned, was that he did not feel out of place among them all. At the end of the training session and set-piece practising, they were instructed to be at their ground for 9am departure on the team coach. When Luke got home and mentioned to Ruth that he was going to be a substitute against *Arsenal* tomorrow, she asked, 'Is that a televised game?'

'I hadn't thought of that,' Luke said.

When he checked the newspaper, he saw that it was in fact going to be televised live on the satellite stations. He phoned his parent's home and told them, and also let Christine know to look out for him, in case he actually got to play.

Luke enjoyed the trip to London on the coach; he was very impressed with the luxury of the coach. Once or twice, he was embarrassed by the behaviour of one or two of the players who were in high spirits, but the manager nipped that in the bud quite quickly with a mild rebuke. Luke was apologized to on two occasions for bad language being used.

Luke realized that the players had been informed of Luke's Christian faith and had probably been warned to kerb their language in his presence. Luke hoped that they did not resent this, but there appeared to be no animosity towards him, and he was included in the friendly banter—like when they asked him when he thought he would start shaving and if there was a supply of nappies in his kit. Luke took it all in good fun and it served to calm his nerves.

On arrival in the away dressing room, Luke saw all the team and the subs' kit displayed on the bench and on pegs, including match programmes. He learnt that his shirt number was 23. He picked up his match programme and opened it to the team sheet page and saw his name as one of the subs. He quickly placed it in his bag to ensure that he had a souvenir of the day. They all changed into their kit and training tops and went out onto the pitch for warm up exercises.

Luke was overawed by the stadium, which was starting to fill up. He could not help but glance over to the *Arsenal* side who were warming up, recognizing players he had only seen on TV before. There seemed to be TV cameras everywhere and he saw several interviews taking place at the side of the pitch. With fifteen minutes to go before kick-off, they were called back to the dressing room, where they were addressed by the assistant to Mr Colluna—basically a pep-talk. The referee came into the room and told them that he expected good discipline from them and would not tolerate any dissent.

A bell sounded and the team lined up in the tunnel, until the officials led them out onto the pitch. The subs followed and took their places on the bench. Luke had never heard such a noise in all his life. One of his colleagues pointed out the area where the *Southtown*'s fans were seated. There seemed to be a good turnout of fans, who were just as vocal as the home fans. The roar increased in volume as the referee blew his whistle to start the game.

For the first twenty minutes or so, *Southtown* were in a difficult situation from the attacking might of *Arsenal*, but they gradually got more into the game. *Arsenal* was limited to two half-chances of scoring but were well defended by the *Southtown*'s defence. *Arsenal* gave *Southtown* no opportunity to score. With ten minutes to go to the end of the first half, *Arsenal* was awarded a free kick out on the right wing. The ball was crossed into the penalty area and an *Arsenal* player met it with his head and it powered past the *Rovers*' keeper for the first goal of the match. They went in at half-time with a score of 1–0 for the home side.

In the dressing room, while tea was being consumed and it was established that there were no injuries or niggles etc., Mr Colluna addressed the players. He was reasonably happy but said they needed to close down the *Arsenal* players quicker and prevent them from playing their usual passing games; they must retain possession of the ball and be sure not to give it away cheaply. He expressed his disappointment at conceding a goal from a set piece after all the work they did in training.

When the bell went for the team to exit, he encouraged the boys by clapping his hands saying, 'Come on now, big effort. We are still in this game.'

The second half proceeded much as the first but with *Rovers* putting more pressure on *Arsenal*'s defence, yet without creating any real scoring chances. With about fifteen minutes to go, Mr Colluna asked two of the other substitutes and Luke to go and warm up.

Within a few minutes, he called Luke back and told him to get ready; he was going on. Luke's heart skipped a beat, but he could not get ready quick enough. Mr Colluna told him he wanted him to play right up front on their defence. The fourth official held up the number board with number 23 on it and number 9 was being taken off. Luke heard his name being announced over the loudspeaker system. His stomach started doing back flips, but when he sprinted out onto the pitch, all the butterflies in his stomach disappeared.

Sensationally, within minutes of him being on the pitch, he received a pass from midfield and spun around the defender who was closely marking him, leaving him in his wake. He ran at the penalty area; then, from 16 yards out, he unleashed a shot at goal which went passed the goalkeeper and was bulging out of the back of the net before he knew it. He turned away with his arms raised and was immediately mobbed by his teammates, ending up at the bottom of a heap of players on the ground.

This goal seemed to spur on the *Rovers* and all the pressure was on *Arsenal* who defended stoically. Their goalkeeper made a superb save in the dying minutes which denied the *Rovers* a winning goal. A corner was awarded to *Rovers* on the right. Luke positioned himself on the 18-yard line and ran in when the ball was floated across. He out-jumped everyone in the area and met the ball perfectly to head it into the bottom nearside of the net. He could not believe how easily he got to that ball and ran to the touchline, where he was hugged and slapped by Mr Colluna and his assistant, as well as his teammates.

Rovers was able to hold out till the final whistle for a very welcome three points. Luke was the talk of the stadium and was quite overwhelmed with the attention he got from the players and staff alike. Mr Colluna denied the TV station an interview with Luke. In fairness to Luke, he quoted Luke's age as the reason for not allowing him to be interviewed. The *Rover*'s fans were ecstatic when the players went to their end to thank them for their support. The club captain raised Luke's arm to fans and the applause increased. On the way back to the dressing room, the captain had his arm over Luke's shoulders and spoke to him:

'Well done lad. What a debut!'

'Thanks,' Luke said. 'Things just happened to fall right for me, I guess. It was a good pass, and the corner came in perfect for me, but it could have been anybody on the end of the pass and the corner-kick.'

'Don't undersell yourself. Take all the credit you deserve when it comes. In this game you can easily be knocked off your pedestal, believe me!'

'I'll try to remember that,' Luke replied.

When Luke entered the dressing room, he was applauded by those present, and Mr Colluna shook his hand and said, 'Well played Luke. You realize it was me that won the game for you, don't you? It was my genius to put you on the field then.'

He was grinning all over his face as he said it and Luke realized that he was joking.

'Yes, Boss, of course,' Luke responded.

Luke's mind was all over the place as he was getting showered and changed. Mr Colluna's assistant told Luke to just take a seat and have a cup of tea to calm himself down. He sat alongside Luke and said:

'Beware Luke. You are going to be the talk of the football world this weekend; the press will have a field day. We will protect you from them. Do not agree to any interview without the say-so of the boss; it is for your own good, believe me. Mr Colluna will tell the media all they need to know; he has vast experience in being interviewed over many years.'

'I wouldn't know what to say anyway,' Luke said.

'Exactly Luke. That is why it is best you just talk with your feet on the field.'

Luke was really chuffed when he was on his way to the coach and the *Arsenal* manager came up to him, shook his hand and congratulated him on his game.

'You have a good future in football,' he said. 'Cherish it.'

Luke thanked him and thought how nice it was of him to do that when Luke had just been responsible for inflicting a defeat on his team.

Luke was indeed the topic of the weekend in all football circles and was virtually a special feature on *Match of the Day* that evening. Luke felt it was quite surreal to see himself play on the TV and then be discussed in the studio afterwards. The pundits agreed he certainly showed great promise; he had pace, he could head a ball and had a lethal shot with his right foot, at least. They said it was difficult to believe he was only sixteen years of age and was still in the learning stage of the game. One of them unwittingly said his future was unlimited. 'Ltd by name not by nature,' Luke thought to himself.

Roger, Ruth and Luke had gone out for a meal that evening as a celebration so, by the time Luke's head hit the pillow, he was ready for sleep, but not before he had given thanks in prayer for a wonderful day.

Luke was the centre of attention at both services the next day and was asked what it was like to be famous: 'Will you be rich and buy a big mansion and a fleet of Rolls-Royces and Ferraris, and have a luxury yacht with a big crew?' They were teasing him, but it did make him wonder what the new offer would be when his new contract would be drawn up in January.

The sports pages on the Monday were singing Luke's praises and had headlines such as, 'Lukeing good,' and 'Luke starts new CHAPTER,' or 'L.T.D. UNLTD'.

There were photos of Luke in action and celebrating. The writers praised him greatly and quotes from Mr Colluna and the club captain both said that Luke had a great future ahead of him.

One writer said Luke's talent belied his age and he could not name anybody in the game today who showed as much promise as Luke. He went on to say that he did not seem fazed by the big occasion but rather, to the contrary, he seemed to thrive on it. A very rare talent indeed he concluded. Other sports writers also wrote in the same vein and Luke became an overnight sensation in the world of football in England.

The team's next match was a home game on the Tuesday evening and Luke was once again named in the squad as one of the subs. The match was against *Stoke City* who were regarded as *Rovers'* 'bogey team' in that they had never beaten *Stoke* in the Premiership, only managing a draw on one occasion.

Luke's parents were unable to get down for the match, nor was Christine for transport reasons. But they wished him well and hoped that he would get a game. Roger said that he would be there and would cheer on *Rovers*; he too hoped that Luke would get on the pitch at some time.

There was a full training session on the Monday and on the Tuesday morning the squad merely worked on tactics and set pieces. They were told to get plenty of rest in the afternoon and ensure that they had a meal no later than two hours before kick-off, which was at 7:45pm and would be televised live on satellite TV. They had to report at the ground at 6:30pm at the latest.

When Luke arrived at the ground, he was about to enter the players car park on his scooter when he was stopped by twelve to fifteen fans who all wanted his autograph. Some produced a match programme for him to sign, others an autograph book and some wanted a photo taken with him. He was a bit overwhelmed by it all but duly obliged. The car park security guard said to him as he let him in:

'You will have to get used to that, lad. You're quite a hero round these parts.'

Luke was on the bench for the first half of a dour, uneventful match with both teams appearing to cancel each other out. The two midfields dominated the play and limited any scoring chances.

In the dressing room at halftime, Mr Colluna was not happy and accused the team of giving up possession too easily. He told Luke that he was coming on for the second half and instructed him to play right up on *Stoke*'s defence, on the last defender whenever possible; he then instructed the midfield to get the ball up to Luke as often as they could and then back him up with forward runs.

When Luke's name was announced over the public address system, there was a roar from the ground and loud applause. The second half progressed much like the first; the ball was not getting through to Luke and he was having little involvement in the game. He unwittingly started to drift back to midfield until Mr Colluna, in an animated rant, called him and signalled him to get back upfield.

Within a couple of minutes, a *Rover*'s defender booted the ball upfield and Luke outjumped the defence to let the ball glance off his head. He spun round and outpaced the defenders and got to the ball just before the advancing goalkeeper, chipping it over his head into the net. His teammates mobbed him, and the crowd were on their feet roaring their approval. When Luke was eventually released by his teammates, he looked across at Mr Colluna who raised a thumb of approval. When the final whistle went at 1–0 for Rovers, Mr Colluna met Luke coming off the pitch, patted him on the back and said, 'Well done.'

Luke thanked him.

Mr Colluna continued, 'Learn from that, Luke. If you had been in midfield, that goal would not have materialized. If I give you instructions, it is with good reason. I know your strengths and how to use them, OK?'

'Yes, sure Boss. I'll remember that,' Luke replied.

'Good,' Mr Colluna said. 'Now listen, the TV company have asked for an interview with you, and I have agreed. I will be with you to chip in if there are any awkward questions, alright?'

'If I have to,' Luke replied reluctantly.

'It is only fair to your fans and supporters of the club; it helps to keep them on our side,' explained Mr Colluna.

The interviewer met Luke and Mr Colluna at the side of the pitch and asked Luke how he felt the game had gone.

Luke replied, 'It was not our best performance but *Stoke* are a tough team to beat. However, we stuck at it, and it paid off in the end for a welcome three points.'

'That was down to your contribution of the goal, which was well taken may I add,' the reporter continued.

'It was a team performance out there. We had to fight hard tonight, and we did that,' Luke replied.

The reporter turned to Mr Colluna and said, 'This lad has suddenly burst onto the scene; will he be a regular in your plans now?'

Mr Colluna replied, 'He will certainly be part of the set up. He is very young and is still learning the game, but the potential is there for all to see. We just have to mature that talent for his benefit and for the benefit of the club.'

'A future England player in the making, do you think?' the reporter asked.

'It's early days yet. Let's not run before we can walk,' Mr Colluna answered.

Luke chirped in with, 'Yes, a future England player!'

All three laughed and Luke and Mr Colluna were thanked by the reporter.

'Cheeky young pup!' Mr Colluna said to Luke as he walked off grinning.

He knew in his heart that Luke would indeed one day play for England—no doubt about it.

Although Luke was happy with his goal, of course, he felt that he otherwise contributed very little to the game and was a bit disappointed with himself. When he confided in the club captain, explaining that he felt a bit of a fraud to be getting all the accolade when everyone had worked so hard, he was told not to be so silly and that is how the boss wanted it.

'He would have been aware that you wanted more involvement when he sent you back upfield; that was the role he chose for you. He's no fool. He knows the game like the back of his hand. As far as he is concerned, you fulfilled the role he asked of you and we did our bit. That's how it works. That's what a team is all about; each to his own.'

'I have a lot to learn, haven't I?' Luke commented.

'Yes, but you will,' his skipper said. 'You will.'

CHAPTER 15

Christmas day was the first time Luke felt homesick since moving down south. Although Ruth had made a lovely meal and he had had a good, relaxing day, Luke missed his parents and Christine. It was always a good time back home with the church activities and friends and celebration, but because of match schedules over that period, it was not possible for Luke to return home, particularly as the third match was scheduled for Boxing Day. Luke even had to be careful about his food intake on Christmas Day, although he enjoyed a good Christmas lunch with all the trimmings; he merely snacked at tea-time after going for a long walk in the afternoon.

He reported to the ground on Boxing Day at 1:30pm for a 3 o'clock kick-off and was spoken to by Mr Colluna, who told him that he was starting the match today and that he was going to be rested for a couple of matches afterwards. He also told him that, at his age, it was not good to play a lot of matches together as his body needed time to recover. Luke said that he felt perfectly capable of playing two or three matches a week if he had to.

Mr Colluna said, 'You may well feel like that, but I can assure you your body will protest eventually, and you will lose your sharpness, believe me. I've been there. Besides, the absence of playing will make you even more eager to get out onto the pitch. Concentrate on today's game, play well, and show us what we will be missing. Do you understand what I'm doing?'

'Yes, I do,' Luke said. 'But I don't have to like it, do I?'

'That is a good attitude, Luke. You're learning,' the boss said.

In the dressing room, Mr Colluna addressed the team and said today would be a tough game: *Manchester City* are a team full of stars and are pushing for a League title. They are in a good run of form, 'but,' he said, 'we are capable of getting three points today if you focus on your role, remember your training, and put it into practice out there. One hundred per cent effort from all of you please!'

Luke got a loud cheer from the crowd when his name was announced and he gave them a quick wave of the hand; he had quickly become a favourite with the fans. He spotted one or two banners saying, 'Lim for England' and 'united' and '@look out for Luke' etc. This gave Luke a big lift and made him determined to make them proud of him to repay their admiration.

The *Rover*'s came under pressure right from the start and the defence had to work hard to keep *City* at bay, but they conceded a goal after half an hour and only a brilliant save by the *Rover*'s goalkeeper prevented a second just before the halftime whistle. In the dressing room at halftime, Mr Colluna told them to keep their heads up and to concentrate. The match is not lost. We have forty-five minutes to turn the game around; you are well capable of doing that,' he told them.

As the team was entering the tunnel to go out for the second half, Mr Colluna whacked Luke on the backside and said,

'Go out there and win the game for us, son.'

You could say that Luke was stung into action because he really showed his capabilities in the early part of the second half. He seemed to take the match by the scruff of the neck and run rings around the city defence, eventually scoring a wonder goal by dribbling past two defenders and slotting the ball past the keeper for the equalizing goal. The crowd went berserk, and so did his teammates who mobbed him with congratulations when they finally caught him, as he had run to the home fans and raised his arms to them.

It was not long before he had another opportunity to score but was thwarted by a good save from the *City* goalkeeper. The match seemed to have swung Rovers' way and they had plenty of possession of the ball. Luke was much involved and began to be closely marked by *City*, but he was unfazed by the close attention and even seemed to thrive on it.

Once again, he received possession of the ball just outside the penalty area. He side-stepped a defender and unleashed a shot at goal which took a slight deflection from a defender; it was enough to wrong-foot the goalkeeper and the ball hit the back of the net, 2–1.

Mr Colluna turned to his assistant and said, 'That boy is a phenomenon, a genius. He is such a mature player for his age.'

The match was nearing its end with only a few minutes to go when Luke gained possession of the ball and dribbled past defenders into the penalty area. He was promptly hacked down with an awful tackle and the referee rightly awarded a penalty; the defender was booked by the referee. The captain picked up the ball and was about to place it on the penalty spot, when Luke went up to him and said, 'Skip, can I have it? I'll score from this.'

The skipper looked across at Mr Colluna, who nodded his head; he knew what Luke had done.

'OK, son. It is all yours,' the skipper replied.

Luke placed the ball on the spot and took several steps back. While waiting for the referee's whistle, Luke envisaged his wall back home and a particular patch on the wall. In his mind's eye he placed that patch in the top right-hand corner of the goal. When the whistle went, he hit that patch dead centre to complete his hat trick. Even some of the *City* players applauded Luke off the pitch.

Football had not seen the likes of Luke for many years and, once again, he was the talk of the football fraternity in the press, on TV, radio and across Europe. His name was being mentioned in all football circles. Luke had well and truly arrived on the scene. When the players were in the dressing room after the match, Mr Colluna applauded them all and said,

'Well done lads, a good performance all round.'

He was careful not to single out Luke in front of the other players for the sake of harmony in the dressing room among the team, but he was fully aware of Luke's major contribution to the win. As he exited the room, he asked Luke to see him in his office before he left. The other players started to tease Luke about why Mr Colluna wanting to see him in his office:

'Perhaps he's going to give you a bag of sweeties?' one said.

Another said, 'Maybe he is going to tell you about the birds and the bees or tell you that there is no Father Christmas.'

Luke took the banter all in good fun; in fact, it made him feel good. He felt like 'one of the lads'—at home even.

Mr Colluna asked Luke to sit down when he entered the office. Once seated, he said to Luke:

'You may or may not realize it Luke, but you have a very special talent; I would even go as far as to say unique talent. In a short space of time, you have established yourself in the football world very early on in your career. I believe you have a sensible head on your shoulders, but you need to be aware that there are those out there who will try to exploit you: agents, media, and commercial enterprises who will want you to endorse their products etc. In a very short time, you are going to be a very rich young man. My advice to you is to get yourself an agent you can trust and a financial advisor to handle your affairs. If you want legal advice, our Mr Simms will be only too pleased to help.'

In those few moments, Luke realized the enormity of his situation. In his naivety, he had not considered the financial implications of a successful career. As far as he was concerned, he was doing what he loved—merely playing football.

Mr Colluna continued: 'Now, what I want you to do is to take a week off. Go home and see your parents and tell them of this conversation. Perhaps your dad may know someone who can act for you; someone who will have your best interests at heart and someone you can trust. Come back on the 2nd of January at 10am for a meeting with myself and Mr Simms and we will talk about a new, updated contract. If you can, bring your father with you and whoever you appoint to act for you. In the meantime, just relax and unwind because you have a busy time ahead of you.'

Luke thanked him and asked him when his next match was likely to be.

Mr Colluna laughed and said, 'You are keen, aren't you? I can't answer that yet; I'll have to check how everyone else is, if there are any injuries and things like that.'

Luke was about to leave when Mr Colluna said:

'One other thing, Luke. There is a strong possibility that the media will try to contact you. I don't want you to have anything to do with them at this stage. The only concession I will make to that is if your local paper or radio station want an interview; then that is OK. But be very careful what you say. Just speak generally about how you feel. Don't mention any future contract or anything we have discussed here today. Do you understand what I am saying?'

'Yes, I do,' Luke replied. 'I don't like interviews, so I won't be saying much anyway.'

'Good, keep it that way,' Mr Colluna said. 'Now, off you go and be careful on that scooter of yours.'

Luke's head was in a whirl as he rode back to the house. The match was going through his head: the conversation with Mr Colluna; the thought of a week back home; seeing Christine again; the forth coming meeting in January. Before he knew it, he was in the driveway of his digs. He was met by Roger as he entered the house, who embarrassed him by vigorously shaking his hand and saying:

'Luke, you were absolutely brilliant this afternoon. I was at the match. I knew you were good but that was an exceptional display of football; it made me proud to know you. I had to tell everyone around me that you were my lodger.'

Luke did not know what to say but managed an embarrassed, 'Thanks.'

During dinner, he mentioned the conversation he had had with

Mr Colluna and, in particular, the bit about having an agent to act on his behalf and safeguard his interests.

'Perfect!' Roger exclaimed. 'I know someone who would be ideally suited to do that for you. He is a member of our fraud squad and is about to retire. As far as I know he does not have anything else lined up after he retires. He is as honest a chap as you could find and a keen football fan too. You speak to your dad and, if he agrees, I will ask him if he would be prepared to do that for you.'

'Well, what a coincidence!' Ruth said. 'It's as if God knew what you would need and has already provided it.'

Luke looked at her and saw a big grin on her face. He could not help laughing. Colin must have mentioned his favourite phrase: 'God will provide.'

Luke phoned home after dinner and told his mum that he would be coming home for a week; she was thrilled and said she had missed him. She said she would organize a celebratory meal and invite Christine too.

'That would be great,' Luke said. 'I'll ride up in the morning; get some teabags in Mum! I'll phone Christine and invite her for a meal at the same time.'

'OK,' Alice said. 'Tell her it's on Wednesday at around 7pm but she can come earlier if she wants to.'

'I will and, by the way, I have some good news to tell you when I get there.'

'Good; I like good news,' his mum said.

'Bye Mum, see you tomorrow,' Luke said.

'Bye,' Alice replied, feeling happy that Luke would be home for a while.

She had missed his presence about the place; he was still her little boy.

Luke was warmly welcomed when he arrived home just before lunch on the Tuesday. Colin was out but was due back for lunch. Luke thought that his mother looked a bit under the weather and asked her if she was alright. She said she had had a bad night and still did not feel too good.

'Is it your head problem?' Luke asked.

'Yes, but it will pass. It usually only lasts for a couple of days, then goes away. Don't you worry yourself about it; I'm fine,' Luke's mum replied.

Luke was not convinced, but let it rest at that. When Colin arrived, he greeted Luke, and said that, wherever he went and whoever he spoke to, all they wanted to speak about was Luke and the publicity he was getting. Luke said that it was not his doing; he would rather stay in the background. He mentioned that it could get even worse because he was due an interview on local radio and most likely *The Daily Echo* would want an interview too.

'I might just emigrate,' Colin said, 'and go somewhere where you are not known!'

'There won't be many of those places soon, if things carry on as they are,' Luke replied.

At lunch, Luke announced his good news. He told them that he was going to be part of the first team squad and would be given a new, full 'pro' contract. He asked his father if he could be at the club on 2nd January at 10am to meet with Mr Simms, the lawyer, and Mr Colluna, the club manager. He also mentioned about the representative that Roger had suggested. Colin said he would make sure that he could be there, and he would contact Roger to find out a bit more about this man he had suggested as an agent for Luke.

'How will this affect your current arrangements as regards your college course and accommodation etc.?' Colin asked.

'Not in any way, I shouldn't think,' Luke replied. 'I will still need to live somewhere, and the club is keen for us to have a 'second string to our bow', as Mr Batson puts it, so I do not think anything will change in that respect. It's just the question of a new contract regarding payment I suppose.'

'We'll see,' Colin said. 'I must put it down in my diary; January 2nd at 10am you said, was it?'

'Yes,' Luke confirmed.

'I'll ring Roger this evening about the other thing, this agent fellow. Do you know if Roger will be working?'

'I don't know,' Luke replied. 'I will phone Auntie Ruth and ask her.'

This he did and informed his father that Roger would ring him about 6pm. After lunch, Luke said he would walk down to the flower shop and walk Christine back when she finished work at 4pm. It suddenly dawned on Luke that his mum was not at work and, when he asked her why, she told him that the doctor had put her off work for a couple of weeks as she needed to relax a little; the stress of managing the shop was not good for her when she was suffering these bouts of headaches.

'But I will be back at work next week, no worries,' she reassured Luke. 'Sally has been able to fill in quite easily, as her husband had taken time off over the holiday period and was enjoying having more time to spend with his little girl. So, things have worked out quite well really. But I do miss the shop, and everybody has been so kind enquiring after my health, and I've had quite a few cards too.'

Luke could not help feeling that he was being kept in the dark a little over his mother's health. He felt he was not being told the full extent of the problem. He knew it would be pointless to ask any more questions as they would only protect him by not giving the full story, but he could not help thinking that she had not been put off work before.

He dismissed all these thoughts from his mind as he left the house to go to the flower shop. He realized what a mistake he had made in deciding to walk it. Every few minutes or so, he was hooted at and waved to by the passing cars. Some even stopped to congratulate him and passers-by, who he did not even know, were greeting him on the street. One or two even asked for his autograph. He remembered the words from the players' car-park security man, when he said,

'You'll have to get used to this, son; you are a hero around these parts.'

Luke thought he would never get used to this sort of attention but resigned himself to the fact that it was going to happen. Christine greeted him at the shop with a hug and a kiss, as did Sally to Luke's surprise.

'My, Luke, how you have grown in such a short space of time. You have certainly filled out and seem so much taller. Something is agreeing with you down south, that is for sure!' she said.

'I still take the same boot size,' Luke said.

'And the same hat size, I hope!' Sally said laughing.

'I don't wear a hat,' Luke replied. 'The only thing I want on my head is an England Cap!'

'You have a one-track mind when it comes to football, haven't you?' Sally retorted.

'Nothing wrong with ambition!' Luke came back.

'Christine, just get him out of here will you. He's giving me an inferiority complex. I'll see you in the morning,' Sally said.

'Thanks,' Christine said and went for her coat to walk home.

When they got outside the shop, Luke stopped and said,

'I think we should get the bus back' and he related what had occurred on the way to the shop.

'No way,' Christine replied. 'I want to walk with you and show you off to the public too, so I can share in your fame. It will also be an announcement that you are spoken for and will keep the local female population at bay.'

'Spoilsport,' Luke replied.

Christine whacked him playfully on the arm and said, 'Come on, let's walk!'

She grabbed his hand and they set off. Within a very short space of time, they were stopped, and Luke was asked for his autograph by a couple of young lads.

He duly obliged and then Christine said,

'Hi, I'm Christine,' and extended her hand for a handshake.

Both boys, in shock, took her hand and said, 'Hello.'

She laughed at the amazed look on Luke's face as they walked on and carried on laughing.

Luke said, 'Will you behave yourself; they'll think I am going out with some sort of nutter.'

'Perhaps you are!" she said still laughing.

Luke was hooted at a couple of times after that but thankfully no one else confronted him the rest of the way home.

Luke told Christine how worried he was about his mother and that he thought she was more ill than she was letting on. Christine agreed with him and said that her and Sally had been discussing it in the shop and they both agreed she had not been her normal self recently:

'Sally is worried in case the running of the shop had been responsible for bringing on the latest bout, but I told her I did not think that was the case as your mum was perfectly happy in the shop and thoroughly enjoyed it. Sally did agree with me.'

Dinner was enjoyed without Alice's condition being mentioned. Christine announced that she would be moving down south in two weeks to commence her course at university. Sally was aware of it and would be able to spend more time in the shop now that Natalie, her little girl, was progressing well.

'Where will you live?' Luke asked.

'In the halls of residence for the first year,' she replied. 'Then I will have to find some digs for the following two years.'

"You could stay with me at Auntie Ruth's,' Luke suggested.

'I'm not sure that would be a good idea, Luke,' Christine said. 'We would probably see too much of each other: "Absence makes the heart grow fonder". The reverse might be the case too.'

'Well said,' Colin remarked. 'Besides, that's a year away. There is a lot of water to pass under the bridge before that.'

'Right, you men, off into the lounge you go. Christine and I will clear up and then join you shortly with coffees,' Alice said.

When they were at the kitchen sink doing dishes, Christine said,

'Luke is very worried about you; he feels you haven't told him the full story. How are you really?'

'I'm not absolutely sure,' Alice said. 'I know my doctor is quite worried about my condition. The test I am due next week will indicate if the growth has changed in the last few weeks. I have deliberately kept it from Luke. I don't want to worry him unduly; he has a lot on his plate at the moment. I must say that I have felt a bit worse recently and am fearful of what the scan will reveal. Do you think I should tell Luke?'

'Yes, I do, but you know him far better than I do. I just think that Luke is mature enough to take it. He is very much like you and not fazed by adversity. I am sure he would much rather know the truth,' Christine answered.

'Perhaps you are right,' Alice said. 'I'll have a word with Colin.'

'OK, enough of this morbid chat. Let's get some coffees to those two before they fall asleep in their chairs, shall we?' Christine suggested.

'I'll make the drinks and you put a few biscuits on a plate from that tin,' Alice said. Then they joined the other two in the lounge.

Colin had taken his first sip of coffee when the telephone rang. Colin came back into the room and announced that Roger and his colleague would be there in half an hour to talk about him representing Luke as an agent and minder.

Christine asked, 'Is Roger that policeman who comes to church?'

'Yes,' Luke replied. 'I like Roger; didn't you meet him when you came down for my birthday meal?'

'Oh yes, of course,' Christine said. 'I forgot.'

'The words dumb, and blonde come to mind for some reason!' Luke said grinning.

Christine playfully thumped him on the thigh and said, 'Alright, Mr Perfect.'

'Hey, be careful; that is the leg that scores all my goals,' Luke scolded playfully.

'Why don't you two go and wash the mugs? I want a quick word with Dad,' Alice requested.

After Luke and Christine had left the room, Alice told Colin that Luke suspected they were holding back regarding Alice's true state of health; he had mentioned it to Christine. She asked Colin if he thought they should let him know the full situation. Colin agreed. He said it was only fair that he should know, especially as Christine knew, and it must be difficult for her when Luke brings up the subject in conversation. They agreed to tell him that evening.

When Luke and Christine returned to the lounge, Colin said:

'We need to update you on Mum's condition, Luke; it would appear that the growth may have increased in size recently. The scan she is due to have next week will confirm that or otherwise. As you know, because of its position it is almost impossible to operate on it. Mum can be treated with painkillers to alleviate the pain but no medication can reduce the growth.'

'So, what will happen if it grows then?' Luke interjected.

'The doctors cannot really say; it may affect her speech or her mobility or both. We also have to be aware that it, of course, could be fatal. That is the current state of affairs and we felt it only right that you should know,' Colin replied.

'Thank you for telling me. It just seems strange to me that in this modern day they cannot do anything,' Luke responded.

'They could if it was in a different position,' Alice said, 'but the neuro- surgeons would be reluctant to tackle it because of the risk involved. Anyway, let's drop the subject now; we will know more after Thursday.'

Luke went across and gave his mum a big hug and said, 'I'll pray lots for you, Mum.'

'Many are doing just that,' she said.

Luke then spotted Roger's car coming into the driveway and said, 'There's Roger now.'

Getting up to go to the door, Colin said, 'We'll go into the study with them. Come on Luke.'

Colin met them at the door and Roger introduced his colleague as Andy Thomas.

'Pleased to meet you, sir,' Andy said.

He was a huge man about 6 foot 4 inches (1,93 metres), smartly dressed and as wide as the doorway.

'How on earth did you fit in Roger's car?' Colin asked.

'With difficulty, sir, I can assure you!' Andy replied.

'Please call me Colin,' Colin requested. 'We do not stand on ceremony at home.'

'Sure,' Andy said.

They went into the study where Andy was introduced to Luke.

'You're only sixteen?' Andy said, questioningly.

'Yes, just,' Luke replied.

'I was that size when I was sixteen,' Andy said. 'Look at me now!'

'He has got another five years of growing yet,' Roger reminded him.

Once they were all seated, Andy said:

'Roger has filled me in on your situation, Luke. I gather you have a meeting due about your future at *Southtown Rovers* and they have advised you, presumably because of your age, to appoint an agent or representative to oversee your affairs and look after your welfare. I would be prepared to do that, but perhaps I should fill you in on myself.

'I'm fifty-six, happily married with two teenaged sons. I have served Hampshire Police since I was nineteen years of age. I currently hold the rank of detective sergeant on the fraud squad. Because I have served sufficient time in the job, I can retire whenever I want to. While I have not been specifically looking around for another job, I have been keeping my eyes and ears open for any opportunities that may present themselves. What Roger has suggested to me sounds very appealing and would suit me down to the ground.

'I have to tell you of course, that I have had no experience in football administration but, along with common sense, my experience on the fraud squad would assist me in safeguarding Luke and his affairs, which would be my priority should you choose to appoint me.'

He then asked Colin if he wanted him to leave the room while they discussed what he had said.

'That won't be necessary,' Colin replied. 'Do you have any questions, Luke?'

'No, sounds good to me,' Luke said.

'Just one thing,' Colin said. 'What about your fee? 'What sort of payment would be appropriate in these circumstances?'

'I was going to mention that,' Andy said. 'I don't want to make a fortune out of Luke,' he said. 'I will receive a lump sum on my retirement and a pension, so I wouldn't starve without a job. I propose that five per cent of Luke's salary would be appropriate. I don't know what other agents charge but would you be happy with that?'

'That is fine as far as I'm concerned,' Colin said. 'What about you, Luke?'

'Yes, sure,' Luke said.

'In that case, you're appointed,' Colin said, and they all shook hands.

'I think we should draw up a formal agreement on this,' Andy suggested. 'But why don't we wait until the meeting with the club and perhaps get them to include it in the contract that is eventually agreed on between Luke and *Southtown Rovers*; let their lawyers do all the work?'

'Good start,' Colin said, and they all laughed.

Andy said that he could be available almost immediately. He had some leave due to him, so he would not have to work a long notice period. He gave Colin his address, telephone number and email address. When they got up to leave, Colin invited Andy to meet Alice and Christine before he went home. He shook hands with both of them and declined the offer of refreshments, saying he had to get back. Colin saw them off at the front door and, as Roger was about to get into the car, he looked at Colin in the doorway and Colin gave him the thumbs-up sign. They had arranged to meet Andy at the club for 10am on the 2nd of January.

Luke and Colin both agreed that Andy seemed to be a genuine

sort of chap and Colin felt confident that he would look after Luke's best interest.

'He looks more like a bodyguard than an agent,' Alice said. 'He nearly crushed my fingers when he shook hands!'

Colin was thinking to himself how fortuitous it was that Andy and Roger arrived when they did, as it gave Luke something else to think about rather than his mother's health.

CHAPTER 16

On New Year's Day afternoon, Luke returned to his digs after reluctantly saying goodbye to Christine and his parents, but not before leaving instruction for them to contact him as soon as they had more information on his mother's condition. He mentioned to Ruth how comfortable he felt with Andy Thomas representing him. She said she had not met him, but Roger spoke highly of him and that he would be very good for Luke. Luke also told Ruth about his mother. She told Luke that she knew and had been praying for her.

'Me too,' Luke said.

Tuesday, 2 January dawned, and Luke was a bundle of nerves when his father picked him up from his digs at 9:30am to go to the club. They met Andy, who was waiting in the car park for them. He drove a Range Rover, very appropriate for a person of his size. Once handshakes and greetings were over, Luke led them into the building and to Mr Colluna's office, where they were greeted by Mr Colluna and Mr Simms. Andy and Mr Simms knew each other vaguely; they had met before when Andy was investigating an incident at the club some years ago. Luke, Andy, and Colin were invited to take their seats in front of Mr Colluna's desk; they declined the offer of coffee or tea.

Mr Colluna opened the conversation by addressing Luke:

'Luke, in the short time you have been with us, we have seen that you have a remarkable talent. After consulting with the owners of the club, we have been authorized to offer you a full-time professional contract. Should you wish to accept our offer, it will nullify your current youth contract and you will be classed as a full time senior professional.

'I have here a proposal which has been drawn up by Mr Simms and approved by the Board of Directors and is as follows:

'We will ask you to sign a three-year contract committing you to *Southtown Rovers*. Within this contract are the conditions which were in your youth contract regarding your behaviour on and off the field and your present accommodation arrangements, which can only be changed with the club's approval. Once again, because of your age, we have included a veto on any media interviews or appearance.

'Also, the chances are that you will be approached to endorse products in an advertising sphere. We will need to sanction any products that you choose to endorse; for example, we would not want you endorsing any tobacco or alcohol products or things like that.

'Your salary for those three years will be one and a half million pounds—roughly ten thousand pounds a week. Your contract will become reviewable at the end of the three years. Have you understood everything so far?'

'We would need to include the clause stating that Luke does not play on Sundays, as in his previous contract,' said Colin.

'Of course,' confirmed Mr Colluna.

Luke could not believe his ears and the shocked look on his face prompted Mr Simms to say:

'That sum of money, Luke, is not an extraordinary amount of money in the world of football. It sounds a lot of money to a sixteen-year-old, but it is pitched at that level because this club feels that you are an asset and want to keep you at the club.'

Colin said, 'It sounds a lot of money to me, let alone a sixteen-year-old. It seems almost immoral, I have to say.'

'That's football these days, Mr Tewkes-Dawson,' Mr Colluna interjected.

'I'll leave you with a copy of the offer for say half an hour; then we'll meet again. You can use that room through there,' Mr Simms said, pointing to a door behind him.

Luke, Colin, and Andy went into the room and, once the door was closed, Luke said, 'I can't believe what I just heard. It sounds too good to be true. I never expected anything like that. I don't know what to say!'

Colin said, 'I've never heard anything like it in my life; there has to be a catch somewhere. How can a sixteen-year-old lad be worth that ridiculous sum of money? Some of my congregation don't earn in a year what Luke would be paid in a week.'

'It's a different world, Colin,' Andy said. 'Can I make a suggestion?'

'Of course, you can. That is why you are here,' Colin replied.

'Well,' Andy said, 'I would ask for a two-year contract instead of three. The reason being that, if Luke is worth ten thousand pounds a week to them now and he is still learning and presumably improving all the time, he is going to be worth more in two years' time and we could renegotiate his contract again.'

'I can see the sense in that, but it seems a bit mercenary to me,' Colin said.

'I'm thinking of Luke,' Andy replied. 'We don't know how long his career will be; take all the advantages you can while you can, is my advice.'

'Will they wear it?' Colin asked.

'If they value Luke they will,' Andy replied. 'What do you think, Luke? Do you agree with my suggestion?'

'You know best,' Luke said. 'I can't think straight at the moment; it's all too much. All I want to do is play football, that's all. I can't do with all these negotiations and stuff; it is beyond me.'

'That's why I am here, so you don't have to,' Andy said, reassuringly. 'One more thing that I will get them to put into the contract is that I will act on your behalf in financial matters, but not without your signature of course.'

'Leave me out of it,' Colin said. 'I trust your judgement and Luke has a level head on him. I am sure you will do the right thing between you, although I would like to be informed of any developments of course.'

'Of course,' Andy said. 'That goes without saying.'

They knocked and re-entered Mr Colluna's office and took their places in front of his desk. Andy presented the proposition to him that the contract be two years instead of three years and asked if the contract could include the fact that he would act on Luke's behalf in all financial issues.'

Mr Simms said that would be acceptable, but he could not guarantee that the financial arrangements would be any different in two years' time.'

'We understand that,' Andy replied.

Mr Simms said he would get the contract formally drawn up and let them have a copy in due course for signing. He told Luke and Andy that, once this was done, they would need to visit the payroll office to make arrangements for Luke's salary to be paid into his bank account. He also explained that it was the norm for the salaries to be paid a month in arrears, but his office would sort that out. There were handshakes all round and Luke, Andy and Colin left the office.

Luke just said, 'WOW!'

Colin and Luke thanked Andy in the car park and said their goodbyes. Andy said he would be in touch. Colin drove Luke back to his digs and went inside with him.

'Can I have a cup of tea urgently please Ruth?' Colin asked. 'If I wasn't teetotal, I'd ask for a big slug of whisky in it too.'

Roger asked, 'What's happened?'

Colin related the last hour's conversations at the club. Ruth was absolutely flabbergasted, saying she had never heard anything like it in all her life. Roger congratulated Luke and said,

'You're on your way, my boy. Fame and riches from now on; embrace it. God has given you the talent; use it to glorify him.'

'Well said,' Colin remarked.

'Can I ring Mum now?' Luke asked.

'She's probably at the shop now,' Colin said. 'I'll fill her in when I get home; you can ring Christine later after four, when she finishes at the shop.'

'Why don't we all go out for lunch to celebrate Luke's good news?' Roger suggested. 'Luke can pay, he can afford it!'

'*Roger*!!' Ruth scolded.

'Only joking,' Roger said.

'I don't feel like eating at the moment,' Luke said.

'What? Did I hear right?' Colin asked.

'Well, I am all in a state,' Luke said.

'Come on, let's go down to your mum's favourite place and have lunch; it's on me,' Roger insisted.

They all agreed and piled into Ruth's car, eventually, with Roger at the wheel.

Roger suggested to Luke that he ought to go and see his bank with Andy to forewarn them of the amounts of money that will be going into his account. The bank could get suspicious of huge amounts of money going into a sixteen-year-old's bank account regularly.

'Yes, that's a good idea,' Colin said. 'And you will need advice from the bank on what sort of account or accounts you should have.'

Luke said he would contact Andy after he had been to the payroll office at the club, as he did not know when or how he was going to be paid yet.

They had a good lunch and Roger duly footed the bill. During lunch, Colin reminded Luke that he had not yet called on Gramps Maynard, who was looking forward to seeing him. Luke agreed he would ride up to his grandpa that afternoon, after he had called at the payroll office.

Once they got back to Ruth's, Colin said his goodbyes, saying he needed to get back as he did not like leaving Alice alone for too long. He promised to let them know the results of Alice's scan as soon as he had the information.

Luke called into the payroll office and was told that his salary was all sorted; the sum of one million pounds would be divided into twenty-four portions and paid into his bank at monthly intervals. Luke confirmed his bank account number and address and was given a sheet of paper with all the information he needed regarding the deductions taken out for tax, insurance, and such like. He was advised to keep these on file or appoint an accountant; he informed them that he had an agent who would be looking after his affairs. In reply to a question from Luke, they informed him that he would have to arrange payment to his agent through the bank. He thanked them for their help.

When he checked the sheet outside the office, he saw that the amount of £37,698 would be paid into his bank every month. He thought to himself, 'I would be happy with the £698 let alone the £37,000.'

He rode up to Gramps Maynard's timber yard and met him in the office. Until Luke took off his crash helmet, Gramps did not realize who he was. He sprung out of his chair and shook Luke's hand with such vigour that Luke thought his hand would drop off.

'It's great to see you, Luke. Haven't you grown,' Gramps said. 'They must be feeding you well down there. Congratulations on how you have done Luke; we are all proud of you. The men in the yard follow *Southtown Rovers* to see how you figure in their matches; they have become big fans of yours. You must meet them before you go.'

'I will,' Luke said. 'By the way, thank you for the scooter, Gramps. It's just perfect for my needs in getting to the ground.'

'You're welcome, my boy. Is it outside now?' Gramps asked.

'Yes, come and see it,' Luke replied.

Luke showed it to him and asked if he had seen it before.

'No,' he said. 'Your dad and that policeman fellow you live with organized it together. It is a smart looking machine. I hope you use it with care, Luke. Two-wheelers were never my cup of tea.'

'Don't worry, Gramps. I can't break any speed records with it and I'm very careful. I can't afford any injuries now,' Luke assured him.

He went on to tell his grandpa of his new contract, leaving out the pay.

'I always knew you would make it, Son,' he said. 'But goodness knows where you get your talent from, I'm sure. None of the family had any sporting prowess.'

'It may be a God-given talent then, eh Gramps?' Luke said.

'Of course,' Gramps replied.

After they had a cup of tea in the office, Luke was taken out to the yard where he was introduced to the men. They were genuinely pleased to meet him and were full of questions about his career. One of them said he had been at the match against *Man City* and thought Luke was brilliant.

'Better than those millionaires on the *City* team!' he said.

'Thanks,' Luke said, smiling inwardly.

When Luke said he had to go, his grandpa said he must not leave it too long before he came to see him again. 'I don't want to wait until you drive into the yard in a Rolls-Royce.'

'You mean driven into the yard in a Rolls-Royce, don't you?' Luke said.

'Yes of course, chauffeur driven I meant.'

They laughed and Luke said goodbye and waived at the men as he rode out of the drive. It was only as he was nearing home that he realized his mum's condition had not been mentioned at all. He wondered if that was deliberate on Gramps' part or not.

When he arrived home, Ruth said that Christine had called and asked for Luke to ring her when he got in. He rang her straight away and she was absolutely astonished at what Luke told her about his contract. She even asked if Luke was 'having her on'. He said he knew it was hard to believe but it was all absolutely true, but he had to keep pinching himself to make sure he was not dreaming.

She informed him that she was getting sorted out to move into the university at the end of the month and was a bit nervous.

'Just think of me being only a stone's throw away and you will be fine,' Luke said.

'I guess I will be alright; there will be many others in the same situation. I expect I'll make friends soon enough,' she said.

'Didn't take you long to make friends with me!' Luke said.

'That's true,' Christine said.

'Perhaps there may be some nice, handsome football players there,' she said.

'Yeah, but not as good as me though. They won't play for England,' Luke replied.

'Time to go, I think!' Christine laughed. 'See you soon.'

'Bye,' Luke replied and finished the call.

He then made arrangements to meet Andy at the bank the next day, after making an appointment with them for 11am.

The bank was extremely helpful and agreed with all Andy's suggestions. They also advised that Luke should consult one of their advisers regarding investments. Andy suggested that perhaps they should wait a few months first, so that Luke could build up a bit of a fund before he went into investments. The bank agreed and also agreed to a standing order of five per cent of Luke's salary to be paid into Andy's account at the same bank. Andy explained that, if Luke gained further payments from endorsements or promotions etc., then he would negotiate that separately and arrange commission from the companies concerned, so only Luke's salary would be subject to the five per cent.

The bank manager said to Luke, 'That is a very fair arrangement; that way you will know where you are.'

Luke agreed.

'Just one more thing before you go,' The bank manager said. 'Can I have your autograph please? My daughter would never forgive me if she knew you had been in my office, and I hadn't got your autograph. She is a big fan of yours and has your picture on her wall?'

Luke duly obliged but felt embarrassed by it. Andy just grinned to himself, thinking how much Luke would have to get used to this sort of thing in a very short time.

CHAPTER 17

The next few months all seemed a bit of a blur to Luke. He played regularly and never once did he have a bad game. He became a firm favourite with *Southtown*'s fans and was the team's leading scorer. He stayed injury free, and the team were pushing hard to gain a place in Europe for the following season.

His replica shirts were the top sellers in the club shop and all Luke's memorabilia were a favourite with the fans. As far as the club was concerned, Luke was a financial asset to them as well as his prowess on the field. The gate money had gone up some thirty per cent since Luke became a regular in the side, and the away game following had increased too.

What pleased Luke the most was that he got on so well with his teammates. There was a great atmosphere in the dressing room and life could not have been better. He saw much of Christine since she had entered university and they were often out together at the cinema or theatre or just out for a meal. Christine spent many an evening at Luke's digs too and became a firm favourite of 'Auntie Ruth' who took on the role of a nagging mum regarding Christine's studies, making sure she did not neglect them.

It was at the end of April when Mr Batson spoke to Luke one day and said that England under-21 squad were going on a tour of

Europe for twelve days in July and had been told to ask him if he would be interested in going. He told Luke that, if he wanted to go, Mr Colluna had given his consent. Luke had no hesitation whatsoever in saying he would like to go.

'Good for you. It will be a good learning curve for you,' Mr Batson said.

'Did you or Mr Colluna recommend me then?' Luke asked.

'No, not at all,' he said. 'We just got a phone call asking us to invite you. Somebody has obviously been watching you these past few months and liked what they saw, I suppose.'

'What do I have to do?' Luke said.

"We will pass on the message, and you will receive something from the Football Association (FA) in due course with all the details of the trip etc. If you have any queries, then just come to me, and I'll sort you out,' Mr Batson replied.

'Thanks,' Luke said.

'Do you have a passport?' Mr Batson asked.

'Yes, I have,' Luke replied.

'That's fine then. Make sure it is up to date, won't you?' said Mr Batson.

'It's brand new,' Luke said.

'I wish I could come with you, but I suspect my wife wouldn't be very happy about that; she doesn't see very much of me now!' Mr Batson added.

Luke suddenly thought that he would be away when Christine would be on holiday from her course. He hoped she would not mind. Would she think it selfish of him? He saw her that evening and told her of the invitation. He was a bit devious in that he did not tell her at first that he had agreed to go, but asked her what she thought he should do?

'You must go, of course Luke. You can't turn down an offer like that. Besides, it's your job; you must further your career as much as you can, while you can,' Christine said.

'You don't mind then?' Luke asked.

'Of course not. Why should I mind?' she replied.

'Well, it is during your holidays,' Luke said.

'But it is only for twelve days you said, and I am off for nearly twelve weeks,' Christine reminded him.

'Phew! Thank goodness for that because I already said yes without thinking,' Luke confessed.

'I don't think any less of you for that; I know what it means to you,' Christine said, reassuringly.

'You're so understanding. I thought you might be mad at me,' Luke told her.

'Luke, you're scared of me!' Christine said.

'Yes, I'd rather tackle a big brute of a defender than face you when you are angry,' Luke admitted.

'You've never seen me angry,' Christine replied.

'No and I want to keep it that way!' Luke stated.

A week later Luke received a letter from the FA informing him that he had been selected for the England under-21's tour of Italy, France and Portugal between 26th June and the 7th of July. The squad would consist of twenty players and each member would be guaranteed at least one game or part of a game, depending on the circumstances. There were instructions on where and when to join the group and to ensure passports were up to date.

The England under-21 manager, Mr Colin Hargreaves, would be in charge, along with coaching assistants and medical staff. There was a list of contact numbers on any given day during the tour, and the names and addresses of the hotels to be used in each location.

When Luke checked the calendar to mark the dates, he noticed that there were two Sundays included in those dates and hoped there would not be a match on any of those days.

The season ended with *Southtown Rovers* just missing out on getting into the European Competitions for the next season. Luke was the top scorer for the team and third top scorer in the Premiership. He was voted, *Young Player of the Year*, by journalists and *Player of the Season* by his club. The sports journalists repeatedly mentioned the unique talent of Luke and he had become a household name and a hero in his hometown.

The *Rovers'* last match of the season was at the end of April and players were then free to go, after being warned to keep themselves fit during the off season, or they would suffer when they returned for training in August. Two of the first team were transferring to other clubs and there were rumours of at least one top player being bought by the club for a large sum of money. The identity of that player had not been announced but it was revealed that it was a foreign player.

Luke went up to Manleigh to stay with his parents for a few weeks before his trip to Europe. He kept himself fit with training runs and visits to the leisure centre where he swam regularly and used the gym on a daily basis. Christine was due to come back up to her mum's place in two weeks' time so he would be able to spend some time with her before the trip.

He noticed that his mother had changed considerably since he had last seen her. It was obvious that her condition had taken its toll on her body: she had lost weight and her face showed pain, especially around the eyes. In answer to Luke's enquiry about her health, she was truthful and told him that a recent scan had shown that there was a small increase in the size of the growth and that the treatment seemed to have no effect in arresting it, but she was grateful that the painkillers she took when necessary did ease her pain somewhat. Luke had to be satisfied with her report but still wondered if she was holding back her true condition from him. However, he did not press her on it.

Luke took the opportunity of visiting old haunts while he was there, as well as church. He attended the youth club, popped into Mr Patel and the flower shop. Nearly everybody he spoke to remarked how much he had changed. They reckoned he was taller and had filled out somewhat; he was never exactly a beanpole but had certainly bulked up a bit and looked every part the athlete that he undoubtedly was. He had recently started shaving regularly, although he liked to think that a bit of 'designer stubble' was the cool thing to have; although not as far as his mother was concerned as she thought it made him look scruffy. He merely told her that she was living in the old days. The only concession Luke made was to attend church clean shaven.

When Christine arrived back home, she and Luke spent much time together. She accompanied him to the leisure centre each day and even swam with him but drew the line at the gym workout and the training runs. She was amazed at how fit Luke was when she watched him in the gym. She also noticed how much attention was being paid to him by other gym users and she felt proud to know him.

She noticed a group of girls watching Luke and obviously discussing him. She strolled over and said, 'Hello, do you know who he is?' None of them did. She said, 'That is Luke Tewkes-Dawson, a professional footballer. He plays for *Southtown Rovers* in the Premier League; I've been going out with him for over a year.'

'Is he rich, then?' one of them asked.

'He's paid well but I don't know if he is rich or not,' Christine said. 'I know he is a Christian so he would not consider worldly goods his priority!'

'What do you mean?' one of the girls asked.

'Well, his priority is to serve the Lord Jesus Christ and to obey his will and his teachings,' Christine replied.

'Weird!' the other girl remarked, and they seemed to lose interest in Luke, all of a sudden!

Christine then wondered off with a grin on her face, thinking to herself, 'That worked.'

When Luke asked her if she knew those girls, she said she didn't but was just making polite conversation. 'They have been there nearly every day,' Luke told her. 'And they seem to go out of their way to watch me train.'

'Oh really?' Christine said, offhandedly. 'I wonder why?'

Luke just looked at her, questioningly, but knew she was teasing him. He flicked the towel at her and caught her on the backside with it.

'Big bully,' she cried. 'Pick on someone your own size.' And they both laughed.

On the way home, Christine said she was going to miss him while he was away on the tour. She did not know what she would fill her time with in those twelve days. Luke asked if she had any studying to do in the holidays. She said she had a bit but wanted to have a break from it for a short time.

Luke mentioned that he was thinking of giving up his course at the college. He was enjoying it and was doing very well but he had no time for himself. He also explained that Andy, his agent, had a couple of sponsorship deals that he was working on. That would take up even more of his time, what with personal appearances, photo shoots and the like, so things were going to get even more hectic than they were now.

'Oh, the pains of being famous, eh Luke,' Christine mocked.

'Yeah, I know. I shouldn't complain, should I.' Luke said.

'No!' Christine scolded.

CHAPTER 18

Luke reported, as instructed, to a hotel near Gatwick Airport on Saturday 26th June at 10am where he was met and ticked off on a clip board. He was directed to a room where he was provided with a smart grey suit, with an England Badge on the breast pocket; a crisp white shirt; and an England tie. Once all the party had been kitted out, they were ushered into the dining room for a slap-up lunch followed by a 'pep-talk' from Colin Hargreaves, the manager of the England under-21 squad. He then told them to relax for the next hour but to be at the reception desk at 2 o'clock for the departure to the airport.

In the hotel lounge, Luke saw one or two of the squad that he had met before and some others he had just read about or seen on TV. He engaged in conversation with a well-known player who had played before for England at the under-18 and under-21 level. Luke asked him what happened with the suits at the end of the tour. He was told that they could keep them. When Luke asked if he had travelled with the squad before, he said he hadn't; he had only played home matches for England, and he was dreading it.

'Why?' Luke asked in surprise.

'You must promise not to say anything of what I am going to tell you,' he said.

'I won't,' Luke said.

The other chap (whose name was Les) said:

'I am absolutely terrified of flying; I've never been in a plane before. I don't want anyone else to know. You know what it is like—I'll be the butt of their jokes for the whole trip if they knew.'

'I won't say a word, I promise,' Luke said.

'Thanks,' Les said. 'I thought I could trust you.'

'I've never flown before either, but I'm not worried about it; millions fly across the world every day,' he said. 'If you like, I will sit by you on the plane.'

'OK, thanks,' Les said. 'I promise I won't hold your hand on take-off and landing.'

'Or in between either, I hope,' Luke said laughing.

They all eventually boarded the coach and, once in the concourse of the airport, all eyes were on the squad as they were shown to the check-in desks. Luke was approached on three separate occasions for an autograph; no other members of the squad were, and this embarrassed Luke a little. There were other, better-known players in the squad than he, as far as Luke was concerned anyway.

The flight was uneventful, and Les was fine and remained chatty on the two-and-a-half-hour flight to Paris. Luke was able to introduce into the conversation that he was a Christian and did not play on Sundays. He said that it was part of his contract with *Southtown Rovers*, but he was concerned that Mr Hargreaves was not aware of his stand. Les said that there were no matches planned for Sundays while they were away so there should not be any problem. Les said he respected Luke's stand on Sunday playing but, personally, could not see what harm there was in it. 'After all,' he said, 'it is your job. That is what you do, just like nurses, policeman and such like.' He could not see the difference.

Luke said, 'We would need a longer flight than this for me to explain it.'

'Does that mean you may miss out on being picked for some matches then?' Les asked.

'Yes, but I am prepared to sacrifice the odd game or two as long as it doesn't rule me out of selection for England in the future; that's my only worry,' Luke said. 'But that is my choice and I have to trust that I'll be selected when I can play, if I am good enough that is?'

'Oh, you're certainly good enough,' Les said. 'We all know that!'

When they eventually arrived at their Paris hotel, they were assigned rooms. Luke was paired up with a young lad from *Arsenal* called Ambrose, who was also a forward player. The manager addressed them all before they went to their rooms and told them that the mini bars in the rooms allocated to the club had been emptied, and they were forbidden alcohol on the evening before any match. They were permitted wine with the evening meal but it would be limited to a maximum of two glasses. The menus were already arranged and were set menus.

Then the words which Luke had been dreading:

'All players will report to the reception area tomorrow morning at 9:30am where you will be taken to the training ground for a light workout. The first match was on Tuesday evening against the French under-21 team. Monday would consist of further training and then the starting eleven would be announced and set pieces worked out.

Luke said to Ambrose, 'You go on up; I need to speak to Mr Hargreaves.'

'What's up?' Ambrose asked.

'It's just something I need to speak to him about; it's private,' Luke said.

'Suit yourself,' Ambrose replied, shrugging his shoulders.

'Boss, have you got a moment?' Luke said to Mr Hargreaves.

'What is it, son?' he replied.

'I can't join the squad for training tomorrow morning. It is a Sunday; do you know my position on that?' Luke asked.

'What are you talking about? Are you injured or something?' Mr Hargreaves asked.

'No, I am not injured but I'm a Christian and I don't play or train on Sundays. I thought you would have been told about,' Luke added.

'It's news to me,' Mr Hargreaves said. 'What good are you to me if you can't or won't play when I want you to?'

'None of our matches are on a Sunday, so I would be available for any of them,' Luke said.

'Oh, I see. You think you can just turn up to play without taking part in the training, do you? The other players work for their places. How do you think they would feel if you were selected without having put in the work that they have?' Mr Hargreaves asked.

'I would still train on other days and would be prepared to make up for the training that I missed,' Luke said.

'That's not the point, lad. You're part of a team and I expect each member to pull their weight. I can't start making allowances for each individual's silly foibles,' Mr Hargreaves continued.

'It's not silly to me, sir; it's what I believe. My club is sympathetic to my feelings and are happy to accept me as I am,' Luke protested.

'This is not your club, son,' Mr Hargreaves replied. 'What do you intend to do tomorrow then?'

'I'll go to a church, if I can find a suitable one, and, if not, I will stay in my room and read my Bible,' Luke replied.

'Well, it is your choice; you will have to bear the consequences,' Mr Hargreaves informed Luke.

'Does this mean I will not even be considered for selection?' Luke asked.

'I'll need to give this some serious thought. I don't like this one bit,' Mr Hargreaves said, dismissing Luke and sending him off to his room.

Luke was completed devastated by the conversation with the manager and was near to tears. He resigned himself to the fact that he would not now be considered for selection and his worse fears had come to pass. Ambrose let Luke into the room and when he saw his face he said,

'I know, don't tell me. You asked to change room because I'm black, didn't you?'

'No, of course I didn't! That's not what I wanted the boss for. I would respect you for who you are, not your ethnic background. This is not about you in the slightest,' Luke assured him.

'I'm sorry,' Ambrose said. 'It's always my worry in situations like this. I've experienced racial prejudice before. Forgive me for doubting you.'

'Of course. No hard feelings?' Luke said and they shook hands.

Luke sat on his bed with his head in his hands.

'What is wrong then, Luke?' Ambrose asked. 'Anything I can do to help?'

Luke related the whole sorry story to Ambrose, finishing by saying he had no chance of selection now. Ambrose reminded him that the letter they all had guaranteed each member of the squad at least one match. 'They can't go back on that.'

'I know you are trying to reassure me,' Luke said, 'but Hargreaves was not very sympathetic; in fact, he was even a bit angry that he had not been told before.'

'That's not your fault though,' Ambrose said. He continued:

'I must say I don't fully understand you though, Luke. Me and my family are Christians and we go to church. My pastor knows that I have to sometimes play on a Sunday and there's no problem with that, as long as I attend when I can. He's happy and my parents are too.'

'But it is not the pastor or minister that makes the rules, Ambrose, its God. The Bible says, "remember the Sabbath day to keep it holy." That is an instruction from God. Anyway, let us drop the subject. We don't want to fall out, at least not until you pinch my place in the team; then you might find strange things ending up in your bed!' Luke joked.

They both laughed and Ambrose said, 'I like you; I think we are going to get on just fine. Let's hope we have a chance to play together in the same team, eh?'

'Yeah, that would be good,' Luke replied. 'Fancy a cuppa?'

'Yeah, black coffee, please,' Ambrose said. They looked at each other and laughed.

Luke made the drinks and they relaxed and discussed other members of the squad who they knew.

After dinner that evening, Luke made enquiries at the concierge desk and asked if there were any English-speaking churches in the area. They were very helpful at the desk, checking their own information leaflets and the internet. There were two churches that had services in English, but both were Roman Catholic. They did not seem to understand the kind of church that Luke wanted, so they agreed for Luke to use the computer and conduct his own search. However, he was unsuccessful.

Luke waited until the squad had left for training before he went down to breakfast. The waitress at breakfast queried why Luke was not with the squad and he briefly explained why, adding that he was unable to find a protestant church which held services in English. She called the restaurant manager over and, in her broken English, explained Luke's problem. His English was excellent, and he knew of a church that was the type Luke was looking for, but he had no information on times etc. He obtained a street map and marked on the map where the church was and explained which metro station he needed to get there.

Luke was a bit nervous about going across Paris on his own as he knew only a little French. Luke changed and armed with the street map and the restaurant manager's information, he set off to find the church. He coped with the metro quite well and, after pointing out on the map where he wanted to go to a passer-by, he eventually found a Baptist church whose service, according to the notice board, started at 10:30am. When Luke checked his watch, he saw that it was 11:05am, so he decided to give it a miss as he did not want to go into the service so late, but he resolved to attend the 6pm service, instead.

By the time he got back to the hotel, the squad had returned, and Ambrose was in the room when Luke entered. He said they had had a light training session in the morning and one or two had noticed Luke's absence and had mentioned it to Mr Hargreaves, who told them he was off 'Bible punching'. Ambrose said that they were free for the afternoon and evening and asked Luke if he would like to explore Paris with him after lunch. Luke welcomed the invite. He said he would like to very much and asked Ambrose if he would like to come to church with him that evening; he agreed.

At lunch, they checked with the hotel staff if there was a specific time for the squad's dinner that evening. They were told that, although there was a set menu for them, they could eat when they liked as long as they booked a table beforehand. Luke asked if they could eat at 8 o'clock and the waiter noted Luke's room number and name and booked a table for them at that time. Luke told Ambrose that the church service was at 6 o'clock so they should be back in time.

After lunch, Luke and Ambrose took a cab and went to the Champs-Élysées, walked along the Seine and then sat for a while watching the river traffic. They decided to do the Eiffel tower but were put off by the long queues waiting to enter.

As they crossed one of the bridges, they stopped to watch some artists who were sketching and doing caricatures of the public. One of them invited Ambrose to sit for a portrait but he shook his head. Luke goaded him to do it and he eventually agreed. Luke stood behind the artist, who was Japanese, and was fascinated by the speed in which Ambrose's caricature was drawn; he was laughing as the portrait took shape. When the artist showed the finished portrait to Ambrose, he was very impressed with how the artist had emphasized his features in a comical way.

They decided it was time to make their way to the church and, after consulting the street map, concluded they had no idea how far away they were or the best way to get there. They ruled out using the Metro and found a taxi who quoted them 20 euros to take them to the church. They managed to ascertain that it would take fifteen minutes to get there, and it was 5:15pm. They took the taxi and very quickly started to wonder if they had done the right thing. To describe it as a white-knuckle ride was an understatement. The traffic was horrendous, and the driver seemed more of a kamikaze pilot. How they did not collide with anything they will never know. The taxi's hooter, and that of the other traffic, was ringing in their ears by the end of the journey.

As they neared the area of the church, Luke recognized where they were and asked the driver to drop them off; he told Ambrose that they were in walking distance of the church. They split the cost of the taxi between them.

After the Taxi had driven off, they both burst out laughing spontaneously.

Ambrose said, 'I've been on smoother rollercoaster rides than that!'

Luke replied, 'The remarkable thing is that there wasn't a scratch on the car anywhere.'

Luke pointed out the direction they needed to go, and they set off at a leisurely pace to the church arriving at 5:40pm. They were welcomed at the door and handed hymn books and asked if they were on holiday. Luke explained their presence in Paris. They selected their seats and listened to a violinist playing beautiful music before the service. By 6 o'clock there were about forty to fifty people in the congregation. Some were English-speaking, French people; others were holidaymakers as well as English people who were resident in Paris.

The preacher, when he took to the pulpit, welcomed everybody and especially the visitors among them and he specifically mentioned Luke and Ambrose as team members of England's football team. All eyes turned to Luke and Ambrose and to Luke's embarrassment Ambrose stood and raised an arm in acknowledgement.

After the service, which was appreciated by them both, some members spoke with them and eventually a couple offered to drive them back to their hotel, which they gratefully accepted. They arrived back at the hotel in good time for their evening meal after having enjoyed a good afternoon. They ascertained that again they needed to be at breakfast for 8am the next day to be ready for the coach leaving at 9:30am to take them to the training ground.

When Ambrose walked into the dining room the next morning, all the members of the squad who were there pointed at him and were laughing. He looked around him wondering what it was all about. Then, someone pointed to the notice board and to his horror he saw that his caricature portrait had been pinned to it. Unbeknown to him, Luke had sneaked it out of the room and had pinned it on the board. Ambrose took it off the board, pointed at Luke and said:

'You have to watch your back for the rest of the tour now, as I will be seeking revenge; count on it!'

Luke laughed.

At the end of the morning training session, which Luke had put his whole heart into and was noticeably trying his hardest to impress, Mr Hargreaves called them all together to announce the team for the following evening. Luke was not included in the starting eleven, nor was he one of the five substitutes named.

Luke was not too worried; he knew that not everybody could play in all the games and there were two more matches to play yet. However, what did worry him somewhat was that immediately after Mr Hargreaves had named the team and subs, he looked directly at Luke, and Luke was sure there was a smirk on his face. Luke immediately dismissed the thought from his mind; Mr Hargreaves was a mature man after all, wasn't he? He surely wouldn't hold a grudge against a sixteen-year-old lad, would he?

At lunch, Luke congratulated Ambrose for being selected and hoped he had a good game. Ambrose detected Luke's disappointment and said the boss was saving the best till last. Luke was not convinced.

In the afternoon, there was another short training session, then a friendly ten-aside game of just twenty minutes each half. Luke shone out above all the other forwards, scoring several goals, and running around the defenders. He could not have done more to show everybody what they would be missing in tomorrow's match.

However, that was not the reason why Luke tried so hard. He just enjoyed playing football and was in a different world when he was on the football pitch. He always played to the best of his ability and his natural skills were second nature to him. Luke was aware that some of the other players were discussing him and were puzzled why Luke was not playing against the French—probably the strongest of their three opponents.

The following day consisted of just light training sessions with the selected team and subs, concentrating on set pieces, free kicks, corners etc. Luke and the three others practised taking penalties, having turns each playing in goal. The afternoon was free, and an early meal was arranged for the team so that they would have plenty of time to digest their food before the evening kick-off at 7pm. The four non-participants were permitted to accompany the team to the match.

Luke and his three colleagues took their seats behind the away team dug out and soaked up the atmosphere of the ground, which was the home ground for Paris Saint-Germain, one of the top French League teams. It was a magnificent stadium, built to seat forty-seven thousand people but, by the time the two teams came onto the pitch, there were probably only six or seven thousand spectators in total—very few English, just a small group of about one hundred in one corner of the ground.

When Luke was standing for the national anthem, he could not help but feel jealous of those out on the pitch, though he knew it was wrong to feel that way. One of his colleagues said to him, 'Don't you wish you were out there, Luke?'

'I am in spirit,' said Luke. 'All the way.'

'We'll get our chance,' one said.

'I hope so,' Luke replied.

'Well, you will for sure. You are our star striker,' he continued.

Luke told him that he had a funny feeling he was not going to be used at all on the tour.

The three were shocked and said that was rubbish. Of course he would be used; everybody was guaranteed one game at least. Then Luke explained to them why he felt that way, mentioning his Christianity and the Sunday morning absence from training and the boss's attitude towards Luke. All three thought that Luke was mistaken and he was imagining it.

'I hope you are right,' Luke told them.

The match progressed with England doing all the pressing. The French seemed content to sit back and absorb the pressure; their defence gave nothing away. Mid-way through the first half, the French broke away and England were caught out and outnumbered by the French attackers, who scored a well-worked goal to take the lead. The English forwards were having a hard time breaking down the solid French defence.

The teams went in at halftime with the French leading 1–0. Luke and his mates analysed the match at halftime and each had several opinions on what Mr Hargreaves should or should not do.

The teams restarted the second half unchanged, and the same scenario was displayed with the English struggling to create goal-scoring chances. The French then started to press more and scored a second goal late on in the half. Mr Hargreaves, then, brought on two forwards, including Ambrose.

The fresh legs seemed to make a difference and only a good save by the French keeper stopped Ambrose from scoring. In another England attack, they won a corner but were unable to take advantage of the crossed ball and the keeper easily gathered the ball.

In a French attack, an England defender was deemed to have fouled a French forward in the penalty area and the French scored from the penalty, eventually ending the match with a 3–0 win. All the English players gathered in the dressing room after the match and Mr Hargreaves ranted and raved at the team.

'There is no need for that. I would not let him talk to me like that; I'd have to say something,' one of the players commented.

'The trouble is,' Luke said, 'he has the final say as to who plays and who doesn't, so you can't afford to get on the wrong side of him or you will be side-lined.'

There was very little conversation in the coach on the way back to the hotel. Information was given out on the next day's arrangements; they would be travelling mid-morning by coach to Italy.

Their base in Italy would be Milan and, on the Wednesday evening, they would be attending an Inter Milan match against *AS Roma* in the Serie A League, then resume training at Milan's training ground on the Thursday morning. Their Wednesday evening meal would be taken at the San Siro Stadium as guests of Inter Milan. They were to wear their England suits and would be introduced to the crowd before the match.

Luke was really looking forward to it. He was aware of how good Inter Milan were and he admired some of their star players. When they were checking in at the hotel, one of the assistant coaches called Luke aside and said he did not want it repeated to anyone what he was going to say; Luke agreed.

'Look,' he said, 'somehow you seem to have upset the boss. He has categorically stated that there is no way you will play in any team he picks.'

Luke was obviously taken aback by this statement and was about to say something when the assistant coach said:

'Wait. Before you say anything, the rest of the staff are not going to let that happen. We know what he is like when he has a bee in his bonnet, but we know how useful you are to the team, and we are going to make sure you get your fair share of football on the tour, OK?'

'Thank you,' Luke said.

'Now, not a word to anyone,' the coach insisted.

'I won't,' Luke said.

Luke was not totally convinced though. He wasn't sure how much influence the assistants would have on the boss, but he felt a lot better after that conversation.

When the squad walked out onto the pitch prior to the Milan-Roma match, they were greeted with loud applause. There were a few boos from one section of the ground and they suspected that those came from the team they were due to play on Saturday, but it was all friendly banter really.

They thoroughly enjoyed the match which was played at a slower pace than the Premier League, but there were some great players on display. The noise from the crowd was unbelievable and many flares were ignited in all areas of the stadium. The home side won 3–0.

Thursday was a full training day and light training was organized for the Friday morning with set pieces and corners etc. being emphasized as usual the day before a match. Luke knew that, at the end of the session, the team and subs would be announced for the following day's match against the Italian under-21s. His heart was in his mouth as Mr Hargreaves called out the names. Firstly, he called out the starting eleven —no Luke! Then, he called out the five subs; Luke's name was called out as the fifth sub.

He tried hard not to show the disappointment on his face, but it was there for all to see. Ambrose came up to him and said, 'Sorry Luke but, as I said before, he's saving the best till last.' Ambrose was also a substitute this time, but at least he had played a match. Luke could only hope he would be used at some time during the match; he so wanted to play at that stadium.

Luke was pleased to be involved in the dressing room before the match, getting changed with the rest of the team and being part of the pre-match warm-up. 'Better than sitting in the stands,' he thought as he took his place on the sub bench.

There was no score at halftime and, although England had more possession of the ball, the Italian defence was resolute, and England had few scoring chances. Italy had a couple of chances, but England's keeper had made two good saves.

The second half continued in the same manner and, with half an hour to go, Mr Hargreaves instructed Luke, Ambrose, and another player to go and stretch and warm up. Luke's heart skipped a beat; he recognized that the England team was crying out for someone who could split the Italian defence apart and score. They were tiring, and it was starting to show. After about five minutes, the boss called them back, pointed at Ambrose and said,

'You're on son, get stripped.'

One of the assistants said to Mr Hargreaves, 'Wrong choice, Boss. Put Luke in and he will get a goal for you; he's fresh and raring to go.'

He turned to his assistant and said, 'Me Boss, you assistant. I'll do my job; you do yours.'

The assistant coach was fuming and stormed off to the dressing room and one of the other coaches followed him. They were absolutely shocked at what the boss had just done, agreeing that Luke should have gone on and he should not let his personal feelings cloud his judgement. Unbeknown to them, when Ambrose replaced the current striker, the team captain came over to the boss and said,

'Is Tewkes-Dawson injured, Boss? Why hasn't he come on? We need him.'

Mr Hargreaves swore at the captain and told him, 'Just get out there and do your job. You've got a fresh striker on the pitch; use him!'

The captain was flabbergasted at the boss's outburst and went back to the game shaking his head. The match ended with no score and there was a stony silence in the England dressing room after the match. When the boss addressed them all, he accused them of lack of commitment and not trying. His language was not the choicest again and heads were bowed as he was speaking. All of a sudden, Ambrose stood up and shouted:

'That is enough! You have no right to speak to us like that. We have to show you respect because of who you are, but we have a right to some respect too!'

He was interrupted at this point by the boss, who said, 'You sit down and be quiet. Don't you dare talk back to me like that!'

Ambrose retorted, 'I won't keep quiet; I'll have my say. I don't care what you do to me as I've had my share of play on this tour.

'You let your personal feelings outweigh your better judgement. Everybody in this dressing room knows Luke should have come on out there and, if you were honest, you would know it too. Don't have a go at us for not trying; look to yourself. We all know you are a good coach, but you let yourself down as well as the team. No one else is prepared to say so; they have too much to lose.'

Mr Hargreaves was totally shocked, as was everybody else in the dressing room. Hargreaves turned to his assistants and said:

'Have you ever heard anything like it before, a player addressing his boss like that?'

One of them said, 'No Boss, because it hasn't been necessary but, on this occasion, I feel it was. However, this is not the place to discuss it. I suggest we have a meeting and discuss this situation away from the players; it's bad for the morale of the squad.'

When the staff left the dressing room, all the players stood and applauded Ambrose. Luke thanked him and said he felt embarrassed by it all. Ambrose said he hoped he had not made it worse for Luke, but he could not contain himself and had to let it out. Later on, in private, Luke told Ambrose that he knew in his heart the boss would not put him on, but he could not explain how he knew.

The players were all on the coach waiting for the coaching staff for about twenty minutes before they appeared; not a word was said!

They were all instructed to be ready for departure to the airport at 10am the next morning for the flight to Lisbon. They were also told that there would be a meeting an hour after they had checked into the hotel, which everyone was expected to attend. There were a few raised eyebrows at this and one or two suggestions and guesses what the meeting would reveal. The boss came up to Luke and said,

'Are these travel arrangements any problem to you, tomorrow being a Sunday?'

Luke replied, 'No, it can't be helped.'

'Good,' the boss replied.

Luke read his reply as being genuine and not sarcastic in anyway.

It was about 4pm by the time they were all checked into their rooms in Lisbon. The meeting was scheduled for 5pm in one of the anterooms, which was laid out with chairs and tables. Once it was established that all were present, Mr Hargreaves stood up and addressed them all. He said:

I am aware there is unrest at the moment among the squad. We are a team, all working for the same goals and aims. My staff and I have discussed the situation and it appears that I have upset some of you with my attitude towards you and to one of you in particular. I mean Luke Tewkes-Dawson, of course. For some reason or other we fell out over something, and I here and now wish to apologize publicly to Luke. I accept I was out of order, but you should understand that I put one hundred per cent into my job and, if I suspect that anybody is not giving their all, I will take action.

I misread his motives for not wishing to train with the squad on that Sunday morning. I had not been informed of Luke's religious convictions, but that was not his fault, though I wish he had mentioned it at the start of the tour. Anyway, that is water under the bridge. I did not use Luke in the last match deliberately to make a point. Perhaps things might have turned out differently if I had put Luke on. No offence to Ambrose, but Luke would have had fresh legs when the Italian defence was beginning to tire.

I want to close by saying I hold no grudge against Ambrose for his outburst in the dressing room. As it happens, it brought things to a head and has allowed the situation to be sorted. I believe we are a good squad and can finish off the tour united and with a win over Portugal to round off a successful tour.

Just one more thing, Luke; you will be in the starting line-up on Tuesday. Thank you for coming to this meeting and hearing me out. Once again, I apologize to you all and hope you can trust me and my staff to lead you in the right direction and to maintain the unity the squad needs to succeed.

Mr Hargreaves sat down again and took a long sip of water. For a few seconds there was complete silence, then one person started clapping and gradually the others joined in. Luke was sure he detected that Mr Hargreaves's eyes were somewhat wet. He stood up and thanked them.

'Now, off you go,' he said. 'See you at dinner and at training tomorrow morning at 10am. As you can see, the training ground is virtually within the grounds of the hotel, so make your own way there in the morning.'

The buzz of conversation after the meeting was centred on how big it was of the boss to do what he just did. They all agreed it could not have been easy for him and they admired him for it. Luke knew that it was the influence of his support staff that caused the turnaround of attitude but as promised, he did not say a word to anyone.

Dinner that evening was a much more relaxed occasion and there was much chatter and friendly conversation. On entering the dining room, Luke was approached by the boss with an outstretched hand and he said:

'Forgive me, Luke, for doubting your commitment. I should have known better. You always give your all, in training; I should have recognized that.'

'No problem,' Luke said. 'All sorted now and forgotten.'

'Thanks,' the boss replied.

Halfway through the meal, Luke noticed that there was a lot of sniggering going on and everybody was looking at him and laughing. He asked the ones on his table what was going on: 'nothing,' was the reply, but the sniggering continued until someone eventually pointed above Luke's head.

When he looked up, he saw that someone had tied a stiff piece of wire to Luke's chair which extended above his head to support a halo of glittery material hovering over him. Everybody laughed out loud, and Luke had to laugh with them. He looked straight across at Ambrose who held out his hands in all innocence but had the biggest grin of all on his face. Mr Hargreaves nodded his approval and turning to one of his assistants said, 'I believe we are a united squad again.'

CHAPTER 19

Training the next day went very well and Luke stood out as the good player he was. He even resorted to a bit of showing off with the ball and amazed many with his skills. The coaches remarked how quick he was on his feet for someone who was so big and not fully mature in body, being only sixteen. They agreed that he had a bright future ahead of him and he was a likeable lad and popular with the rest of the squad. At the end of the training session, the starting eleven for the next day's match was announced and, of course, Luke's name was included. They were told that there would be just a light training session the next morning, the day of the match, to brush up on set pieces etc.

Luke was chosen to take all free kicks near the penalty area, but the team captain would be the penalty taker. The squad was again told to have an early evening meal, which had been arranged with the hotel, and to relax in the afternoon. They were categorically told to stay out of the sun, even with sun block applied, as the sun was deceptively fierce at this time of the year and they could easily get burned.

The match venue was half-an-hour's coach ride away and en route Luke's nerves started to kick in. He had butterflies in his stomach, which was unusual for him as he usually only felt excitement before a match. But this match was the biggest he had ever played in, and he knew there were great expectations on his shoulders. He hoped he would not let the team down.

Once Luke was changed and ready to go out onto the pitch for the warmup, his nerves had gone and he was excited about playing. He soaked up the atmosphere as he looked around the stadium at the large crowd. He looked across at the area occupied by the English supporters and saw England flags and banners with one or two saying, 'Go Lim Go'. He gave them a wave and received a loud roar in return. He felt good.

They lined up for the national anthems and Luke sang out enthusiastically; he was fired up and raring to go.

Soon after the kick-off, Luke obtained possession of the ball and ran at the Portuguese defence. He evaded three tackles and, as he entered the penalty area, he let fly with a powerful shot at goal and saw the ball sail into the net with the goalkeeper unable to stop it, despite getting one hand to it. The match was just three minutes old!

Luke leapt about four feet in the air and raised his hands towards the English fans who were on their feet and cheering. Luke's teammates mobbed him and succeeded in knocking him to the ground; it was an unbelievable start to the game. Luke got a thumbs-up sign from the boss at the touchline; he was shaking his head in disbelief.

As the match continued, Luke became more closely marked but was causing the defence all sorts of problems. It became obvious that Luke was the star player on the pitch. He did not put a foot wrong and had two good scoring chances which were saved by the keeper. Then, England was awarded a corner on the right-hand side.

Luke took up a position on the edge of the penalty area and raised his arm to the corner taker, pointing towards the penalty spot. As the ball came over, Luke ran forward, outjumped everyone in the area and powered a header into the net. Again, Luke was mobbed by his teammates. The first half ended with the score of 2–0.

Luke received congratulations and 'well-done' from the coaching staff in the dressing room.

Mr Hargreaves said, 'Well done everybody. Be aware that in the second half they will be coming at you. Keep your shape. You all know your job; make sure you are focused on what you should be doing. Luke, the chances are that you will be closely marked. They will probably delegate someone to closely mark you. If that happens, you must go and stand alongside another of their defenders, which will take two of them out of the game. The midfield can take advantage of that and press forward when the occasion arises.'

Sure enough, right from the start of the second half, one of the midfield players latched on to Luke and followed him everywhere. Luke did as instructed and went alongside another of the Portuguese players. Within a short place of time, the two were obviously arguing among themselves, although Luke did not understand what they were saying. The English side pressed forward and Luke went wide, taking his marker with him. As the English pressed towards the opposing goal, one of their players was fouled about 25 yards from goal and England was awarded a free kick. Luke quickly ran across and grabbed the ball and placed it to take the kick.

The referee instructed him to wait for the whistle while he ensured that the defensive wall of defenders were the requisite 10 yards away. When the whistle blew, Luke stepped up and, anticipating that the wall would jump up to block his shot, he drilled a hard low shot underneath them and into the bottom corner of the goal, giving the goalkeeper no chance; he could but stand and watch as the ball rocketed past him out of reach. Again, there were great celebrations on and off the pitch.

Mr Hargreaves turned to his assistants and said:

'That boy is sheer genius. He not only has great talent, but he also has a good football brain—a maturity far beyond his age. A footballer like him comes around once in a blue moon. The world is his oyster.'

His assistants agreed, one saying, 'I've never seen anything like it in one so young and he's only going to get better as he grows too.'

Later on in the match, Luke showed his genius once again by gaining the possession of the ball and outsprinted all the opposition. As he got into the penalty area, he was one-on-one with the Portuguese goalkeeper, who rushed out to him. Luke slipped the ball past the keeper on one side of him, ran past him on the other side and merely toe-poked the ball into the empty net. There were gasps of admiration from the bench and rapturous applause from all around the ground.

With two minutes to go, Luke saw that he was to be substituted and, at the next break in play, he jogged to the touchline amid a standing ovation from the crowd, both English and Portuguese. Luke acknowledged the applause with overhead clapping and waving to the crowd. He received handshakes and pats on the back when he got back to the dugout. When the final whistle blew, Luke returned to the pitch to shake hands with his colleagues and the opposition.

One of them said to him, 'Do you play for *Southtown Rovers*?'

Luke said, 'Yes, why?'

'I also will be playing for *Southtown* next season; they have bought me. I look forward to playing with you. I would prefer to play with you than against you; you play too well!'

'Thanks,' Luke said. 'I will look out for you when we start training again.'

Once Luke got into the dressing room and sat down, he felt absolutely shattered. He had not felt even a bit tired on the pitch and guessed that the adrenaline had kept him going. He could not remember when he had last enjoyed a game so much.

When Mr Hargreaves came in after doing the TV and press interviews, he said to Luke:

'I just don't know what to say to you, Luke. "Well played" doesn't seem adequate for what we have all witnessed out there; you were just at a different level. You have a well-earned rest now before the next season starts. You are going to burst onto the scene like the premiership have never witnessed before. Enjoy it!'

'Thank you, Boss,' Luke said. 'And thanks for your coaching and advice.'

'My pleasure,' Mr Hargreaves replied.

On the way back to the hotel in the coach, instructions were issued for the departure to the airport and the flight back to Gatwick airport the next day. Luke could not believe how quickly these twelve days had passed.

CHAPTER 20

As Luke walked into the arrival hall at Gatwick Airport, he was surprised to hear a familiar voice calling his name. When he looked at the waiting crowd, he saw his father waving and beckoning him over.

'Hello Dad, what are you doing here? I never expected to see you at the airport?'

'Hello, Son, Colin said. 'I came to meet you because I have some bad news. Mum is in hospital here in London; she had a bad turn at home and the hospital has sent her up here to Guy's Hospital for more tests. Come with me and I will take you to see her. Can you do that?'

'I'll have to tell the boss that I won't be going back with them on the coach. Wait here and I will go and tell him,' Luke instructed.

Mr Hargreaves said of course it would be alright; he was a free agent. He hoped everything would be alright and his thoughts would be with Luke and the family.

When Luke returned to his father, he told Luke that his mum was virtually in a coma and was heavily sedated to keep her movements to a minimum; she had collapsed at home a week ago. Colin explained that he was in accommodation provided in the hospital grounds, but he did not think Luke would be able to stay. He would keep him informed of his mum's condition, if he went back home or to Ruth's house.

They boarded the Gatwick Express to Victoria Station and then took the underground to Westminster, where they just had to cross the bridge to get to the hospital. They first went to Colin's room, where Luke dropped off his luggage and changed out of his England suit before going across to the hospital.

Luke was visibly shocked when he saw his mother in the Intensive Care Unit, she was all wired up with an endotracheal tube down her throat, a drip in her arm and monitors and bleeps sounding all around her. Luke kissed his mother on the forehead and said:

'Hi Mum, it's Luke.' He was in tears and said to his dad, 'What's going to happen? What are they going to do?'

Colin said he would be speaking to the doctor in charge soon as he would be in to check on Alice shortly. He was waiting for the result of the scan she had this morning. In order not to impede the nurses, they both went into a small waiting room down the corridor, asking the nurse to inform them when the doctor arrived. The waiting room was empty and, at Luke's request, they both got down on their knees and Colin prayed for Alice and for a guiding hand upon those who were caring for her. He also prayed for Luke and himself for strength in their situation and for help in trusting in God's wisdom during this time of concern for a loved one.

Luke then told Colin that he would not go back home while his mum was here in hospital and suggested that they both check into a hotel nearby. Colin protested initially on the grounds of the cost, but Luke persuaded him that money was not an issue and reminded him of the salary that he was now earning. Colin eventually agreed that it was a good idea, and it would free up his room for some other patient's worthy relative. Colin informed the hospital authorities later, once they had found a hotel.

The physician in charge of Alice came into the waiting room and was introduced to

Luke and sat down with them. He said to Luke, 'I suppose you realize by now that your mother is a very sick lady?'

'Yes, Dad has filled me in,' Luke replied.

The doctor continued, 'My colleagues and I have studied the scan. The tumour is in a very difficult position and only an operation can make any difference. Although we can operate, there is a huge risk involved because of its location. We cannot remove all of it and what we can remove will only have a small effect on Alice's quality of life. We cannot be sure how mobile she would be if she gets through the operation; unfortunately, there is no other alternative in this country.'

Colin interrupted, 'Are you saying there is a danger she may not get through the operation?'

'Yes, I have to tell you that there is always that risk in major intrusive surgery,' the doctor responded. 'But Alice is fit and well otherwise and has no blood pressure or breathing problems, so that all goes in her favour.'

'You said there was no alternative in this country; do you mean there is something else that could be done in another country?' asked Luke.

'Well, there is a surgeon in Boston, Massachusetts, who does a procedure whereby he uses laser treatment on the tumour once the skull has been opened. He has had some success with it, but it is still in the experimental stage. The only thing I will say is that, when it has been successful, the results are quite remarkable, and even if the results are not totally successful there is still an improvement in the quality of life,' the doctor explained.

'Well, let's go for it,' Luke said.

'Whoa, wait a minute,' Colin said. 'I take it this is not something that can be done on the NHS, can it?'

'Indeed not!' The doctor replied. 'The cost would be in the region of 80,000 U.S Dollars, approximately £60,000.'

'I'm afraid that is out of the question,' Colin said.

'No, it is not Dad! I can easily afford that, no problem,' Luke exclaimed.

The doctor looked quite shocked at Luke's statement and looked at Colin questioningly.

'My son is a highly paid, professional footballer,' Colin explained.

'Oh, I see,' the doctor said. 'Let me go and have a word with my colleagues while you discuss it. I will come back to you shortly and we can discuss it further.'

With that, the doctor left the room.

Colin turned to Luke and said, 'I can't let you do this Luke; it doesn't seem right somehow.'

'Right for who? It's right for Mum. She deserves the best we can do for her. It is only six weeks' wages for me; what else am I going to do with that much money? Earlier on, you prayed for God's guidance in this and you always say, "the Lord will provide.' Well, perhaps he has done and that is why I have this contract. The Lord has provided it for this time when we need it; can you deny that?' Luke asked.

'You put up a strong argument, Luke. We must give Mum every chance we can. Are you sure about this?' Colin replied.

'Of course I am sure,' Luke retorted. 'You would do it too if you could, wouldn't you?'

'Yes, yes of course,' Colin said and gave Luke a hug. 'Thank you, Son. I'm so proud of you.'

Luke was slightly embarrassed; he was not used to his father showing his emotions so openly.

When the doctor re-entered the room, he told them that he had contacted the surgeon in Boston, and he was prepared to do the operation, subject to him seeing the scan and x-rays. These would be sent to him via the internet that very day. The doctor asked Luke and Colin if they had come to a decision. They told him that they wanted to go ahead with it. They were asked to leave a contact number so that the doctor could inform them of the situation when the surgeon contacts them again.

Colin and Luke found a reasonably priced, decent hotel within walking distance of the hospital. They checked in for one week initially with the option of extending that, should they need to. The hotel was very understanding and sympathetic and readily agreed to that arrangement.

Colin returned to his room in the hospital grounds to collect his belongings and check out of the accommodation, while Luke unpacked and got some hot drinks ready.

He then telephoned Ruth and updated her on the situation and asked for her to remember his mum in her prayers. She said she always did and enquired after Colin and himself and how were they coping with the situation. Luke said they were very worried, of course, but it helped that they were together. He did not know yet if his mum would be going to America, but hopefully they would find out more in the morning and would keep her posted.

He then phoned Christine and told her he would not be coming back home just yet. She fully understood and told him he must stay as long as necessary.

When Colin returned to the hotel room with his things, Luke noticed how haggard he looked and asked him how he was.

He replied, 'I must say it has been a tough couple of weeks, a big upheaval and a worry, even if I did not know how seriously ill Mum was. She was so good at hiding her pain. She kept things so close to her chest for the benefit of those around her and so as not to worry us. I am fine in myself though, just worried that's all.'

Luke said, 'If Mum has to go to America, we'll have to go with her of course.'

'No, not you Luke, there is no point in both of us going. Apart from it being extra expense, you have your career to think about. You don't know how long you would be away, and your new season will be starting in a few weeks' time.'

Luke saw the sense of that and did not dispute Colin's reasoning, but he knew it would be hard.

'Anyway, this is all conjecture. We don't even know if Mum will be going yet,' Colin said. 'I'm going to have a little rest now; I haven't been sleeping too well lately. We will find somewhere to eat later.'

Colin stretched out on his bed and was soon fast asleep. Luke decided to go out and get a newspaper and left a note for his dad before creeping quietly out of the room, closing the door very gently. He found a newspaper stand and bought the late edition of a paper and, on turning to the back page, saw his photograph with big headlines which said, '*Lim out on a limb on class*'.

He read the article which reported on the Portugal match in particular and they said that he had set Europe alight with his display. The article went on to say that his coach at national level had described him as the most exciting prospect in English football for decades and suspected that, even at his age, it would not be long before he was considered for the England first team. The reporter also wondered how long *Southtown Rovers* would be able to hang on to him before the big clubs starting sniffing around. 'English football needed someone like Luke to give it a lift,' the article concluded. Luke was quite taken aback by the accolades in the article and thought that the writer had gone over the top somewhat. Luke was not aware just how good he was; he just thoroughly enjoyed playing football.

When Luke returned to the room, his dad was awake and had showered and changed. He told Luke he had checked through the hotel literature and suggested that they eat in at the restaurant, which seemed to be priced quite reasonably. Luke agreed and Colin phoned down to reception to book a table. Luke showed his dad the article in the newspaper. After reading it, Colin said, 'Quite the hero eh!'

'Bit embarrassing,' Luke replied.

'It looks like you might have to get used to that sort of thing in the future. Don't let it get to your head now,' Colin warned.

'I won't,' Luke replied. 'I think it is all a bit over the top if you ask me. There are plenty of good players about in the Premiership.'

'Yes, but not at sixteen years of age; I think that is what they are saying,' Colin added.

'To change the subject,' Luke said, 'what is happening back at Manleigh with the churches while you are away?'

'Oh, Reverend Wills has made arrangements for cover with lay preachers for now. And then, when we have more idea of how long I will be away, he will appoint a more permanent incumbent,' Colin answered.

After Luke had showered and changed, they went down for dinner and Luke demonstrated that, even with the trauma of his mother's illness, he had not lost his appetite and they enjoyed a good meal together, giving thanks before eating.

They went for a short stroll afterwards along the embankment before returning to their room. After watching the news on TV, they prayed together and then turned in for the night at the end of an extraordinary day.

When they visited Alice the next morning, they were informed that the doctor wanted to see them. The nurse said she would let him know they had arrived. The nurse said that Alice appeared to have had a comfortable night and as far as could be ascertained, there was no change.

When the doctor arrived, he suggested that they go down to the waiting room. There he announced that the surgeon had looked at the scan etc. and had agreed to operate on Alice if that was their wish. He pointed out that there were great risks involved even flying Alice to America. She would be accompanied by nursing staff and an airline that had vast experience and specialized in medical cases would be used.

He further explained that the risks involved in the operation itself were no greater than if she was operated on in England; the only extra risk was the flight which added to the risk of complications, but he assured them she would be in good hands. They both agreed that they should go ahead with the operation in America as there was a chance of a better outcome for Alice than the local procedure. The doctor said that he agreed with their choice.

He also explained that he had inadvertently misled them on the cost of the operation. He had converted £60,000 to $80,000 when, in fact, it was $60,000 which was about £40,000, so that was good news, but the price did not include flights etc. Therefore, it would probably still be £60,000 in total. Luke assured the doctor that was no problem.

They were told that things would move very quickly now. The hospital would make all the arrangements and would contact them with the details of when Alice would be flown over as soon as they had them. It should be in the next two or three days.

'The sooner the better, eh?' The doctor said.

Colin asked about the payment, and he was advised to contact the hospital administration office and they would liaise with him regarding making the payment. This was sorted and arrangements were made to transfer money from Luke's bank account to the hospital.

When Luke and his father were in the canteen having a little bit of lunch, Luke said he would see his mum off at the airport and then return to Ruth's rather than go back to his home in Manleigh, as at least he would have company there rather than being in an empty house. Colin thought it was a good idea and said he would feel better knowing that Luke was not alone. Colin then remembered he needed to phone Gramps Maynard to update him on the situation; he had not been informed of the American trip as it had all happened so fast.

Gramps Maynard said he wanted to come up and see Alice before she went to America. He would get one of his men to drive him up to London, so arrangements were made to meet him the following day. In fact, he arrived in London by train and Luke and Colin met him at Victoria Station and accompanied him to the hospital. At Alice's bedside he broke down and wept, saying he never expected to see Alice look so ill.

After spending half an hour or so at the bedside, they adjourned to the hospital canteen and there Colin informed Gramps more fully on the situation regarding the choices for Alice. He was overwhelmingly supportive of the decision to go to Boston. When the cost involved was mentioned, he insisted that he make a contribution. When he was told that it had all been sorted out and Luke was more than able to cover the costs involved, he persisted and said it was not fair on Luke; besides he wanted to get more involved.

'She is my daughter after all,' he insisted. 'Here Luke, let me give you a cheque.'

He reached into his pocket, but Luke placed a hand on his arm and said,

'Gramps, there is no need really.'

'I insist,' Gramps said, and he wrote out a cheque and handed it to Luke. Luke saw that it was made out for £25,000; he just shook his head and thanked his grandpa. Gramps asked Colin if he needed any money for eventualities while he was in America. Colin said he would be fine; bed and board were provided for him by the clinic in Boston and he could not foresee that he would need to spend much money otherwise.

Gramps Maynard popped in to say farewell to Alice and then left to return to his business in Manleigh. He asked to be kept updated on Alice; Luke assured him that he would contact him whenever there was more information to pass on.

Two days later they left the hospital, bound for Stansted Airport. Alice went in an ambulance with two nurses, who were going to accompany her to America. Luke and Colin followed behind in a car provided by the hospital. The airport authorities were very helpful, but Luke was not allowed to accompany the ambulance and Colin up to the aircraft. He boarded the ambulance and kissed his mum and gave his dad a hug. He waited at the airport until he saw the plane take off, then made his way to the coach station for his journey back to London, where he took a train down to Southtown.

He felt thoroughly drained, more exhausted than if he had played his toughest match ever. But, perhaps for the first time in his life, football was not on his mind. He could not rid his mind of the image of his mother when he first saw her in the Intensive Care Unit at Guy's Hospital and the haggard look on his father's face when he met him at Gatwick Airport on his return from the European Tour, which now seemed to be somewhere in the distant past. He thought at least it was a blessing that he had a few weeks before he needed to get involved in football again, but then he thought that it might be better if he did, rather than centre his thoughts solely on his mother's health. It might be good to have a distraction from the worry of it all.

CHAPTER 21

Ruth was so pleased to see Luke when he arrived back home, she gave him a big, motherly hug and said:

'You poor thing, Luke. You must be so worried. I have not been able to think of anything else lately. How have you and your dad coped? Your dad has kept me updated and we have all been praying for the family at church.'

Luke saw that there was a huge pile of cards on the sideboard, all addressed to him. Ruth explained, 'The poor old postman has been kept busy around here. Every day more cards arrive. Here, let me take your bags upstairs while you read them and then we will have a cup of tea together.'

'No way,' said Luke. 'I'll take them upstairs while you put the kettle on.'

'OK,' Ruth said. 'Bring down any laundry you may have, and I'll put the machine on. I guess you have not been able to do any washing have you?'

'No, that was the last thing on my mind I'm afraid, both on the tour and in London with Mum,' Luke explained.

Luke took his bags upstairs and returned with a big armful of laundry.

'There's quite a lot, Auntie Ruth. I am sorry about that,' Luke said.

'That's no problem, Luke; I don't have to do it by hand you know!' she quipped.

'Thanks Auntie Ruth, you are so kind. I do not know what I would do without you; it's like a home from home here,' Luke explained.

'Oh, stop it, Luke. You've brought tears to my eyes now. I do enjoy having you here; I really missed you about the place. Roger is in and out like a yo-yo, even more so since his recent promotion. I suppose you don't know about that do you? He's "Detective Sergeant" now. He's really chuffed about it. Is "chuffed" a cool word to use these days?' she said.

Luke laughed and said, 'That'll do.'

Ruth replied, 'Whatever—let's just say he's pleased. Ah this is what I've missed, this sort of banter.'

As she was pouring the teas, Luke started opening the cards. Most of them were from the churches at Manleigh and Rushton and also from the flower shop customers and from Sally, herself. They all expressed their best wishes for a full recovery for Alice. Luke was greatly surprised to have received one from Mr Hargreaves, as well as from *Southtown Rovers'* staff. He remarked how kind people were to think of him and his family and to take the trouble to send cards.

'Your parents know a lot of people Luke,' Ruth said, 'and are obviously well thought of. Of course, you are getting well known too, being spread all over the newspapers; you have even got me reading the sports pages these days!'

Luke drank his tea and then asked to be excused, as he wanted to ring Christine.

'Use the house phone Luke. 'I will go into the utility room and sort out this pile of washing,' Ruth insisted.

Christine was so pleased to hear Luke on the phone. She told him not a day had gone by without him being mentioned. It was also reported that Alice was very ill and that it was a trying time for Luke.

'How are you coping with it all?' Christine asked.

'Well, to be honest, and I haven't said this to anyone, I'm very scared as to what is going to happen. I've never seen anybody sick like that before and it was a bit of a shock to see Mum like that. I keep thinking if she dies because of this trip to America, I will never forgive myself; I will feel responsible. Gramps Maynard and I have financed this trip and I keep wandering if we have done the right thing?'

'Of course you have,' Christine responded. 'You have to always remember the reasons why you did it: because you considered it the best thing for your mum, regardless of the outcome. You and your dad obviously weighed up the advice from the doctors, and they themselves said they thought you had made the right decision, so don't you go and beat yourself up about it.'

'Yeah, I know. I suppose I just needed reassuring; you always seem to talk sense. I value your opinion,' Luke replied.

'And so, you should. I am a woman!' Christine said, jokingly, trying to lighten the conversation.

'I think perhaps it is time to finish this phone call!' Luke replied, laughing. 'I have one or two things to sort out, then I will come up at the weekend, probably on Sunday.'

'I'll be counting the hours,' Christine replied.

When he came off the phone, he asked Ruth if she minded if he went to his room for a bit of a lie down as he felt absolutely exhausted.

'You do that,' she said. 'I'll call you for dinner. What would you like for your dinner today, Luke?''

'Anything you like, I am just looking forward to some home cooking for a change,' he replied.

'How about a homemade steak and kidney pie, chips, and mushy peas?' she asked.

'Yes please, a big one!' Luke requested.

'But of course. I wouldn't dare give you a small portion when you are out of training!' Ruth retorted.

'That's something I must get back into. I'll start my morning runs next week; we will be back in full training in about three weeks' time,' Luke emphasized.

Luke went upstairs and lay on the bed. He was fast asleep within minutes. With Mum, Dad, Christine, the hospital and the airport all rolling around in his head, he felt he had packed two years experiences into just two weeks. 'Growing into adulthood was so tough,' he thought. 'Surely things can't always be like this, can they?'

There was a knock on the door and Ruth called out that dinner would be ready in twenty minutes. Luke aroused him from a deep sleep. It took a minute or two for him to get his bearings before he called out, 'OK'. He looked at his watch and saw that it was nearly 7 o'clock; he had slept for almost three hours!

He went downstairs to a wonderful smell emanating from the kitchen.

'That smells worth waking up for,' Luke announced as he entered the kitchen.

'You're looking better; you needed those forty winks, Luke,' Ruth replied.

Luke saw that there were three place settings on the large kitchen table and asked who else was here for dinner.

'Me,' came a voice from behind him as Roger walked into the room. He extended a hand to Luke and welcomed him back.

'So sorry to hear about your mother, Luke. I hope everything turns out alright. Modern medicine is so advanced these days; it's amazing what they can do. I'm sure she is in good hands. We have to trust that our prayers will be answered,' Roger continued.

'Yes, thank you for your concern,' Luke replied. 'By the way, congratulations on your promotion, Sarge.'

'Thank you. I am not the only one that is due congratulations. I gather from all the newspaper reports that you had a good tour?' Roger added.

'Eventually I did,' Luke replied. 'But can we eat please! It seems to me that all this chat is keeping us from some delicious food. I'll tell you all about it at the table.'

'Well, you haven't changed that's for sure!' Ruth interjected. 'You have retained your love for food through the entire trauma.'

'It is your cooking, Auntie Ruth,' Luke retaliated.

'You're learning,' Roger said. 'You know which side your bread is buttered; flattery will get you everywhere.'

'And a bigger slice of pie too, I hope!' Luke said, and they all laughed.

Ruth served up the dinner.

'This is the most delicious food I have ever tasted in my life,' Luke announced.

Roger just shook his head and laughing, said, 'Don't overdo it Luke, or you will have to say it every time you are fed!'

Ruth turned to Luke and said, 'Tell us about the tour, Luke. There is obviously a story to tell, judging by what you said earlier about enjoying it "eventually".'

Luke proceeded to tell them the whole story (between mouthfuls!). They were quite shocked at the initial attitude of the coach but gave him credit for his apology and the remorse shown. Luke left out the bit about the match he played in Portugal, but Roger brought it up and commented on how the reporters had raved about his performance in that match. He had also bumped into Andy Thomas, Luke's agent, who had bought every paper he could that had a report or comment on the match. Andy had also said he would be in touch shortly, as he had some propositions for Luke.

Roger told Luke that he had explained to Andy about the situation with his mum and said it might be better to leave it a few days before getting in touch. However, if Luke felt up to it, he could call Andy. Luke said he would leave it until after the weekend, when he had come back from Manleigh.

Luke rode up to Manleigh after having received a phone call from his dad, saying they had arrived safely, and Alice was quite stable, after having endured the flight very well. The surgeon was due to see her the next day and he would update Luke afterwards. Luke went straight to church as he did not have time to go to the house first. As he expected, the people were very kind and were all asking about Alice. The younger element in the church wanted to know about his football life and, in particular, about the tour as they had read the papers and the rave reviews.

Finally, Christine got a word in edgeways, gave him a kiss and said it was good to see him. He told her he had been thinking about her and wished she had been there when he was in shock over his mother's illness. She tried to reassure him by saying she was in good hands and that there was much prayer being offered on her behalf. She also told him he was invited to her house for lunch—an invitation which Luke readily accepted as he had not made any plans. Besides which, he had not yet met Christine's mother.

Luke was welcomed during the service and was informed that Alice was very much in their prayers, as was he and his father. They all hoped there would be a good outcome from the operation in America. Luke mouthed a 'thank you' to the preacher.

Once again, at the end of the service, Luke was surrounded by well- wishers and enquirers. Christine eventually had to tear him away. They decided to walk to Christine's house and leave Luke's scooter at the church, since they would be attending the service in the evening.

Luke was made to feel very welcome by Christine's mum who said all the right things about Alice's condition and hope she would be alright. They enjoyed a good lunch of roast beef with all the trimmings. Christine's mum had obviously been forewarned about Luke's appetite because there was plenty food, and Luke ate well! Christine's mum remarked how good it was to see someone enjoy their food as Christine was a nightmare to cater for as she had such a small appetite.

Luke declined a tea or coffee after lunch as he wanted to go to the Manse and generally check up on things. He knew that a steward from the church was a key-holder and was keeping an eye on the Manse, but he wanted to pick up a few things from his room.

He and Christine went for a long walk together, holding hands as they walked. Christine told Luke how much she was enjoying her course at university, and she thought it was going really well. Luke was pleased for her but told her he was thinking of giving up his course on architectural drawing at the college. He was getting on really well, but he felt he had no time for himself what with training and matches etc. And, apart from Sundays, his only free time was taken up with attending the college or studying. Also, because of the ridiculous amount of money he was being paid, he would not need another trade as a backup as he could invest for any future eventuality, and the chances are he could earn a lot more as time went on.

Christine said, 'What if you get an injury which puts paid to your football career before you have had time to invest sufficient funds? You would be in trouble then without having something to fall back on.'

'If that happens, I'll just get an ordinary job. Other people manage without qualifications, so why can't I?' Luke replied.

'You need to think it over carefully before you decide; maybe you should talk it over with your dad?' Christine advised.

'He's got enough on his plate at the moment,' Luke responded.

Luke collected a couple of items from his room and then they caught a bus into the town and had a coffee in one of the cafés there. They could see the flower shop from where they were sitting and, on seeing the shop, Luke's mind went to his mother. He pictured her in the shop and tears formed in his eyes. Christine noticed and reached across for his hand and said,

'She'll be fine Luke; she is as strong as an ox. She will be back in the shop before you know it.'

'I do hope so; I would give up everything just to see that happen,' Luke replied.

They finished their coffees and sat on one of the seats in the square. Luke had to sign his autograph two or three times for fans who approached him, which helped to distract his mind from more serious thoughts.

'Do you realize that I don't have your autograph?' Christine said. 'Perhaps I should get several from you and then I could sell them when you are famous.'

'I am famous!' Luke retorted. 'Don't you read the papers?'

'I don't actually!' Christine responded. 'But people are always sticking them under my nose when you are in them, so I am well informed of how you are doing.'

They strolled back to the church and took their places early, so as not to 'hog all the limelight' as Luke put it. He didn't mind the attention, but he did not want to be a distraction to the other church goers. Roger did come across and said, 'Hello,' and asked Christine how she was. Once again, with a different preacher, Alice and her family were prayed for. Luke felt there was a genuine concern among the congregation, and he took some comfort from that.

After church, Luke decided he would ride back to Southtown that evening rather than stay overnight at the Manse. He wanted to be at Ruth's when his dad phoned on the Monday. He and Christine chatted in the car park for half an hour or so before Luke kissed her goodbye and set off on his scooter. Christine watched him disappear down the road with a heavy heart. She felt so sorry for him; she knew how close he was to his mother and how worried he was.

On the Monday morning, Luke went for his usual run and spent an hour at the gym and swimming pool, as he knew his dad would not have any information at that time since they were five hours behind Greenwich Mean Time. Luke then telephoned Andy Thomas to say that he was available that afternoon if he wanted to meet up. Andy met up with Luke that afternoon and informed him of two sponsorship deals that were on offer, if Luke wanted to take them.

The first one was to appear in newspaper adverts for a travel agency on a three-year contract, which was worth half a million pounds. This would involve several photo shoots a year over that three-year period. Andy said he had sought approval from *Southtown Rovers* should Luke decide to take the offer and they had no objection. Luke was flabbergasted at the amount of money offered and he asked Andy for his advice. Andy informed Luke that there were huge amounts of money involved in advertising and this was just the tip of the iceberg.

'Go for it,' Andy said. 'You have nothing to lose. It will also help to raise your profile which could work in your favour.'

'I've never done anything like that before; I may not be any good at it,' Luke answered nervously.

'You don't need to worry about that. You would be handled by professionals who have vast experience in dealing with all sorts of people, and you would have a say in what photographs were used and what the adverts would actually say,' Roger re-assured him.

'OK, I'll give it a go,' Luke said.

'Good,' said Andy, 'I'll set up a meeting with them and they will fill you in on what they will require; then you can say "yea" or "nay".'

'What's the second one?' Luke asked.

'This one is not quite so lucrative, but I think it is something that you might like to get involved in. The government is about to launch a countrywide, anti-drugs campaign using young people from all walks of life. This is for TV and will be a thirty-second advert and will run for a year. It will mean one half day of filming and that is it. Once again, professional film makers will be producing it so you will not need any previous experience. You have been selected from the world of football to represent young people in sport. The fee is a one-off payment of £15,000 with no royalties or anything, regardless of how many times the advert is shown,' Andy explained.

'Yes, I would like to do that; it seems like a good thing to do,' Luke replied. 'But what is in it for you? Do I pay you a percentage of my fees?'

'No, that's sorted; I charge a commission to both agencies, so you get all the money from the contract that you sign,' Andy explained.

Luke asked when these things would be taking place and Andy explained that some of the filming for the anti-drug campaign had already started, so they will be in touch with him shortly. Andy would let Luke know the date when he heard back from them. Andy also told Luke that the filming would take place at *Southtown Rovers*'s ground and Luke would be in his *Southtown* kit. The club had approved this also.

With that sorted, Andy said he would draw up the contracts and arrange for them to be signed at the agencies. Luke's mind was in a whirl after Andy left and he hoped he would not regret agreeing to do these things. He preferred to stay in the background rather than be a high-profile person.

Soon after dinner that evening, Roger answered the phone and called Luke, saying his dad was on the phone from Boston.

'Hi Dad, what's the news?' Luke said as he took the phone from Roger.

'Mum has had the operation; she is in recovery at the moment. She smiled at me and waved her hand. The surgeon said he was happy with what he was able to do. He zapped more of the tumour than he had expected to but had to leave a small amount due to the proximity of important nerves. He said the next twenty-four hours will be important in learning how well she will recover and whether any of her faculties will be impaired or not. She is doing fine Luke; our prayers have been answered, so don't you worry any. I'll keep in touch,' his dad assured him.

'That's good news, Dad. I've been so worried. Where are you now?' Luke asked.

'I'm at the hospital. It's 1:30pm here so it must be about 7 o'clock in the evening there, is It?' Colin enquired.

'6:30,' Luke replied. 'We've just had dinner.'

Luke told Colin about Andy's visit and the two promotional projects he had agreed to do. When he mentioned the sums involved Colin said:

'It doesn't seem right that that sort of money should be used to promote a product. Just think how much good that money could do in third-world countries.'

'I knew you would say that, but some of it will go to charity as part of my tithe,' Luke replied.

Colin rang off with a promise to ring again tomorrow about the same time. Ruth and Roger expressed their delight at the good news and hoped Alice would now make a full recovery. Ruth reminded Luke that he should phone his grandpa and Christine. He decided to do that straight away. He phoned Gramps Maynard first and then he spoke to Christine for ages on the phone. When he told her about his two contracts, she laughed and teased him about being a male model. She added, 'There can't be many ginger-haired male models?'

She laughingly suggested it might be an idea for a second career after football. He threatened to put the phone down if she persisted in her teasing. She thought he sounded in a better frame of mind than yesterday; he had not been himself yesterday, but she also understood how worried he was over his mum. She also mentioned that he had made a good impression on her mother. She said, 'He seems a nice lad.'

'Your mum is a nice lady too,' Luke said. 'I can see where you get your good looks from!'

'Oh, she will be pleased when I tell her that,' Christine replied.

'Don't you dare,' Luke squealed. 'I will never be able to face her again.'

When Luke came off the phone he felt on top of the world and when he rejoined Ruth and Roger in the lounge, Ruth said, 'We can tell who you have been talking to by the look on your face!'

'Young love, eh?!' Roger added.

Luke just mockingly glared at him. Roger held up his hands in submission and said, 'Sorry, just stating the reason for that glint in your eye. That's all!'

Ruth added, 'She is a lovely girl, Luke; it is no surprise if you have fallen head over heels in love with her.'

'It's time I went to my room, I think! There's something I want to watch on the TV,' Luke replied.

Ruth and Roger laughed and wished him goodnight.

After breakfast the next morning, Luke told Ruth he was going for his run and then to the gym. Within five minutes of leaving, he was back again in a panic. He had just gone down the road when an L-plate on a car reminded him that he had his driving test for his scooter at 10 o'clock. He had forgotten all about it.

'Oh Luke, you'll have to go as you are; you've no time to change. Can you get there in twenty minutes?' Ruth asked.

'Yes, it's just ten minutes away. No problem,' he replied.

He was dressed in his tracksuit, so he just needed to put his crash helmet on. He told Ruth he would go straight to the gym after his test but would be home for lunch.

'You may have lost your appetite after the test,' Ruth quipped.

'No way; the result of the test will have no bearing on my appetite. I can promise you that,' Luke retorted.

'Off you go, and good luck,' Ruth shouted as he left.

When Luke got back home, he walked into the kitchen with two L-plates in his hand and said, with a big grin on his face, 'Roger can have these back now.'

'You passed?' Ruth exclaimed.

'Yes, it was so easy, it was hardly a test at all; nothing like I expected. I merely rode my scooter with two other candidates and the examiner just followed us on a motorbike,' Luke explained.

'Did the others pass as well?' Ruth asked.

'Yes, we all did. We will get our licence in the post. In the meantime, I have a "pass" certificate which I have to carry with me when I drive my scooter,' Luke explained.

'Well done,' Ruth said. 'I suppose you are hungry now, are you? I have made some pasties. Would you like a couple with some chips for lunch?'

'That sounds great,' Luke said.

Ruth asked Luke if he wanted to shower first after the gym. Luke explained he had not been to the gym but had popped in to see his tutor at the college instead. He wanted to tell him that he was thinking of quitting his course and explain why. His tutor was half expecting it, as he had read up on Luke's footballing activities and Luke had missed two evening sessions and a full day recently. He was very understanding though and asked Luke if he was sure about it and that he would not regret it sometime on the future. Luke explained that he had thought it out and would make provisions for the future with his financial advisors at the bank. If the worst came to the worst, he would find a job of some sort, but he would have more time for himself without college.

Luke took a short rest after lunch and then went for a run and a session at the gym. He was determined to maintain his fitness for when the new season started. After dinner that evening, the telephone rang and Ruth answered. It was for Luke. When Luke answered the phone, he heard, 'Hello Luke.'

'*Mum*!' He exclaimed. 'It's you, how are you?'

'I feel fine Luke; I'm sitting in a chair alongside my bed. I've just been for a short walk along the corridor and saw a reflection of myself in some glass; not a pretty sight, I assure you. A partly shaved head does nothing for a woman's dignity! But I suppose that is a small price to pay.

'Talking of price, I owe you and Gramps a big hug. Thank you for paying for this. Dad and I could never have done this without you both,' Alice explained.

'I'm just so glad I was able to do it,' Luke said. 'I have nothing else to do with my money at present and there's lots more on the way, anyway.'

Luke explained his two promotional contracts he had just agreed to and reminded his mum of his salary at *Southtown Rovers*. He asked her when she was likely to be coming home and learned that a decision on that would be made by the surgeon in the next forty-eight hours; they had to make sure that the pressurised cabin of the aircraft would not have any effect on her, especially after several hours under anaesthetic. Luke asked if he could speak to his dad and said his goodbyes to his mum. He told his dad about his decision to quit his course at college and the reason why. Colin was not sure it was a good idea but respected Luke's decision.

CHAPTER 22

It had now been several weeks since Alice and Colin had returned home. Alice was getting over the operation very well but just wished her hair would grow back more quickly. Luke had gone up to Manleigh and had stayed a few days until Christine left for the new term at university. Then, he became bored and returned to Southtown a few days later—a day before he was due for his filming session for the anti-drugs campaign.

The filming went a lot better than Luke expected. He was instructed on what to do and then had to say a line into the camera. He performed some tricks with a football several times and was told this would be edited and put together, along with his few words; this would form part of the government's anti-drug campaign. He was thanked for his contribution, and he responded by saying he hoped it would have the desired effect, as he was totally against drug-taking—both performance-enhancing drugs in sport and for recreational use.

While at the club, he called in to the office and informed them that he had quit his college course, so they could stop their payments towards it. They told him they already knew as the college had been in touch. He got a bit of a flea in his ear for not informing them and had to apologize. He did not tell them that he had other pressing things on his mind; he was not sure if they knew of his mother's traumatic situation, and he did not want to start explaining it at this time.

Luke felt so at home when he reported for training at last; he felt this is where he belonged and where he wanted to be. In the dressing room, he met Paulo from Portugal. He remembered Luke from the match and came over to greet him and shook Luke's hand. There were one or two other new faces in the squad as well and they made a point of saying hello to Luke and congratulate him on his game in Portugal. One said he felt proud to be in the same team as him and looked forward to playing alongside him. Luke was a bit embarrassed by the attention being paid to him and was pleased when Mr Colluna summoned them all outside onto the pitch.

He gathered them altogether for a pre-season chat, stating that while he did not expect them to win the Premier League this season, the very least he expected was to qualify for European football next season. He urged them to give their all in every game. They had the talent; it was down to everyone to pull their weight if they wanted to succeed.

He then told them that he, along with his assistants, was going to conduct a series of tests this morning to assess their fitness levels prior to getting into serious training before the season started. He also told them that there were two pre-season, friendly games arranged and all members of the squad would be used in these games. After this, they were separated off into various groups and Luke was with the other strikers and midfield players. He was disappointed that no footballs were used as he had itchy feet.

When Luke got home from training that morning, there was a

message for him to contact Andy who wanted to know if he was free Thursday afternoon to do some photo shoots for the travel firm's advertising campaign; He was. Andy said he would pick him up at 1 o'clock and take him to the studio. Luke immediately began to regret agreeing to do this and was dreading Thursday afternoon. Ruth said she thought he would do very well. He was a fine figure of a lad and was handsome; besides, with clever photography they can make anybody look good!!

On the way to the studio, Andy suggested to Luke that he should make an appointment with the bank to sort out what to do with his money in the way of investments. They would have financial advisors there who would help him and tailor his accounts according to his wishes. Andy also said he would be happy to go with him if Luke wanted him to. Luke said he would appreciate that very much as he was out of his depth with those sorts of things.

When Luke got to the studio he was introduced to the photographer and a representative from the travel company, who told him that he would be photographed against a backdrop of various well-known tourist attractions from around the world, including the Taj Mahal, the Leaning Tower of Pisa, the Pyramids, the Eiffel Tower, Sydney Opera House, and several beach locations. It would also involve several changes of clothing, including beachwear for the seaside shots. All the clothing would be provided from the studio's extensive wardrobe.

A dresser was appointed for Luke who had a list of all the shoots and the order they would be in. He was first sprayed with fake tan from his face to his torso and then his legs. After this, he was handed a pair of swimming trunks for the first shoot. He glanced across at

Andy who was hiding a big grin behind his fist, which was in front of his mouth. Luke glared at him, threateningly. He felt so self-conscious in such an alien environment to him. The consolation was that the studio staff were very professional and went about their work without batting an eyelid. Luke followed their instructions and stood or sat as requested and, before he knew it, the beach shots were done.

There was a short break while Luke was cleaned up and different make-up applied to his face. He was given a very welcome cup of tea before he was dressed for the location shots, each one requiring a change of clothes. At just after 6 o'clock, the studio manger said:

'That's it, folks. All done.'

He thanked Luke for his patience and told him he was a natural: 'You were so easy to work with; you could make a career out of modelling.'

'I don't think so,' said Luke.

As Luke was about to leave, he was handed an envelope by the rep from the travel firm who said, 'This is your first year's payment. We will contact you in about twelve months' time for another session like this, when we will probably use different locations.'

There were handshakes all round and when Luke got to Andy's car, Andy was laughing hysterically and held his hands up in self-defence. He said to Luke,

'If you could have seen your face, especially when they said they were going to apply make-up and fake tan.'

Luke said, 'That was the worst experience I have ever gone through. In a year's time when they contact me, I might just be on the other side of the world!'

'Sorry Luke, you're committed to another two sessions—a three-year contract, remember?' Andy told him.

'Don't remind me,' Luke pleaded.

Luke opened his envelope and took out a cheque for the sum of £200,000.

'Wow,' Luke exclaimed, 'look at that!' as he showed the cheque to Andy.

'Not a bad afternoon's work, eh?' Andy replied. 'Now wasn't that worth all the hassle?'

'I feel I have earned every penny of this,' Luke said. 'Once a year is plenty.'

Andy laughed and said he was looking forward to seeing the adverts and posters everywhere.

'More embarrassment!' Luke remarked.

When Andy dropped Luke off, he reminded him to make an appointment with the bank and let him know the time. In response to Ruth's questioning when he got in, Luke told her all about it and that he now felt totally exhausted—more than if he had done a full training session!

'So too exhausted to eat then?' she teased.

'No way,' Luke said emphatically.

'How does spaghetti bolognese grab you?' Ruth asked.

'Perfect. I'll just go up for a shower first; I'm sure I am still covered with make-up and stuff,' he said.

After dinner, he rang Christine and told her all about his afternoon. She said she wished she could have been there.

'Perhaps you could invite me along next time?' she said.

'Not a chance,' Luke replied.

When Luke turned up at the grounds of *Shirley Football Club* on Saturday afternoon for the friendly match, he was met by Mr Preece, his old sports master from school. He shook hands with Luke and congratulated him on his progress; he said he always knew he had it in him. Luke learned that Mr Preece was connected to *Shirley F. C.* on the coaching side. Even though they were a semi-professional team, Mr Preece helped out on a voluntary basis when he could. He was assistant coach today.

He said to Luke, 'Tell me Luke, ever since I learned that you had turned professional, I have been wandering what happens when *Southtown* have a match on a Sunday. Do you play?'

'No, I have an agreement with the club that I do not train or play on a Sunday; it's written into my contract,' Luke replied.

'They must think highly of you if they are prepared to sign you with those conditions,' Mr Preece commented. 'But, from all accounts, it was worth it from their point of view. I suppose they have a strong enough squad to leave you out on Sundays.'

'There are only two or three Sunday matches in our season, so I won't miss many matches,' Luke replied.

'Anyway, good to see you, Luke. Enjoy the game,' Mr Preece said as he went to his seat.

'Thanks,' Luke replied.

Not very long after the match had started, it became obvious that *Shirley F. C.* were outclassed by *Southtown*, who were 2–0 up within twenty minutes. But *Shirley* was making a game of it and almost scored a goal themselves. Luke received the ball on one occasion and proceeded to run rings around their defence. He was showboating and doing tricks with the ball until he was heavily tackled by a *Shirley F. C.* player, who followed through and caught Luke with his studs on Luke's ankle. Luke went down in pain and the ball was kicked into touch for the physio to come on. Luke's boot and sock were removed and the physio said:

'That's your match over young man!' and he signalled to the bench for a substitute to come on.

'I'll be alright,' Luke said. 'Give me a minute and it will be fine; it's only a knock.'

'No, come on, up you get; I'll help you off,' the physio insisted.

Luke limped off the field with the help of the physio and went straight to the dressing room where he received further treatment to the ankle. The half-time whistle went before Luke could go back out to watch the match, so he waited for all the players and staff to come into the dressing room. Mr Colluna asked the physio how Luke was, and received the reply that there was nothing broken, just bruising and a bit of swelling. Mr Colluna turned to Luke and angrily said to him:

'You brought that on yourself. I don't like showboating; it's unnecessary, unproductive, and disrespectful to the opposition. They felt you were making fun of them and so took retribution on you. You may have ended up with a broken ankle. Don't you ever do something like that again! Leave it on the training ground, do you hear?'

'Yes, sorry Boss,' Luke said a bit embarrassed. 'It won't happen again.'

'See that it doesn't,' Mr Colluna said.

'Should I go and apologize to them after the match?' Luke asked.

'No, leave it. Perhaps they should not have reacted in the way they did, although it was only one player who lost his rag and he was booked for the tackle anyway,' Mr Colluna advised.

Luke watched the rest of the match from the touchline and felt a bit sorry for himself. He had learned a harsh lesson. Luke was rested for the next friendly and his training sessions were restricted to sessions in the gym. The swelling had subsided within twenty-four hours but his ankle was still sore, so he was not allowed to put too much weight on it for any length of time. A week later, he was able to resume normal training with no ill effects on the ankle.

The new season came upon them, and Luke was a regular in the side. He resumed his goal-scoring ability immediately and received rave reviews in all the newspapers, with many requests for personal interviews and TV appearances. Thankfully, from Luke's point of view, Mr Colluna refused permission for him to do many of these, although pitchside 'after the match' interviews were permitted in the presence of either the team captain or Mr Colluna, himself. Luke hated them and his comments were very limited.

As the season progressed, Luke was enjoying his football more and more, particularly when he had had a good game and scored goals, which was quite often. He soon became the League's top scorer, and the pundits were all earmarking him for an England place before long. Their remarks were quite prophetic because when the first England qualifying match for the European Championships came about in December, Luke was mentioned in the initial squad of twenty-three names. He had turned seventeen in September and, if picked to play, would be one of the youngest players to play for England.

The first match was against Croatia with the first leg to be played in Croatia. A week or so before the match, the squad had been whittled down to a final squad of sixteen players. Luke was absolutely thrilled to be in that sixteen and hoped to play in the match, even for part of the game. Mr Colluna congratulated Luke on his selection and said that he had studied the squad of sixteen. He knew the manager, Mr Barry, very well and his philosophy on football and, while he did not want to raise Luke's hopes too much, he felt that Luke had every chance of being in the starting line-up and wished him good luck.

The squad left for Croatia on the 10th of December and Luke felt elated to be in the company of so many well-known players, many of whom he had only seen on TV and had not yet played against but merely admired from afar. The day before the match, the squad trained on the pitch they were due to play on and, after the morning training session, the starting team was announced by Mr Barry. Luke was the last name mentioned and he could hardly contain his joy when he heard his name; he was in seventh heaven when he learned he would be wearing shirt No. 9. He ran his mind through some of the famous wearers of England's No. 9 shirt in the past and felt humbled to be selected to wear one—a dream came true as far as he was concerned.

On the afternoon of the match, Mr Barry called Luke aside and said:

'Luke, you have been selected on merit because we believe in you. You are going to be nervous, but you must get as involved as you can early in the game. You will be one of two strikers and Croatia will have done their homework on you. They will know it's your first England match and that you are only seventeen years of age; the chances are they will try to bully you and close mark you. Do not react to the rough treatment, keep your discipline, and play your game and you'll be fine.'

'I'm not nervous,' Luke said. 'I'm just excited and can't wait to get out there on the pitch. If they want to rough me up, they will have to catch me first!' he added.

Mr Barry laughed and said that Luke had the right attitude and hoped he would have a good game.

Just before Luke left his room to assemble in the foyer and board the coach to the ground, he excused himself from his roommate, the reserve goalkeeper, and knelt down by his bed to pray. Les, his roommate, said,

'Do you always do that before a match?'

'Yes, I do. I ask God to help me to do the right things on the field, not to play well necessarily, but to keep my discipline and behave in a proper manner, befitting that of a Christian,' Luke replied.

'Each to his own, I suppose,' Les said, but not in a mocking way.

Luke was restless during the presentations before the match and the playing of the national anthem. He wondered if nerves were kicking in or if he was impatient to get on with the game. When they dispersed to take up their starting positions, Luke glanced at the England supporters' part of the crowd and was pleased to see a couple of *Southtown Rovers'* banners and one or two with his name on. He gave them a quick wave and received a loud roar of approval in return.

Croatia kicked off and it was several minutes before Luke received the ball. He was aware of a Croatian player coming at him and he cleverly side-stepped him and passed the ball out to the wing and ran into the penalty area. Luke jumped to meet the crossed ball, but it was too high for him and was cleared upfield.

He noticed he was given close attention by the defenders when the ball was crossed, and he logged that in the back of his mind. He had several touches of the ball, none of which were wasted as he made good passes each time. He was starting to feel good about the game. Croatia had created a couple of goal-scoring opportunities but they had come to nothing.

Then, after about half an hour, Luke received a through pass down the middle and he dummied his marker and ran with the ball towards the goal. His speed took him well away from his marker and, having side-stepped another defender, he played the ball out to the wing. He hesitated to run directly into the penalty area until the ball was crossed; then he ran forward, jumped way above all the defenders and powered a header into the top corner of the goal, giving the keeper no chance. The England supporters went wild, as did the bench and his teammates, who pounced on him and knocked him to the ground, almost knocking the breath out of him.

When they assembled for the restart, Luke felt good to see the scoreboard illuminated at 0–1. Just before halftime, Luke had another goal-scoring chance which was well blocked by a defender, but it was obvious that he was causing problems for the Croatian defence, none of whom could match his speed. Luke was happy with his game as was Mr Barry who told him so at halftime.

Luke said precociously, 'Don't take me off, Boss; I've got the beating of that defence. I'll get you another goal, you just wait and see.'

'I've no intention of taking you off at the moment, Luke,' Mr Barry said, 'but I will if I have to. Don't you worry about that.'

'After I've scored my next goal though, eh?' Luke said, cheekily.

'If you score another goal, you mean,' Mr Barry replied.

'No, that's not what I mean. I mean WHEN I score my next goal and I will, you just watch!' Luke responded.

'You are a precocious little brat, aren't you?' said Mr Barry. 'But I hope you are right.'

'I am right, I'm telling you. I am going to score another goal in the second half,' Luke said, emphatically.

Mr Barry shook his head and turned away, laughing and shrugging his shoulders.

The second half was well under way with no further goals until, with ten minutes to go, Luke received the ball in the centre circle and sped off towards the Croatian goal. He outran a midfield player, who gave up the chase. When a defender confronted Luke, he side-stepped him and brushed off the challenge, continuing on. In the penalty area, he evaded another tackle, then flipped the ball about two feet into the air and let fly a shot which rocketed into the net, leaving the goalkeeper rooted to the spot. It was in the back of the net before he could move. Once again, his teammates mobbed him, and one said to him:

'You're a genius,' with an expletive for good measure and then said, 'Whoops, sorry about the language mate. I forgot.'

Luke extracted himself from his teammates and looked across at the bench. Mr Barry merely bowed to Luke with outstretched arms and a huge grin on his face. The match ended with a score of 2–0 to England. What a debut for a seventeen-year-old's introduction to national football. He was certainly the *Man of the Match* and was given an interview pitchside with Mr Barry in attendance. He played down his role and insisted it was a team performance, but everybody concerned knew how big a part Luke played in the win.

At the end of the interview, he was told that he would be named the *Man of the Match* and Mr Barry was asked to present him with a magnum of champagne. Mr Barry said he could not do that, due to Luke's age, but the team would make good use of it.

Luke laughingly said, 'Perhaps I could have five litres of petrol for my scooter instead?'

All three laughed and the interview ended. Just before Luke entered the tunnel to the dressing rooms, he raised his hands in applause towards the England fans and was greeted with a loud roar from them. In the dressing room there was a mood of elation at the win and Luke was the centre of attention. He tried to play down the accolades, but he knew he had played well because he recalled how much he enjoyed the match. The assistant manager said to him:

'You would have looked a bit silly had you not scored your second goal, after your prediction at halftime, wouldn't you?'

'There was never any danger of me not scoring a second goal. I knew I would,' Luke replied.

'How can you say that?' the coach asked.

'I just knew. I told myself I was going to and I went out with that in mind. When the first opportunity came, I went for goal; that's my job,' Luke replied.

'And you're very good at it, young man. I've never seen anything like it in my life. I can't believe you are only seventeen! Goodness knows how much better you are going to get as you mature!' the coach added.

'I'll score three goals instead of just two, I suppose!' Luke said, laughing.

'Well, you can do that in the second leg at Wembley!' the coach said.

Mr Barry chipped in and said, 'If he's picked to play that is!' However, he had a big grin on his face.

On his return to England, Luke was confronted with headlines over all the sports pages of the newspapers, calling him a phenomenon, a genius, the new Pelé and the new George Best. He was the talk of the pundits on all sports channels on TV and featured in all the sports programmes. They analysed his game minute by minute and could not fault him. He was deemed the most gifted player to come on the scene in decades. Only Luke knew where the gift came from and appropriately gave thanks for it often.

There was a break for *Southtown Rovers* over the Christmas period and Luke was able to go up to Manleigh for a few days to stay with his parents. It was no coincidence that Christine was on a break from university too and had returned home for Christmas, so they saw a lot of each other. Luke found that his mum was not looking as well as she had done the last time he saw her, but she assured him she was fine and that, just occasionally, she would have a bit of a headache but nothing abnormal.

On Christmas Eve, Luke invited his parents, Christine, and her mum out for a meal at an expensive restaurant. It was the first time that Christine's mum had met Luke's parents; they got on very well. Christine's mum was not a shy person and Alice was a good conversationalist. The meal was excellent, and Luke refused to let anyone else see the bill, let alone contribute to it. When Colin asked

Christine's mum if she would like to come to the special Christmas Service in the morning, Christine butted in and said:

'You've got no chance, Mr Tewkes-Dawson. I've been trying to get her to come to church for ages.'

'Excuse me!' Christine's mum said. 'I can answer for myself thank you.' Then she turned to Colin and said, 'Thank you, I'd be delighted to come.'

Christine, mockingly, made out to faint and they all laughed. They thanked Luke for a lovely evening and Luke walked Christine home, hand in hand. Colin sounded the horn as he drove past them to take Christine's mum home. When Luke and Christine arrived at her house, they saw that Colin's car was still there and that they were inside drinking coffee and deep in conversation. Luke was pleased to see them as he wanted a lift home.

Colin welcomed Christine's mum at the church door on Christmas morning; she then sat with Alice and Luke in the pew with Christine. After a couple of carols, a prayer and a Bible reading, Colin announced that someone special was now going to come forward and give a talk to the children. Luke got up from his seat and went forward, much to the amazement of Alice and Christine who knew nothing about this arrangement. Alice said to Christine, 'Did you know about this?'

'No,' replied Christine. 'Luke hasn't said anything to me.'

Luke got all the children to come and sit on the floor at the front. There were about fifteen of them. He asked them what gifts were brought to baby Jesus in the manger and they were able to answer him correctly. He then asked them to raise their hands if they had received a gift that morning; they all put their hands up. Luke said he hoped they all remembered to say, 'Thank you.' He went on to say that he was given a gift when he was a young boy, although he did not know it until he started to grow up. He continued:

'I was given the gift of being able to play football and I am constantly thanking God for it. However, the greatest gift that was ever given was given by God and that was his Son, Jesus Christ. He gave Jesus to the world to save them from their sin. Baby Jesus grew up and did wonderful things: he performed miracles; he healed the deaf, the blind and the lame; and then he gave himself as a gift to sinners when he died on the cross for us. The Bible says there can be no greater gift than this: 'that a man lay down his life for his friends' (John 15:13, KJV).'

He concluded by saying that whenever they play with or use the gift that they have been given today, remember the greatest gift of all and give thanks to God for him.

He then dismissed the children and returned to his seat. Colin thanked Luke and said that this applied to all of us of course: 'This is why we celebrate today the coming of the Lord Jesus to earth.' As Luke took his seat, Alice looked at him and silently applauded him and mouthed, 'well done'.

After the service, Luke was the centre of attention, particularly with the younger element, but not because of his talk but because of his football achievements. He was fielding questions left, right and centre about playing for England, and what it was like scoring for England and playing with all those famous players etc. Luke was quite overwhelmed by it all and Christine noticed his discomfort and whisked him away, saying it was home time. The kids shouted, 'Bye, Luke,' and they waived as he left.

Luke's season progressed very well. He maintained his goal-scoring record and started every game. He hated it when he was substituted, as he was in most matches when *Southtown* were in a good winning position. When he summoned up the courage at one training session to ask Mr Colluna why he was taken off so often, Mr Colluna said:

'Firstly, it is not down to you to question my decisions young man, but I will answer your question. I am paid to run this football team. I am also paid to look after those in my charge. You are only seventeen years of age, and your body is still developing. I know you are very fit but too much football and exertion at your age can be harmful later in your career. What I am doing is protecting you, in order to prolong your playing career as long as possible. Does that satisfy your curiosity?'

'Yes, thank you,' Luke replied. 'I wasn't questioning your judgement, Boss. I was just curious, that's all.'

'That's OK,' Mr Colluna said and dismissed Luke.

As he was walking away, Mr Colluna called, 'Oh Luke?'

'Yes,' Luke answered.

Mr Colluna pointed to a large advertizing board at the side of the ground, which had been erected and said, 'Nice pictures!'

Luke noticed a huge picture of himself in the flimsiest of bathing trunks, on a sun-kissed beach, posing with a beach ball. The photograph had obviously been computer adjusted to reduce the size of the trunks to the skimpiest size and yet remain decent.

'Oh no!!' Luke shouted, actually blushing with embarrassment.

Mr Colluna wolf-whistled at Luke and laughed. Luke shouted at his teammates,

'Don't any of you say a word!'

Luke was thankful that there were several other posters around that were less embarrassing and the beach ones were few and far between, although, as far as he was concerned, one was too many.

The time came around for the second leg of the Croatia match at Wembley and all Premiership matches were postponed on the weekend beforehand. Luke got an email to report to the English training ground on the Monday morning; the match was due to be played on the Thursday evening. When Luke knew he was in the squad, he obtained match tickets for his mum and dad, Andy, and Ruth and, of course, Christine. The training sessions went well, and Luke was informed on the Wednesday morning that he was in the starting eleven. He told his dad at the first opportunity who was thrilled.

Luke was restless on the Thursday morning light-training session due to the excitement and anticipation of playing at Wembley—the home of football as far as he was concerned. The team relaxed in the afternoon with a game of crazy golf at the hotel and, after a light meal, they boarded the coach for the short trip to the stadium. Luke's nerves started to kick in when he saw all the crowds approaching the ground.

When the team went out onto the pitch for a warm-up before the game, Luke scanned the stand and spotted his family there. He gave a wave and received one back. His nerves had disappeared, and he just could not wait for the kick-off. Luke sang out at the top of his voice during the playing of the national anthem, especially when the camera passed within inches of his nose.

Luke had been forewarned that, after his performance in the last game, he would be closely marked by the Croatians. Sure enough, soon after the kick-off, one of the Croatians stuck to him like a shadow and Luke initially had little opportunity to show his skill to any effect.

As the game went on, he began to get frustrated, and he looked across at the bench. Mr Barry signalled him across and said he had seen what was happening. He told Luke to pick out another opponent and stay with him; this would confuse the marker. It worked a treat; the defenders were confused as to who should stay with Luke. Soon afterwards, Luke received a pass, slipped by both defenders, and ran for goal. Unmarked now, Luke rounded an approaching defender and unleashed an unstoppable shot, which buried the ball in the back of the net: 1–0 to England.

As Luke turned away in celebration, he saw the two defenders arguing and was grateful he did not understand the Croatian language. He looked across and got a thumbs-up sign from Mr Barry. Luke applauded him, nodding his head at the same time.

The score remained 1–0 at halftime. In the dressing room, Luke said to Mr Barry,

'That worked, Boss!'

Luke was warned that it may not in the second half. They would have discussed it and formed some other plan, and he was just to play his normal game.

When Luke came out for the second half, he noticed his family group were not yet in their seats. He assumed that they were still partaking of the hospitality provided for player's families etc. Luke had a little more of the play at the start of the second half and was not particularly marked by any one player. Ten minutes into the match, his attention was brought to the home dugout, where a sub was waiting to come on. When he looked at the illuminated board held up by the fourth official, he saw the No. 9 in red and a green No. 23. He looked at Mr Barry's assistant in shock and was signalled to come off. He could not understand it; he was not playing badly or anything and felt he had not been given a chance. It was too soon to bring him off.

As he slunk across the pitch, he noticed that his family were still not back in their seats. He came off the pitch and made as if to sit with the other players on the bench but was guided away by Mr Barry towards the dressing room. Mr Barry placed his arm across Luke's shoulders and said:

'Luke, I am sorry to have to tell you this, but your mother has been taken to hospital; she collapsed in the hospitality suite at halftime. Your dad and the others have gone with her to the hospital. We have laid on a car for you. Get changed and do not worry; I'm sure she is in good hands.'

Luke was stunned and in complete shock. While he showered and changed, one of the PR men stayed with him and, although he tried to comfort Luke with words of encouragement, it had no effect. When Luke was ready and about to leave the dressing room, he said to the PR man, 'Just a minute please.'

Luke knelt down in prayer and asked God to be merciful towards his mother so that she may overcome this affliction and be made well.

As the PR man saw Luke into the car, he said to him, 'I hope your prayers are answered Luke and everything turns out alright.'

'Thank you,' Luke replied.

Luke could not get to the hospital quick enough. The journey seemed so slow. Every traffic light was on red; every slow-moving vehicle was in front of them; and the driver appeared to have no urgency about the situation, although there was very little he could do to hurry the traffic along. After what seemed an eternity, they finally arrived at the hospital on the bank of the River Thames. Luke dashed off without even thinking to thank the driver.

He entered the hospital reception area and was directed to the Accident and Emergency department. As he strode down the corridor, he saw his father, Christine, Ruth and Andy all seated on chairs outside a ward. His father spotted him and went to meet him. Luke looked at his father's face and knew straight away what the news was going to be.

Colin said, 'Luke, there was nothing they could do. Mum died about half an hour ago. She had a massive bleed on the brain.'

Luke sank to his knees and broke down in tears.

'*No, no!*' he cried. 'This cannot happen; she was so well. Why couldn't they do something?'

Colin helped Luke to his feet and hugged him.

'Luke,' he said, 'we have to be strong in this. God has a reason for this; he called her because he wanted her with him. I know it is difficult to accept, but we are not privy to God's ways. We can be grateful that Mum suffered no pain and slipped away peacefully.'

'Can I see her?' Luke asked.

'Of course, you can. Come with me,' Colin said, taking Luke into the private room where Alice lay.

Luke burst into tears again when he saw her and leaned over and held her. He gave her a kiss and said:

'Bye Mum. Love you.'

He turned to his dad and said, 'She looks so well.'

'Yes,' Colin said. 'No more pain, no anguish, no sorrow and forever with the Lord. We will meet her again one day, Luke. You know that don't you?'

Luke replied, 'I will cling to that belief more than ever now.'

Before they left the room, they hugged each other and shed tears for several minutes.

When they came out, Christine and the others, who were still in a state of shock, greeted Luke. They were still able, though, to offer sympathy and words of comfort to Luke as they had done to Colin earlier.

Colin was showing much presence of mind and strength and, with the assistance of the administration staff, got down to practicalities. He told the others he would deal with the situation and that they should arrange to get home. Luke offered to stay and help but Colin just hugged him, saying that he would rather deal with the arrangements himself. He would meet them at Ruth's when he had finished. After they had all been in and said one more goodbye to Alice, they left Colin and assembled on Westminster Bridge to assemble their thoughts.

Luke remarked, 'Look at all these people going about their business, totally unaware of this group of people having experienced such a loss.'

Ruth said, 'That's how it is Luke; life goes on. We are only just passing through. We can take comfort in knowing that Alice had faith and she knew in her heart that death is not the end for us who believe.'

'But it still hurts,' Luke added.

'Yes of course it does. Your mum was much loved and will be sorely missed, but time will heal the hurt,' Ruth replied.

Eventually they made their way to the railway station and made tracks for home. Unknown to the others, Andy had purchased an evening paper at the station, realizing that at some point Luke would wonder about the result of the match. The back page headlined: 'England moving forward to qualification with a 1–0 win over Croatia.'

Colin called in on his way back home to update them on the situation as far as Alice was concerned. The local undertaker at Rushton would collect Alice from the hospital and then he would make the funeral arrangements once she was home. Ruth invited him to stay the night, but he declined, saying he had much to do and wanted to make an early start in the morning. He also said he wanted to call and see Gramps Maynard on the way and make sure he was alright. Before Colin left, they had a short prayer together.

After Colin had gone, Ruth expressed concern for Colin, saying he did not appear to want to take time to grieve his loss and she was concerned that it might suddenly come upon him and break him, particularly as he was going to be alone.

'He won't be alone,' Luke said. 'His faith is strong, and he can cope better than most with such a loss.'

'I hope you are right,' Ruth replied.

Later that evening, Roger said:

'Luke, congratulations on your match. Yours turned out to be the winning goal you know!'

'Yes, I know. Thanks. I saw the headlines on the paper Andy

bought at the station. It appears they did not know the reason I was substituted, because the writer questioned Mr Barry's decision. I bet the crowd thought it odd too.'

Luke had little sleep that night. He could not get the image of his mother lying so serene in that hospital bed out of his mind. Although he had moved away from home, he knew he was going to miss her. She had always been there for him when he needed her.

In the morning, he remembered to thank everyone for their concern and help yesterday. He decided that he would go for a run after breakfast to clear his head and then ring his dad at lunchtime, as he was a bit concerned for him after what Ruth had said last night. On the return from his run, Ruth told him of the dozens of phone calls she had received. She had noted down each one and gave Luke the list.

'I'm so sorry, Auntie Ruth; I should have been here, shouldn't I?'

'Not at all,' she said. 'I don't mind at all. It's probably better for you this way and then you will not get upset by the calls.'

'You are so wise, Auntie Ruth; you always seem to say the right things.' Luke said.

'Oh, get away with you. It is only common sense that is all,' she responded. 'I'll make you a nice cup of tea and then you can ring your dad, OK?'

'Yes. Thank you,' Luke said, gratefully. 'I'll just pop and have a shower.'

When Luke came down, Christine was in the kitchen being comforted by Ruth, although they were both in tears. She hugged Luke and said she could not believe that Alice had gone just like that. She was so shocked yesterday that it only just hit her this morning. Mugs of tea helped to ease their sorrow and they were all able to hold a conversation and discuss Alice and her life without further upset. Luke fielded one or two phone calls and handled them well, before he phoned his dad.

Colin seemed fine and was more concerned about Luke. Luke discovered that the funeral would take place in Rushton on Friday morning and David Wills, the circuit superintendent, had agreed to conduct the service. Luke asked about Gramps Maynard. Colin said he was in shock but was doing OK.

Luke received calls of condolence from many sources including Mr Barry and Mr Colluna, who told Luke he did not want to see him until after the funeral.

By the Tuesday lunchtime, Luke had become bored and phoned his dad to ask if he thought it would be OK for him to go in for training. His father said there was no reason why not as his mum would have understood.

The people at the club were surprised to see Luke on the Wednesday morning, but he was greeted well and received much sympathy and condolences. Mr Colluna asked him if he was sure this is what he wanted to do. Luke assured him that it was.

Mr Colluna said, 'Luke, we have an away game on Saturday. I think it is best if you don't play. You should be with your family so soon after the funeral.'

'I accept that, Boss, thank you,' Luke said. 'Everyone has been so kind. I'm really grateful.'

'OK, get your kit on and prepare to sweat; it's going to be a heavy session this morning,' Mr Colluna said.

'Bring it on,' Luke replied with a smile on his face.

Luke travelled up with Ruth, Roger, and Christine on the Thursday evening for the Friday morning funeral. Colin was pleased to have their company overnight. He appeared to be handling his loss very well and said how kind and sympathetic everybody had been.

The church was packed. All the pews were full, and the service was relayed into one of the anterooms as an overflow. Reverend Wills beautifully conducted the forty-minute service. Colin himself gave a tribute to Alice, only breaking down at the very last minute. This set everyone else off and there was much weeping in the congregation.

The interment was a private occasion, but all were invited into the hall afterwards, where the ladies in the church had prepared a sumptuous buffet lunch. Many took advantage of the invitation and talked fondly about Alice and how she would be missed in the community.

Afterwards the family all returned to the Manse, along with Reverend Wills, who told Colin that, as far as his ministry was concerned, nothing would change unless Colin wanted it to. Colin said he could see no reason why anything should change but he would wait and see how things worked out, as Alice had been a big support to him and he would miss that greatly. He also said that the ladies of the church had offered to arrange a rota system to help with the housekeeping and cleaning etc. which he most gratefully accepted. It did not go un-noticed by Revd Wills how popular Colin was with the congregation.

CHAPTER 23

O nce things got back to a 'new normal', Luke knuckled down to his football again and had a very good remainder of the season. He ended up the top scorer in the League and was a household name across Europe, let alone the UK. In all football circles, he was deemed a genius. He was in much demand for opening fetes and appearing on TV chat shows and, although this sort of thing was not Luke's forte, he grew into it and was quite articulate. He always jumped at the chance to promote his preferred charity and took every opportunity to remark on his faith and how important it was to him.

In September, there were two more matches in the European qualifying group: home and away against France—a bigger test than the Croatian matches. Luke was an automatic team choice. England drew 2–2 in France, Luke having scored the equalizer late in the game and was once again the England hero.

In the second leg at Wembley, he scored in the first half and then, in the second half, he scored the goal of the tournament when he collected the ball on the halfway line and just ran for goal. He evaded three tackles on the way and then rounded the French goalkeeper. From just 3 yards out, he whacked the ball with all his might into the net. His teammate mobbed him, and he was awarded the accolade of *Man of the Match* once again.

That was the last match of Luke's season and he had booked a holiday with Christine in the Algarve; this was at Ruth's suggestion as she felt he needed to unwind after his first real season in top-level football and after the trauma of losing his mother.

Some days before they were due to depart, Christine suggested that Luke should go and visit his mum's grave. He emphatically refused; as far as he was concerned, he could not see the point, as his mother was not there. He said he did not need to go to the grave to remember her as she was always in his thoughts.

They returned from the Algarve in time for Luke to celebrate his eighteenth birthday. Colin came down to Southtown and they all went out for a meal with Ruth and Roger. Luke was embarrassed when the head waiter brought out a candle-lit birthday cake in the shape of a football pitch and, even more so, when the staff sang 'Happy Birthday' to him with all the other diners joining in. At the end of the meal, Luke dropped a bombshell when he said he had something important to say. He produced a little box from his pocket, left his chair and knelt down at Christine's chair. Holding out the opened box towards Christine he said,

'Christine, will you marry me?'

Christine just gasped with shock and held her head in her hands. She was dumbstruck, as was everyone else at the table.

'Well?' Luke asked.

'Yes, of course I will,' Christine said and she stood up and hugged Luke. They all applauded, and the other diners also clapped and cheered. Ruth was in tears and was the first to congratulate them, followed by Colin. Luke placed the magnificent ring on Christine's finger, which was admired by all. Colin became quite pensive after the celebrations calmed down and Luke noticed this and said to him,

'Don't worry, Dad; the wedding won't be just yet. Christine has a course to finish first!'

They all laughed, and Colin was perhaps a little embarrassed that his thoughts had been so obvious. Christine's mum was thrilled with the news, as were the tabloids, which somehow got news of Luke's engagement. Messages of congratulations started rolling in from all directions.

Just before Luke was due to resume training for the coming season, Andy, his agent, contacted him and said he needed to speak to him; they arranged to meet the next morning for coffee. Andy told Luke that Mr Colluna had informed him there was another club interested in buying him. Mr Colluna did not want to see Luke go and would fight to keep him but felt duty-bound to put the offer to him.

The offer was from *Benfica* of Portugal and was for the sum of £24 million. Luke's wages would be doubled in the first year of a three-year contract and then reviewed in subsequent years. *Benfica* would virtually guarantee a place in the starting line-up for each match and would also provide a luxury apartment for him to live in over there. Luke was taken aback by this offer; he truly had not realized his worth and never even thought of being sought after by another club. He told Andy that he was perfectly happy as he was and would not even contemplate playing abroad.

Andy said to him, 'Luke, as your agent, I have to advise what is best for you. It would be good experience for you to play in another country and your wages would be enhanced considerably. It would not affect you playing for England, and you would be living in a good climate too. Portugal is only a short flight away and you would be able to come back often.'

'But I like playing for *Southtown Rovers*,' Luke replied. 'We are improving in the League and could get into the Champions League next season. Besides, my friends and family are here, and I have just got engaged to Christine. I cannot just uproot and go off to a foreign country. No, I'll stay here. I'm perfectly happy to continue with things as they are at the moment.'

'OK,' Andy said. 'You seem to be pretty adamant about that, so I'll not press you anymore but let me do one thing which can be to your benefit. Don't say anything to Mr Colluna yet; I'll see him tomorrow and tell him you were impressed by the offer from *Benfica*. That's true, isn't it?'

'Yes, it is an impressive offer, but I am still not interested in going,' Luke replied.

'I know that but let me speak to *Southtown*. I think I may be able to squeeze a salary increase out of them in light of this offer,' Andy remarked.

'That seems dishonest,' Luke said. 'I would not want to be part of any deception to increase my salary.'

'I would not do anything dishonest,' Andy insisted. 'But they should certainly consider a salary increase if other clubs think you are worth £24 million and twice the salary you are getting now! I would negotiate on that basis alone.'

'Alright, that's up to you. I suppose that is your job, right? I am just not into these negotiation things. I just play football!' Luke remarked.

'You owe it to Christine to get the best deal you can, and I owe it to both of you to get the best deal I can; and that is what I intend to do. Do not forget that is how I make a living now! My percentage helps me to buy a loaf of bread now and again!' Andy said cheekily.

'Do what you have to do,' Luke said. 'But please keep it honest.'

'That is a promise, Luke. I would not have it any other way either. I know your principles and would never compromise them, trust me,' Andy replied.

'I do,' Luke said. 'Thanks for the coffee.'

'No need to thank me; you're paying!' Andy replied, laughing.

Within a week, Andy had contacted Luke to announce that he had been favourably received by Mr Savilla and Mr Simms of *Southtown*. They had expected Luke to turn down the offer from *Benfica*, after speaking to Mr Colluna who informed them that he did not think Luke would be interested. They had foreseen that a salary increase may be requested and had already formulated an offer that was based on a solid three-year contract from this season. It would bind Luke to *Southtown* for those three years. They were prepared to treble Luke's current salary, which would also stand for those three years.

'An offer I can't refuse,' Luke joked.

Andy informed Luke that all the paperwork was ready for Luke to sign when he next went to the club. Luke thanked Andy for his acumen and hoped he was now able to buy a loaf of bread!

'Yes, and some butter for it too!' he said, laughingly.

Luke duly signed the paperwork when he went in for his first day's training. Mr Colluna told him that he had made the right decision, for as good as he was, he was still developing. Eighteen years of age was too young to contemplate playing abroad. To uproot and get used to a new environment may well affect your play. A three-year contract is just right for you now. It will take you to twenty-one years of age and then you will be ready to play anywhere in the world. I think *Southtown* will have difficulty holding on to you then. In the meantime, concentrate on your football and both you and *Southtown* will reap the benefits.

The new season started well for Luke. He was picked for each match and was being substituted less and less as the season went on. His first setback came in late November when he was subjected to a serious foul tackle and went down in agony. He was convinced his leg was broken, as were some of his teammates who quickly rushed over to him, giving him all sorts of advice like, 'lie still', 'do not move', 'take deep breaths' etc. When the club physio got to him, he immediately called for a stretcher.

Luke asked straight away, 'Is it broken?'

The physio, not wishing to alarm Luke, replied, 'No, it is just a bad knock. You will be fine.'

As a precaution, they splinted Luke's leg and carried him off on the stretcher to the dressing room, where the club doctor examined him. He was given oxygen and a painkiller and then told he was to be taken to hospital for further examination and a scan. The offending player had been sent off and was booed by the *Southtown*'s fans.

The x-ray and scan showed no broken bones, but badly damaged ligaments. A splint was placed on Luke's leg, he was given crutches and told not to put any weight on that leg for a week. Then he would be reassessed.

In answer to Luke's question, the specialist said it could be six weeks before he would be able to kick a ball again. As far as Luke was concerned, that news was as hard to bear as the pain in his leg. He broke down in tears and started wondering if he would ever be the same again on the field after this injury. He asked to go home but the specialist said he wanted to keep him in overnight to monitor the swelling and to keep his leg raised for the next twelve hours or so.

Because of whom he was, Luke was given a private room with telephone and TV etc. He fielded several calls from Christine, Mr Colluna, his dad, some of his teammates and the press, who asked for an interview but were turned down. Luke was a little annoyed that the press had been put through to him and asked the hospital if they could vet his calls and not put any reporters or such like through.

Christine came to see him that evening and realized how upset Luke was about not being able to play for several weeks. She tried to comfort him by saying that he would be back to his old self in no time at all; there were no bones broken and he would be as good as ever. Luke hoped she was right.

The surprise visitor was the opposing player who committed the foul. He apologized profusely, saying he never intended to injure Luke; he was a great admirer of his and would never intentionally injure any player. Luke saw in his eyes genuine remorse and held out his hand saying, 'No hard feelings.'

'Thanks,' the player replied and then said goodbye, wishing Luke a speedy recovery.

'That was good of him,' Luke said to Christine when the player had gone.

'He was probably made to do that by his boss,' Christine remarked.

'I don't think so,' Luke replied. 'But even if he was, I think he was genuinely sorry. He's an old pro and must know what it is like to be off injured when all you want to do is play football.'

'You always see the better side of people Luke, which is why I love you so much,' Christine said smiling.

'That's the best medicine I could have right now,' Luke said. 'It has taken at least a week off my recovery time.'

Luke's doctor arrived in the room and suggested that Luke be allowed to rest now. Christine agreed and said goodnight to Luke with a kiss.

The next morning, after being examined by the specialist, he was allowed home with strict instructions not to put any weight on that leg for at least a week. If he did, it would put his recovery time back by three weeks. Luke did not need telling a second time; he wanted to be fully fit again as soon as possible.

Andy Thomas collected Luke from the hospital and told him that arrangements had been made for Luke to stay with his dad for a couple of weeks, rather than at Ruth's, as the media had been pestering the house. Luke reluctantly agreed, even though it would mean he would see a lot less of Christine. Andy also told him that he would issue a press release saying that Luke had gone away to recuperate.

Luke had weekly check-ups with the *Southtown*'s club doctor and physio, who came to his house, and was making good progress. He was no longer in pain by Christmas and decided to stay at the Manse until the New Year, when he would be able to resume light training.

Christine visited every week and stayed over during the Christmas period.

When Luke returned to the training ground in January, he was warmly welcomed back by everyone. He was carefully nursed back to fitness but had to be held back from over doing his training; he was so keen to be up and running again. He was very aware that, in a few weeks' time, the World Cup qualifying matches would begin, and he wanted to be fully match-fit so as to be considered for selection to the England squad.

His first participation in a match was at the end of January, when he was sent on as a sub for the last twenty minutes of a game which *Southtown* were winning 2–0. As was his want, Luke scored a goal in the closing minutes and celebrated by shouting:

'I'm back!'

That was the headline on the sports pages the next day. Luke played his first full game ten days later in a home fixture, which *Southtown* lost 3–1; Luke had scored their only goal. Luke was surprised to read in an article in the local newspaper that he had scored in every one of his last seventeen matches. He had not realized that but hoped his run of scoring would continue, especially with the World Cup looming.

A couple of weeks later, Luke was told by Mr Colluna that the England manager had made enquiries about Luke's fitness, and that he had informed him that Luke was back on form. Luke thanked him and hoped it would mean a call-up for the national squad.

The call duly came within a week and Luke was invited to join the England squad in mid-February for training for the first World Cup qualifier against Georgia in Georgia. Luke was selected for the eighteen-man squad to travel and, on the evening before the match, was told that he had been selected to play.

Luke had a good game. It was a 1–1 draw, but his scoring record was broken; he failed to score for the first time in twenty-one games. He was not too disheartened; he was satisfied with the way he had played. Mr Barry told him he was pleased he had not shirked any tackles and that his recent injury had not left any physiological problems for him.

After the match, some of the team decided to go into the town and Luke was invited to go with them. He declined at first but was persuaded to join them when he was told he did not have to drink if he did not want to. He decided it would be good to see other places. They visited a couple of bars and ended up at a table outside one of the most popular bars of the town. Luke only had soft drinks, but the others were drinking alcohol and were getting a bit raucous.

Luke started to feel a bit uncomfortable, especially when a few girls started hanging around their table, trying to make conversation with them. There was a lot of banter and playful teasing going on and, suddenly, one of the scantily clad girls plonked herself in Luke's lap with her legs kicked up in the air. The flash bulbs popped, and photographers had a field day. Luke's protestations had no effect and demands for the film fell on deaf ears.

Luke could not get away quickly enough and arranged for a cab back to the hotel; he arrived at 1 am feeling very sorry for himself. He immediately sought out Mr Barry and told him what had happened and asked if anything could be done to stop the photos being published. Mr Barry did not think that he could do anything, and Luke learned a valuable lesson.

Luke spent a restless night tossing and turning, asking himself how he could have been so stupid. He was so worried of what Christine and his father would think. He got up really early and tried to contact them before he left for the airport with the team. He was unable to do so and resigned himself to the fact that the newspapers would be out before he got back to the UK.

When the team entered the arrival hall at Gatwick Airport, the media was there in abundance; the camera flashes were quite blinding and all sorts of questions were being fired at the players, especially Luke. He covered his face as best he could and hurried through to the waiting coach.

The coach drove off with photographers in pursuit. Mr Barry produced some of the tabloid newspapers and distributed them throughout the coach. Prominent, as was expected, was the photograph of Luke with the scantily clad woman on his lap. Luke was devastated when he saw the headline, 'New CHAPTER in Luke's life.' The media had pounced on Luke's Christianity to scandalize the incident even further. Luke was in tears and isolated himself at the back of the coach. He used his mobile and contacted his father to explain what had happened.

To say that Colin was angry was an understatement. He told Luke he had shamed his family. Luke was so hurt when his father said that he was glad his mother was not around to see this. Luke tried hard to explain that he was a victim in this and that he felt the media had set him up, but his father would not have any of it. He told Luke he should not have gone out to those sorts of places in the first place.

As hard as Luke tried, he could not appease his father and the conversation ended with Luke apologizing for letting him down and claiming naivety, with a promise that something like that would never happen again.

Before Luke could attempt to contact Christine, Mr Barry joined him at the back of the coach and said:

'Look Luke, I have learned from the others what happened here. I can only say that the more experienced players should have known better, and I have rebuked them for it. I have decided to clear this up once and for all. I will call a press conference when we get back. I will do the talking, but you will need to be present.'

'I am not sure I want to do that,' Luke replied.

'It is the only way; it will knock it on the head once and for all. Otherwise, the media will have a field day with it,' Mr Barry explained.

'OK, if you think that is best.'

'I do.'

Luke then tried to contact Christine, but she was not answering her phone; that is when he really began to worry. He sent her text message asking her to contact him urgently.

Once the squad were back at the Football Association's (FA) headquarters, Mr Barry addressed the whole squad and, in no uncertain terms, told them what he thought of them. He said that this would never happen again while he was England manager; the whole England set up had been disgraced by the behaviour of a few who ought to have known better. Luke became a victim of their stupidity, and they could have ruined his young life.

A press conference had been set up and he hoped that would be the end of it. One of the senior players, who had been part of the group in the town, stood up and said that he would like to apologize for what had happened. The intention was just to go out and have a quiet drink together but the locals turned it into something else. We all deeply regret what happened to Luke and that you feel we have let you down.

Mr Barry thanked him and said he was pleased that they were at least showing some remorse and hoped they had learned a valuable lesson. Mr Barry then dismissed the squad after telling them there would not be a debriefing on the match, as he was happy with the way they had all played. Many shook hands with Luke as they left for home.

After Mr Barry had quizzed Luke on exactly how the evening had progressed, they went into the room that had been set up for the press conference. Luke was visibly shocked when he saw how many reporters, photographers and cameramen were there in the room. The lights were blindingly bright, and it took a minute or two for his eyes to adjust to them. There was a bank of microphones attached to the table they were to sit at. Mr Barry just sat for a minute to allow the cameramen to make their adjustments before he began. He was obviously very experienced at this sort of thing, Luke thought to himself.

Mr Barry started out by saying that Luke would not be taking any questions at the end of the statement he was about to make. He explained that he had called this conference to give the facts about what actually happened to allay any speculation. He went on to say that a few of the team had gone into town to have a quiet drink together to relax after the match:

'They knew that Luke was a Christian and teetotal, but invited him along as part of the team, insisting he did not have to drink if he did not want to. The mistake they made was to wear their national team blazers, so were easily identifiable as England footballers.

'The local fans soon surrounded them, including girls of dubious reputation. We believe that at least one of the reporters, present, knew of Luke and his lifestyle as a Christian and, in order to get a scandalous story, arranged for Luke to be compromised by persuading one of the girls to pose on Luke's lap. The incident was over in seconds and that is all there was to it. Immediately after the incident, the players returned to the team's hotel. None of them were drunk.'

Mr Barry said, 'Thank you gentlemen. That's all I have to say.'

The questions then came thick and fast as Mr Barry and Luke rose to leave.

'Have you disciplined the players concerned?' asked one.

'There is no need; they did nothing wrong,' Mr Barry said as a parting shot, then left the room.

Luke thanked Mr Barry, who said:

'Just doing my job, but I do not want to have to do that again.'

'You will not have to on my account, that is for sure,' Luke replied.

Mr Barry turned and laughingly, said, 'Ah, so you expect to be picked again, do you? You did not score in Georgia, you know.'

Luke laughed and shook Mr Barry's hand and said, 'Touché!'

On the train down to Southtown, Luke again tried to contact Christine, without success. He was becoming extremely anxious, wondering what her reaction would be.

He need not have worried; as he entered Ruth's gate, Christine ran out to him and hugged him.

'You poor thing,' she said. 'You must have gone through purgatory itself.'

'Aren't you angry with me?' Luke asked.

'No, of course not. I saw the press conference; I know what happened, not that I doubted you in anyway,' Christine reassured Luke.

'Phew, thank goodness for that! I've been so worried, especially as I could not get you on the phone,' Luke said.

'I turned it off when I was being pestered with calls. Auntie Ruth has had to have calls intercepted too. By the way, you need to ring your dad. He left a message for you to ring him when you got in,' Christine explained.

'I'll do that right away; he wasn't too pleased last time I spoke to him.'

'That's not surprising.'

Colin had calmed down considerably when Luke phoned him. He had seen the press conference on TV and he thought that it had a positive outcome, as it had been a witness to Luke's Christianity on national TV, although he still pointed out that it was a mistake for Luke to go 'on the town' in the first place. Luke did not argue the point but felt that at least he was vindicated in his father's eyes regarding any misdemeanour on his part.

Luke at last was back in his comfort zone, feeling that the whole incident was behind him. The incident was hardly mentioned at dinner, except when Roger jokingly asked Luke if he had managed to get the girls number. This earned him a good playful slap from Ruth. Luke was comfortable with it being treated as a joke now, but he expected to take a bit of ribbing when he next went to training.

Sure enough, he was the butt of many jokes on the Monday morning but, if anything, it helped with the camaraderie of the team, and he was grateful that Mr Colluna thought no less of him.

CHAPTER 24

The rest of the season went very well for Luke. He continued with his prolific goal scoring and more and more he was making the headlines and had quickly become a household name. He had played in the return match against Georgia and made headlines again, this time by scoring a hat trick in England's 3–0 win, which meant they would go through to the next round with a 4–1 aggregate. He ended up as the League's top-scorer and was nominated for the 'Young Player of the Year' award —something that had never happened before in the history of the awards. Luke had truly reached a high peak in his career.

At the age of nineteen, he had become well known all over the world and was compared to some of the best players ever. Pelé, Charlton, Best and the like were mentioned in the same breath as Luke. He could have walked into any football team, anywhere; such was his talent. His salary went up in leaps and bounds and he was an extremely wealthy young man.

Companies were falling over themselves for him to endorse their products and, when it was learned that he was taking driving lessons with a view to purchasing a car, manufacturers were almost following him around to give him one of their cars; such was the prestige they would have if Luke Tewkes-Dawson drove one of their cars.

It was at this time that Andy, his agent, came into his own. He was brilliant at relieving Luke of all the pressure and was making a tidy little sum for himself of course. He was worth every penny though, as far as Luke was concerned. Eventually, with advice from Andy, Luke chose a very nice car, but not flashy. Christine too had put in her pennyworth of advice in choosing the car. She wanted to make sure as far as possible that it would not stand out in the crowd, so to speak.

England had now qualified for the final stages of the World Cup, although, as the host country, they automatically qualified. Because they headed their group at the qualifying stage, they were one of the eight seeded teams. They were in group 'A', along with Portugal, Ivory Coast, Peru, and Italy. It was felt that England should go through to the next round as runners up at least but should win the group. They duly did by winning all three matches and, therefore, were through to the last sixteen.

Luke had played in all the matches and had failed to score in only one of them. He had seven goals to his name and was the top scorer in the competition so far. He had failed to score in the 2–0 win against Portugal, but this was put down to his teammate, Paulo from Portugal, who at *Southtown Rovers* had inside knowledge of Luke's play! There was a possibility of England playing Portugal again in the competition as they were through as runners up in their group.

England's next match was the one everyone wanted to see; they were down to play Brazil, the favourite for the tournament, although they were only through as runners up in their group. There was speculation among the pundits that Brazil was not the team they were, but Mr Barry told his team that you can never underestimate Brazil. In the team talk before the match, he told the team to make good use of Luke, who was playing out of his skin now. Luke appreciated that comment; he knew that he was playing well and was living his dream, playing football with and against the best players in the world.

The Emirates Stadium, *Arsenal*'s ground, was the venue for the Brazil match and was a sell-out; there was not a spare seat in the ground. For the first time in the tournament, Luke was nervous before the match. He put this down to the fact that they were playing Brazil. He knew how good they could be, and he feared that he might not be able to realize his dream of scoring the winning goal in the final. This was the first time any doubt had crept into his mind since he was twelve years old, and it worried him. He was even too nervous to sing the national anthem before the match and he usually sang with gusto.

His nerves eased somewhat when the match kicked off but slumped again when within two minutes of the start, Brazil scored a freak goal. Brazil did not have things all their own way and England were more than holding their own, when Brazil was awarded a dubious penalty, with which they scored. Luke had just one chance to score in the first half but failed to take it, scuffing his shot. The Brazil keeper easily gathered the ball. The first half ended in 2–0 for Brazil.

In the dressing room at halftime, Mr Barry told everybody to keep focused. He reminded them that Brazil was ahead only because of a freak goal and a dubious penalty. England was a match for them. He noticed Luke sitting quietly on his own, sipping from a bottle of water. He asked Luke if he was all right.

Luke said, 'It is all over isn't it, Boss. We are going out?'

Mr Barry swore at Luke—something Luke had not heard him do before—and said, 'Don't you dare talk like that! If you feel like that, I am not sending you out for the second half.'

This shook Luke and he pleaded with Mr Barry to send him out.

Mr Barry said to Luke, 'Didn't you once tell me that, as a kid, you told your mother that you would score the winning goal for England at the World Cup final?'

'Yes, I did.'

'And how are you going to do that, if we don't get there? You get out there and score the goals we need; you know you are capable of doing it. Now, pull yourself together. Your teammates are fired up for it; we can do this,' shouted Mr Barry.

Mr Barry sent Luke out with a final word of encouragement:

'Get out there and roast those Brazil nuts!'

The team ran out onto the pitch with shouts of encouragement for each other. Luke felt good. He looked up into the stands and picked out Christine, Roger, and his father. He grinned broadly and gave them the two-thumbs-up sign. Christine turned to Roger and said:

'Something's happened to Luke; he's on fire. I know him so well.'

'I hope you are right,' Roger said. 'England needs him to be!'

Right from the start of the second half, England were putting the pressure on Brazil. Brazil's defence was looking a bit ragged when Luke ran into a superb through ball from midfield, outpaced the Brazil defence and rounded the goalkeeper to slot the ball into the back of the net. The crowd, his teammates and the bench went wild. Luke raised an arm in salute and then found himself at the bottom of a pile of his teammates. Once he emerged, he looked across at Mr Barry who just shrugged his shoulders at Luke as if to say:

'You see, it's as easy as that!'

Soon afterwards, Brazil made a substitution and brought on a defender who had a reputation as a hard man. This was a huge mistake because he was much slower than the player who had gone off. Luke's captain went up to Luke and warned him that this defender was dangerous. Luke said he knew of him, but he would have to catch him first.

The next time Luke received the ball, the big defender made a beeline for Luke, who cleverly flipped the ball over him and ran around him. He recollected the ball and side-stepped another defender. Then Luke unleashed a shot at goal which flew past the goalkeeper before he even saw it: 2–2.

Luke liked that one and ran for the bench pursued by his teammates. He hugged Mr Barry and said: 'Thanks Boss.'

'One more,' Mr Barry said.

'How about two more?' Luke replied.

'Get out of here,' Mr Barry said, laughing.

He turned to his assistant and said, 'Is that boy a genius or what?'

His assistant shook his head in disbelief and said, 'I don't know if it is just his talent, but he's got something going for him that is for sure!'

The team physio interjected with, 'He's a Christian you know?'

'Well, if that's what it is, I'm picking eleven Christians in future.'

With ten minutes to go, England was pressing for another goal and a cross was made towards Luke from the right wing. He was aware of the big defender bearing down on him and just stepped over the ball to let it run on to a teammate who scored.

The defender's momentum caused him to clatter into Luke, sending him flying. Luke's teammates were furious and several of them ran to the defender to remonstrate with him. Luke saw this and quickly got to his feet and stood between the defender and his teammates, sending them away saying:

'Leave it, I'm alright. Don't go and get yourselves booked.'

This had the desired effect and his mates backed down. The referee duly sent the defender off, showing him a red card. Luke shook his hand when he started to walk off and the crowd warmly applauded this. Luke's father shouted, 'That's my boy!'

Roger and Christine looked at each other and grinned. It was so unlike Colin to show any emotion at a mere football match.

Luke did manage to score yet another goal before the end of the match and, not surprisingly, was named *Man of the Match*. Many of the Brazilians sought out Luke at the final whistle to swap shirts, but Luke decided to keep his as a souvenir. It is not every day you get to score a hat trick against Brazil after all.

The next day, Dr Dennis, the team doctor, asked if he could accompany Luke to church, to which he readily agreed—Colin had recommended he attend the Metropolitan Tabernacle. On the tube to the Elephant and Castle, Dr Dennis told Luke that he used to attend church regularly up until five or six years ago. He had a busy general practitioner's surgery back then and had also decided to do a three-year course in Sports Medicine. With one thing and another, including a broken marriage, he had neglected his church going.

'So, what has caused the change of mind?' Luke asked.

'You, actually!' Dr Dennis replied.

'How come?' Luke asked.

'Well, I have been watching you since you came into the England set up and you seem to have a contentment about you. You never get angry; you are popular with the other players; and you have not let your undoubtable, exceptional talent go to your head. You are always ready to talk about your faith without being pushy about it. I admire that and this has caused me to realize what is missing in my life.'

'Wow!' Luke exclaimed. 'I never realized I had that sort of influence on anybody.'

'Exactly, that is my point; it is so natural to you.'

At that moment, they reached their destination and joined large numbers entering the church. During the giving out of the notices, visitors were welcomed from many countries as were two or three politicians and TV celebrities. Some well-known sportsmen were also welcomed and there was a special welcome for Luke, who they said was currently playing for England in the World Cup. Luke was so surprised, as he had not introduced himself to anybody on the way in and, as far as he was concerned, had entered unrecognized. Dr Dennis saw the look of surprise on Luke's face and whispered:

'You should expect this now you know; you are famous and well known.'

They both appreciated the service very much and, on emerging from the building, Dr Dennis said to Luke, 'I felt as if the preacher was preaching just for me.'

'I know what you mean,' replied Luke.

Dr Dennis then asked Luke if he had any plans for the rest of the day. Luke replied,

'No, not really. I was just planning on going back to the hotel and relaxing after lunch.'

'I don't feel like going straight back,' Dr Dennis said. 'Would you like to go for a meal? I know a brilliant steak house in the city; they serve the most succulent steak you could wish for.'

'Sounds good to me,' Luke replied eagerly. 'Lead the way.'

They caught the tube, and, after one change of line, they emerged into the city near Oxford Circus. Dr Dennis pointed the way down a small side alley where they came across a small restaurant, which was busy but not crowded. They were welcomed and shown to a table for two. On the way to the table, Luke saw one of the diners with a sumptuous looking steak on his plate and his hunger pangs kicked in.

When he was perusing the menu, he said to Dr Dennis, 'Boy am I ready for this.'

They eventually placed their orders. Dr Dennis ordered fries with his steak, but Luke ordered a side salad and onion rings.

'What, no chips?' Dr Dennis exclaimed.

'No, I am being very careful with my diet during the tournament. I could easily over-eat with all the energy I am expending during these matches,' Luke explained.

'Very commendable I must say,' the Dr replied. 'I hope you are not just doing it because you are with the team doctor!'

'No, not at all. I learned a long time ago about sportsmen's diets and I have always been very careful. I know what I am like with food and could easily slip into a bad eating regime. I have a landlady back in Southtown, who is a marvellous cook and watches my diet like a hawk. So, I have got used to it.'

After their main meal, Luke thanked Dr Dennis for bringing him to this restaurant, adding,

'You certainly were not exaggerating about the steaks. It was the finest steak I have ever eaten.'

They both decided against a dessert and Dr Dennis asked for the bill.

'I'll get it,' Luke said.

'No way,' replied the Doctor. 'It is my treat as a thank you for taking me to church with you this morning. I feel as if my spirit has been fed as well as my body.'

Luke thanked him and agreed to go for a stroll before catching the tube back to the hotel. While strolling along the embankment, Dr Dennis turned to Luke and said,

'Can I ask you a question?'

'Go ahead,' Luke said, looking puzzled.

'Are you aware of how good a footballer you are?' Dr Dennis asked.

'That is a strange one,' Luke replied. 'I know I can play football well I suppose, otherwise I would not be in the England team. But I cannot say how good I am; that is for other people to judge.'

'Well, let me tell you Luke, at the risk of embarrassing you. If you analyse how much you have improved in a very short space of time and that you are only nineteen years old, you have the potential to be one of the best footballers the world has ever known. I am talking about the near future and not some time in years to come.'

'Whoa, steady on,' Luke said. 'That is a bit over the top, isn't it?'

'No, not at all. You should hear some of the conversations from the backroom staff of the England set-up and the remarks made to Mr Barry from other national team managers. I mention this Luke because you are a great lad, and I would not want anything to change you. Often players with even half of your talent go off the rails and end up with ruined lives, through either drinking excessive alcohol, womanizing etc. I would not expect that from you, but the danger is always there when you get the fame you are going to have.'

The conversation took Luke aback, but he quickly realized how genuine Dr Dennis' concern for him was. He reassured him that there was no danger of that happening to him. His faith would keep him firmly on the ground and besides, he had good family and friends around him, as well as a strong, steady relationship with Christine, to whom he was engaged.

'I'm glad to hear it,' the Dr said. 'I hope you were not offended by my fatherly-type warning?'

'Not at all. I appreciate your concern and thank you for it,' Luke said.

After a further half-an-hour stroll, during which Luke had to give half a dozen autographs to passers-by, they got the tube back to the hotel where Luke lay on his bed deep in thought about his day and eventually nodded off. He woke in time for his evening meal. Luke telephoned Christine and his dad before going in for the meal, telling them of the great day he had just had and asking if they would be at the next match. Christine said she would be there with Andy and Roger, but his dad could not make it because of an important meeting at Rushton, which he was chairing.

'Do you know if you will be playing?' Christine asked.

'Don't ask silly questions,' Luke said, laughing. 'Of course, I will be playing. There are goals to be scored! If we win on Thursday, we will be just two matches away from the final. Bring it on!'

Luke then went in for his evening meal—not steak!

Monday morning's training went very well and consisted mainly of light training and practising set pieces. It was here that Mr Barry dropped a bombshell by telling Luke that he would not be in the starting eleven, but on the bench. When Luke asked why, he was told that he needed to be rested; he had played every match so far and there were very important matches to come if they got through this one, i.e., the quarter-finals and semi-finals.

Mr Barry said that England were playing the weakest team of the last sixteen and had an excellent chance of winning and that Luke would still be available off the bench if things went wrong. While Luke did not agree with this decision, he had to accept it of course and did so with good grace, but he could not hide his disappointment. Dr Dennis approached him and said:

'The Boss knows what he is doing Luke, trust him.'

Luke replied, 'I find it so hard to sit on the bench and watch a match I want to be playing in. I seem to see moves that other players do not and I want to be out there.'

'Perhaps being held back from playing, helps you when you eventually get on the pitch to use all that pent up energy in a short space of time. And, if you do not get on the pitch, it carries forward to the next game when you are itching to get out onto the field.'

'Yeah, I suppose you are right,' Luke said. 'I guess the best scenario would be that I am not needed in the match. That would be good.'

Luke contacted Christine after training and gave her the news. He asked her to ring his dad too. She said she would still come to the match anyway.

As it happened, England won through to the quarter-finals by beating The Netherlands 2–0, without Luke playing a part in the match. That evening they learned they would be playing against Spain in the quarter-final. Luke clearly wanted to play against Spain, a team whose football he greatly admired. The match was scheduled for Saturday afternoon; England would certainly be the underdogs in that match. Surely, Luke would not be left out of that line-up, would he?

The media were very surprised that Luke had been left out of the match against The Netherlands. Surely, this would not happen against a team like Spain. The pundits were fearful whether England could beat Spain, given Spain's current form; they had only conceded one goal in the whole tournament and that was from a penalty. They were boasting that even 'Super scorer' Luke Tewkes-Dawson would have his work cut out to score against them.

The day after the Netherlands match, Luke learned that he would be playing on the Saturday and heaved a sigh of relief. He certainly missed not playing in the previous match and Saturday could not come quickly enough. That week, Mr Barry singled him out for training and gave him special instructions for the Spanish game. He told Luke not to play up front so much in the first half at least, but to drop back more into midfield to help out there, where Spain was very strong.

At the beginning of the second he was to do the same, as Mr Barry thought this would lull the Spanish defence into a false sense of security. He would signal Luke when to go up and press the Spanish defence. These instructions were also relayed to the rest of the team, who were told that, when Luke was signalled, they were to use him as much as possible.

The teams were evenly matched in the first half, which ended goalless with both teams only making half chances to score. After about twenty minutes of the second half, Luke was starting to get frustrated at not having any goal-scoring opportunities. He looked across at the bench, but Mr Barry shook his head and, with both hands, signalled Luke to stay where he was.

The Spaniards too were getting a little frustrated at not making any progress to England's goal and their manager signalled their two full backs to move forward. Mr Barry noticed this and signalled Luke to move forward. Within minutes, Luke received a pass and, after beating one defender with sheer pace, and before any other defender could get to him, Luke fired a shot at goal. The goalkeeper parried it but, such was the velocity of the shot, that it rebounded off him for Luke to follow it up and slide it passed him into the net.

The crowd, his teammates and the bench went berserk. After Luke extracted himself from the melee of his teammates, he looked across at Mr Barry and applauded him. Mr Barry gave Luke the two-thumbs-up sign with a huge grin on his face.

That proved to be the only goal of the match. The Spanish team were devastated. Their manager approached Mr Barry at the end of the game and congratulated him on the win. He said:

'Your striker was not your match-winner, you were. You outfoxed me with your tactics.'

He wished him all the best for the semi-final.

In the dressing room after the match, Luke remarked to his mates what a clever move that was on the boss' part. Mr Barry heard the remark and said,

'Thanks Luke, that is what I am paid for. Let me remind you all that it was your discipline on the field as well as your talent that won you the match. If you all obey the instructions given, all pull together in the same direction with the same aim, that is half the battle. You become a team and not eleven individuals. That is what won you the game today; carry it on in the next match. Well done!'

Before the next match, Luke had reluctantly agreed to appear (with the boss' permission) on a popular TV chat show. Luke hated this sort of thing, but Mr Barry told him he owed it to his fans who, week after week, paid hard-earned money to watch him play.

When Luke arrived at the studio (in a car provided by the TV company), he was met by one of the show's producers who went through the format of the show with him. She told him that he would be the third guest to appear and, when he went on, guest number two would still be on the set; she was a famous actress and had been briefed on who he was.

The producer also asked Luke if there was any part of his life that the host should avoid in the interview. Luke said that there was not and asked how long he would be on set. He discovered that he would be on for the rest of the show, which was about fifteen minutes. His interview would end after ten minutes, when a pop group would be introduced to end the show. Luke was then taken to a make-up area where powder etc. was applied to his face and his hair was tidied up.

After this, he was taken to an anteroom to wait for his turn, where he met the band who were closing the show and had a nice cup of tea. The band was excited to meet Luke, as they had been following

England's progress in the World Cup. The boys put Luke's nerves at ease, and he enjoyed their company. He told them that his fiancée, Christine, was a fan of theirs and they gave him a signed photograph of themselves for her. Luke was then collected by one of the studio staff and made to stand in the wings until he was introduced to the audience by the host.

'And now, ladies and gentlemen, it is time to meet my next guest. He is the young man who has become a household name in a very short space of time. He has caused a sensation in the world of football with his goal-scoring ability and has been likened to Pelé, Best, Charlton and the like. Please welcome Luke Tewkes-Dawson.'

Luke was then gently pushed forward and walked onto the set to be met with a handshake from the host and shown a seat alongside the actress, who also shook his hand. The audience had rapturously applauded Luke's entrance. The host asked Luke if he had set out to be a professional footballer.

Luke replied, 'Yes this is always what I have wanted to do from an early age and for as long as I can remember I just loved playing football and took every opportunity to do so.'

The host continued: 'I understand that when you were twelve years old, you told your mother that you would score the winning goal for England in the World Cup final, and have maintained that ever since? Isn't that a bit pretentious?'

'Not at all,' Luke replied. 'It will happen!'

'So, are you saying that England will win their semi-final and then you will score the winning goal in the next match: the final?' the host asked.

'No!' Luke replied. 'All I am saying is that I will score the winning goal in a World Cup final. Remember there is a World Cup tournament every four years and I am still only nineteen.'

'How can you say this? I know you are a committed Christian; did God tell you this? Did you have a vision or a dream or something?' the host asked.

'No, nothing like that. I have just always known it is going to happen. I can't explain it, I just know,' Luke said.

The actress interjected here:

'I can understand what Luke is saying. I also knew from a very young age that I would have a successful acting career. I must admire Luke because his success is due to his love of the sport and his willingness to work at it. What is admirable about this young man is that his obvious success has not phased him. He is a likeable young man; in fact, I would go as far as to say that, with his physique and looks, he is a loss to the acting profession. I am sure that women would have fallen for him in a big way.'

This caused much applause and cheering from the audience, much to Luke's embarrassment.

The show's host asked Luke, 'Is your dedication to your faith a handicap or a help to you? I understand that you will not play football on a Sunday, for instance. What happens when your team, or indeed the national team, has a match on a Sunday?'

'I'm not picked to play, that is all,' Luke said. 'Both Mr Barry, the England manager, and my manager at *Southtown Rovers* understand my situation and accommodate me accordingly. Does it handicap me? I am the top scorer in the Premier League at present and in the current World Cup tournament. I guess that answers your question!'

Again, rapturous applause came from the audience and the actress.

The host announced that time had beaten them. He thanked Luke for being his guest tonight and wished him well in the rest of the tournament. He shook Luke's hand and motioned to him to stay seated. He received a hearty round of applause from the audience and gave them a wave and a big grin. He was just glad the interview was over.

When the band began to play, the actress put her hand on Luke's knee and said, 'I hope I did not embarrass you with my remarks?'

'Not at all,' Luke said. 'It was kind of you to say that, but cameras and I have never been good friends!'

She laughed.

After the show, Luke was invited for drinks in the green room with the other guests. He decided to go because he was rather thirsty. The host approached him and thanked him again saying he was a natural. Luke was not quite sure what he meant by that but took it as a compliment. Luke was later driven back to the hotel.

When Luke walked into the lounge of the hotel, he was cheered and given a round of applause from the England boys who had watched the show. They teased him about being a TV celebrity now and asked when he was going to have his own show and could they appear on it please and sit next to a beautiful actress. Luke took the teasing all in good fun but did throw a couple of cushions at them as he went off to bed.

Reflecting back on the evening, Luke decided that it was not as bad as he had expected it to be; he had even enjoyed it. The questions put to him were not hostile in anyway or confrontational and he was happy to answer them. He welcomed the opportunity to mention his faith too, and, quite apart from that, the 'boy band' had a new fan.

Columbia was to be England's opponents in the next round. The other semi-final was between Germany and Argentina. Most of the pundits wanted to see a European/South American final; they felt an all European or all South American final would be a dull affair with two teams having the same style of play, cancelling each other out. Luke did not care who played in the final as long as they got there. The England/Columbia match was due to be played on the Saturday afternoon with a 3pm kick off. The other semi-final would be at 6pm on the same day.

Columbia were actually the favourites to win the match, but England had other ideas.

England were fortunate enough to be playing their match at the Emirates Stadium, *Arsenal*'s ground, as it was a short distance from their hotel, and they would be in good time to watch the second semi-final from the hotel. Even if their match went to extra time and penalties, they would still see some of the match.

There were no surprises in the selection of the England team as training had gone well with no injuries or niggles to worry about. A good portion of time was taken up with watching videos of Columbia's recent matches. Luke was much encouraged to learn their defence was not the best in the tournament, but they had a formidable striking force. In fact, their top striker was just one goal behind Luke in the running for the 'Golden Boot Award'. There was, therefore, a strong possibility of a high-scoring match and so it proved.

There was tension in the dressing room before the match; none of the England team had played in such an important match before. Although many had played in European Championships, this was different; they desperately wanted to get to the final. Mr Barry worked hard to relax them; he had detected their nervousness and reminded them that Columbia was a relatively new team and would probably be even more nervous as they had the reputation of Columbian football to maintain. They knew what their nation expected of them.

Mr Barry said, 'Go out there and pressurize them right from the start. Put them off their guard and don't let them settle; close them down immediately when they get possession of the ball and don't let them build up confidence. I can assure you; an early goal will break them. Go for it!'

The team went out on a high and lined up before the match with arms around each other's shoulders. They sang the national anthem with gusto and then huddled together before lining up for the kick-off. The roar of the ground was deafening when the whistle went to start the match, and this lifted the England players even more. Every England player seemed to have a hunger for the ball; Columbia did not know what had hit them. England seemed to attack in waves and Columbia was straight away on the back foot. The Columbian defence nervously kicked out England's first shot at goal after twelve minutes for a corner. Luke met the corner with his head, outjumping the Columbian defence. The ball bounced off the far post for another England Player to place it inside the post for the first goal of the game.

Mr Barry got a message onto the pitch for England not to ease the pressure and sit back, but to keep the pressure up while Columbia was still reeling from the early setback. England continued to do that and, after half an hour, a nervous mistake by a Columbian defender gave possession to Luke, who played a quick one-two with a colleague to go through the Columbian defence and then score with a rasping shot into the bottom corner of the net, giving the goalkeeper no chance. It was 2–0 to England at halftime.

The team got a 'well done' from Mr Barry in the dressing room at halftime but also a warning that, in the second half, Columbia would come at them right from the start. They had no choice but to get a goal early on to get back in the match. He told them to keep their shape and be disciplined, retain possession of the ball and be patient. 'Frustrate them,' he said, 'and they will lose patience, throw caution to the wind, and concentrate on trying to get that goal. We will have scoring opportunities on breakaways; we must make the most of these chances.'

Sure enough, when Columbia was fully committed to attack, a long clearance upfield found Luke with two defenders. He let it glance off his head, turned towards goal and ran into the penalty area where his legs were knocked from under him by a chasing defender—penalty for England. England's captain took the penalty and took it well. The keeper could not even get close to the ball; game over.

England concentrated on keeping possession for much of the last twenty minutes of the game. Columbia was soundly beaten by skill on the field and the tactics employed by the manager. Needless to say, the English supporters went wild in the stands and, to the credit of the Columbians, they accepted that they were outplayed by a superior side on the day. The celebrations in the England dressing room were unprecedented and were awash with champagne. Mr Barry was delighted to be interviewed by TV out on the pitch. He said he had no preference as to whom he wanted to meet in the final. He spoke well of Columbia, who did not resort to foul tactics when they were struggling in the match as they may have done in the past.

The World Cup final – England vs Germany at Wembley Stadium

Germany had reached the final due to beating Argentina in a penalty shoot-out after a 1–1 draw at extra time. Argentina finished with ten men after their goalkeeper had been sent off for denying an obvious goal-scoring opportunity to a German striker just before the end of the first half. There were doubts by many of the commentators and pundits whether Germany would have beaten a full Argentinian team, which bode well for England in the final. Had they not just beaten the allegedly best South American team in the compctition? And soundly so?

On paper, having to play Germany in the final looked an easier proposition than the Brazil match; at least that is what the pundits were saying. Mr Barry was quick to poo-poo their thoughts and told his squad to remove that sort of thinking from their heads. Germany is an extremely well-disciplined team and would not be as vulnerable as Brazil.

When the team came back from their warm-up session, Mr Barry addressed them with his final pre-match team talk. This brought Luke out of his thoughts as to why he could not see his family and friends in the stands when they were warming up. Then he remembered that his dad, Christine, Roger, and Andy had decided to lunch at a nearby restaurant rather than in the hospitality suite at the stadium; they felt they would be less of a distraction to Luke by doing that. There was still plenty of time before kick-off, which was the part that Luke hated: meeting and being introduced to dignitaries.

Mr Barry said loudly:

'Right! Listen up everybody. First, I want to tell you that I have received a message from the King. He says that regardless of the outcome of the match, you have all served your country proudly and we thank you. We are right behind you and wish you good luck.

'I would like to endorse those sentiments,' Mr Barry said.

'I am proud of your achievements so far. To get to the final of a World Cup is an achievement in itself. I cannot say how the match is going to pan out; the Germans are a good side and well disciplined, but so are we. One thing which can tip the balance is team spirit. We have that. I like what you did spontaneously in the line-up before the Brazil semi-final, with arms across each other's shoulders during the singing of the national anthem. I want you to do that again today as well as the huddle before you take up your positions for kick-off. I also want all of you singing the national anthem. If you do not know the words, you have two minutes to learn them. You all know your jobs; now get out there and do them. Good luck.'

There was a rousing cheer from the whole dressing room. They were ready and up for it.

The team walked out and lined up together. Luke saw his family and friends in their seats and felt good. Firstly, came the national anthem and, with the team all closed up together, each one sang with gusto. Then the welcoming committee walked out onto the red carpet. In turn, they were all introduced to the King, the president of FIFA (the President of Football Associations), as well as the UK prime minister and the German chancellor. The end of the palaver could not come quickly enough for Luke; he was raring to go.

After the toss up, the England team huddled together, and the captain said,

'Come on lads, maximum effort. Let's make history this afternoon; we can do this.'

Germany kicked off and, with their second touch, they put the ball into touch for an England throw-in—a sign of nerves several England players thought. This was a fillip to them, and they settled down first and played good possession football. The teams, as expected, were evenly matched and the game proceeded with neither team showing any advantage over the other. Then, horror of horrors, Germany was awarded a free kick just about 20 yards from England's goal. The ball sailed over England's wall and into the net. England's goalkeeper seemed rooted to the spot, making no effort to save it. Mr Barry signalled to his team to keep their heads up, but they were unable to make any impression on the solid German defence. The first half ended 1–0 to Germany.

In the dressing room at halftime, Mr Barry said he was making no immediate changes to the line-up and for them to carry on as they had been doing. He said an equaliser would lift us and dispirit the Germans. He was right.

Within ten minutes of the restart, England was level with a headed goal by Luke from a corner kick. This guaranteed Luke as the recipient of the 'Golden Boot award' for the top scorer in the tournament. The goal really did lift England and they were on top and outplaying the Germans with possession football. However, the German defence was very strong and they were denying England any good scoring opportunities. It was stalemate with minutes to go and looking like it would have to go to extra time, when Luke got possession of the ball just inside the German half. Dr Dennis leaned forward, tapped Mr Barry on the shoulder and said,

'Here's his goal!'

Luke ran towards the Germans with the ball, kicked it past them and raced after it, outpacing the chasing defenders and getting to the ball before the advancing goalkeeper. Luke sidestepped him, avoiding his futile dive for the ball and side-footed the ball into the middle of the empty goal. The roar from the crowd was deafening. The Germans were on their knees, many with their head in their hands. Luke sprinted for the corner flag and skidded to a halt on his back just before he was mobbed by his teammates. He looked up into the sky and merely winked.

THE END